AN YE HARM NONE

ALSO BY SHELLEY TSIVIA RABINOVITCH

*The Encyclopedia of Modern Witchcraft
and Neo-Paganism* (with James Lewis)

The Compleat Dagger-Licking Good

AN YE HARM NONE

Magical Morality and Modern Ethics

SHELLEY TSIVIA RABINOVITCH
and   MEREDITH MACDONALD

CITADEL PRESS
KENSINGTON PUBLISHING CORP.
WWW.KENSINGTONBOOKS.COM

CITADEL PRESS books are published by

Kensington Publishing Corp.
850 Third Avenue
New York, NY 10022

All Kensington titles, imprints, and distributed lines are available at special quantity discounts for bulk purchases for sales promotions, premiums, fund-raising, educational, or institutional use. Special book excerpts or customized printings can also be created to fit specific needs. For details, write or phone the office of the Kensington special sales manager: Kensington Publishing Corp., 850 Third Avenue, New York, NY 10022, attn: Special Sales Department; phone 1-800-221-2647.

CITADEL PRESS and the Citadel logo are Reg. U.S. Pat. & TM Off.

First printing: December 2004

10   9   8   7   6   5   4   3   2   1

Printed in the United States of America

Library of Congress Control Number: 2004109744

ISBN 0-8065-2577-0

Contents

Acknowledgments   VIII

Introduction   I

1 Environment   19

2 Lifestyle and Health   55

3 Relationships and Sexuality   94

4 Children   128

5 Money   171

6 Community   198

7 The Magic Connection   225

Afterword: Choosing Wisely   236

Selected Bibliography   239

Index   243

Acknowledgments

As is the case with any project that spans the kind of breadth we have undertaken here, there are a great many people without whose guidance, feedback, and support this book would never have happened.

Meredith would like to thank David Corbett, Geri Weitzman, Marna Nightingale, Ian Clysdale, Louise Gingras, R. Michael Harman, Nikki Murphy, Vicki Robinson, Anne Robotti, Nicole Lavigne and Peter Marmorek for help, advice, support, and services rendered. Each of you knows what I mean.

Shelley would like to thank WindTree Ranch's Jacquie Zaleski Mackenzie and Don Mackenzie; Allyn Wolfe of the New Wiccan Church International; Adrian Harris and David Rankine, Dragon Environmental Network; and Joe Bethancourt, for all the wonderful music while I worked.

We would both like to thank our editors, Margaret Wolf and Amanda Rouse, for their patience and seemingly endless faith in us.

Introduction

This is a book about ethics, morality, and neopagan witchcraft. It is a book about living a life that is deliberate, considered, and deeply pagan. It is not filled with rules and checklists and guidelines. This is not a "how to" book. There is no one best way to live one's Craft. There are as many ways as there are practitioners—a reflection of the diversity of possible beliefs and practices that is both one of the Craft's greatest strengths and one of its greatest appeals. This book is an invitation to reflect upon the way you *do* live. It is designed to help you become more aware of the everyday choices you make.

Ethics and Morality

Ethics and morality are not the same thing. Ethics are about one's worldview. They arise out of how one understands the relationships between human beings, the natural world, and one's notion of the divine, however conceived. Ethics come out of a person's worldview because how one sees the world always informs his/her ideas about "right" and "good." Values are the abstract statements about goodness, beauty, and relative worth that underlie the judgments one makes about how one wishes to live.

While values and beliefs often reinforce one another, the more abstract nature of values means that any given value can be shared with people who do not necessarily share your beliefs. A belief is simply a specific statement that an individual can accept or not. So both Christians and pagans can value tolerance, but where the belief underlying that value for the Christian might be that Jesus said "Do unto others as you would have them do unto you," the corresponding pagan belief might be that intolerance is likely to produce bad karma.

Neopagan witches, like any other practitioners of a spiritual or religious path, possess a shared ethical framework. Participating in this ethical framework is one way that neopagans recognize each other, even if their respective styles of practice differ wildly from one another. There is a sense in which they are able to recognize that the assumptions underlying the various styles are the same. Scholars who have attempted to construct definitions based on what religion does tend to agree that the presence of a shared ethical/value orientation is one of the essential components of "religion."

Morality, on the other hand, is the sum of the choices a person makes. It comes out of a personal set of values, that is, one's way of living inside a worldview and the ethical framework it implies. Where one's ethics will give a person an idea about what the ideal type of "good" might be, given his/her worldview, the concrete decisions a person makes about good and bad, appropriate and inappropriate, right and wrong, define his/her moral outlook. One of the grounds on which outsiders often criticize witchcraft is that there are few explicit and prescriptive pronouncements about morality that specify the exact nature of right and wrong. There is nothing comparable to the 613 laws in Judaism, or the Ten Commandments. When witches say that they do not recognize the concept of sin, many people hear it as "everything is okay, nothing is bad," and fear an outbreak of total anarchy if these attitudes become more prevalent.

Following a set of rules, however, is different from moral action. A rule leaves the individual with only two choices: either to follow the rule or to break the rule. Most situations are more complex than simply black and white, and the range of possible choices is almost invariably larger than two. Also, simply following the rules can make people lazy about moral reflection. They act in accordance with the rules without pausing to think about whether those rules actually reflect what they believe would be "good" or "appropriate," or they break the rules simply because they can, and after all, other people do it all the time. Modern rule-based, legalistic morality is flawed and inadequate, in part because it removes the responsibility for moral decisions from individuals and instead transforms that responsibility into a set of absolute rules that do not refer to either the individual or his/her specific situation. The imposition of laws creates universal rule-dictated *duties*, which are meant to be universally applicable regardless of the context in which one finds oneself. However, where duties tend to make people alike in that each person owes the same duty of following the rules, it is moral responsibility that makes them into individuals. The confusion between law and morality in modern culture has acted to produce a certain "moral numbness" in many people, a state in which they move through their lives without thinking much about why they do what they do.

The heart of moral action is conscious choice, meaning that one understands why he or she makes choices, what the possible consequences of those choices are, whether s/he is comfortable with those consequences or not, and what compromises the decisionmaker is willing to make. This is especially important for neopagans, because most embrace a *situational morality*, in which they make decisions on a case by case basis rather than a prescriptive (when in situation X you must always do Y) or a proscriptive (when in situation X you shall never do Y) form of morality. Neopagan witchcraft is not organized in a way that would permit enforcement of centralized or fixed moral standards. While there is a sense of shared community among pagans, it is a different kind of community from that characterized by sharing physical space or face-to-face social activities.

Community as Neo-Tribe

Michel Maffesoli (1996) uses the concept of the *neo-tribe* to describe a type of group structure and self-identification that has emerged in developed Western countries as they head into the twenty-first century. The neo-tribe replaces in importance the more traditional groupings by kinship, class, ethnicity, occupation, etcetera, at least in the sense that the more traditional groups are seen as communities that one acquires without choosing them, by virtue of being born in a particular place or of particular parents, or through the pursuit of a particular occupation. The idea of community as neo-tribe, a vaguely outlined and constantly changing constellation of individuals united through a sense of shared aesthetic and "feeling"—rather than being a necessary result of geography, class, or political participation—is useful in understanding how neopagan practitioners can see themselves as part of a community, even when they may have few in-person contacts with other neopagans.

For many people involved in neopagan witchcraft, their contact with other witches comes as much through reading the same material, visiting the same websites and participating in the same chat rooms as it does from face-to-face interactions. Neo-tribes are concerned with maintaining the "ambience" that defines them—the sense that everyone shares in a collective sensibility and the shared symbolic, rather than physical, territory that identifies the broad contours of the community. Most witches will talk about the God and the Goddess, the Wheel of the Year, and the cyclical nature of time. These elements, embedded in the ways in which witches talk about themselves and the world around them, are part of the symbolic territory of the Craft. Neopagan groups, despite their incredible variations in specific beliefs and practices, can be said to comprise a neo-tribe because there are recognizable aesthetic, moral, and emotional links and similarities among these groups.

One of the key elements in the concept of the neo-tribe is that of self-identification based upon individual choice. The choice involved here is not considered to be an expression of an isolated individual, but of the desire, arising from sentiment rather than reason, to construct oneself in relation to something broader, as is the case with one small piece in a mosaic. There is, at the same time, an individual piece with a recognizable shape and defined borders, and a large, complex picture of which that piece is a part. In this way, involvement in neopaganism can be seen not as the self-centered withdrawal into the self that some of its detractors claim it is, but instead as a creative attempt to dissolve some of the boundaries separating the self from the "other" and, more generally, from nature. The logic of participation that prevails for the participant in this type of community is not based on outcomes for the individual as much as it is focused on maintaining the deepest concerns and beliefs of the neo-tribe.

Why is the concept of neo-tribe relevant to a discussion of ethics and morality in neopaganism? People choose to identify with a neo-tribe based on a perception of shared sentiment and experience. There is no structured authority in neopaganism that can discipline or punish you for immoral or inappropriate action except in a very limited way—such as expulsion from an event or a coven. In essence, you become your own sanctioning authority, a concept that is exciting to some people and frightening to others.

Putting Choices into Action

Morality, as it works in contemporary neopagan witchcraft, is focused around two central concepts: 1) that there are causes for and reasons why things happen, and 2) that every action you take will have effects. Neopagans behave in a pro-social fashion for many reasons. One key concept is the originally Eastern notion of karma. Simply put, you will eventually (in this life or another) experience the consequences of your actions. Hinduism views karma as a process of learning lessons, while witches view this action/reaction relationship as important in and of itself.

Neopagans believe that one is fully responsible for acting in accordance with one's values. The only "doctrinal" guidance neopagan witchcraft provides is generally known as the Wiccan Rede, which states simply "An ye harm none, do what ye will." The values upon which one draws to guide his/her actions are those of the emotional community chosen, and thereby produce the pro-social effect from the group's point of view. However, there is an underlying sense in neopaganism that neither the individual nor the group is the final arbiter of right and wrong. There is a notion of a final judgment, of a reckoning for harm done. The fact that someone does not believe that pederasty is wrong, and that they deny that it causes harm, would not exonerate their involvement in it in the eyes of most neopagans. Therefore, the ultimate enforcement of karma (or the Law of Return, as it is often called) lies somewhere outside the human realm, although human actions may be the means through which karma is exacted. The precise nature of this extra-human moral force to which we are all answerable is left unspecified, as is its exact operation, but the idea that it exists acts to deter the most socially harmful effects of complete moral ambiguity or anarchy.

All situational morality is concrete, and is expressed through one's actions in a given situation. An appropriate moral action is 1) well-considered and 2) grounded in the group's ethical framework. It is neither a matter of good and evil nor of right and wrong, but more of consonance (when something "feels" right) and dissonance (when something "feels" wrong). The shared sentiment that defines the neo-tribe creates an ethical bond, a sense of solidarity that arises out of the desire to nurture and protect the group. Abstract statements of "rules" are produced by institutions in the business of social control (for example, governments, police, and hospitals), and are therefore both less relevant and less effective in both defining and producing moral human interaction where no legitimate enforcement mechanisms exist, such as in neopaganism. In the end, the individual alone must answer for his/her choices.

Although everyone has the same inherent capacity for self-awareness, some people are more constrained in their choices than others. In modern North American society in general, those people who have more education, more money, and higher social status have more choices than other people. Money can buy a lot of choice. It is only those with sufficient funds who can stand in a new-car showroom and deliberate between buying a traditional, gasoline-powered vehicle or a more expensive yet more environmentally friendly hybrid. If you are not sure that your grocery money is going to stretch all the way to the end of the month no matter *what* you do, the debate on how much better for you and the environment organic produce might be—at anywhere between half again and twice the regular produce cost—is somewhat academic. This book is not intended to condemn those people who do not make certain kinds of choices because they *cannot*; in fact, it is not meant to condemn anybody's choices. Sometimes what might appear to have been a bad choice on the surface has been well considered. Perhaps the decisionmaker needed to make some trade-offs and understood their consequences.

Making moral choices does not mean having to give up all the things you like to do or the material goals you have or your personal comfort and safety. It is about making well-considered decisions about *how* to attain the desired outcome.

The Ethical Building Blocks of a Witch's Worldview

Because there are no overarching sets of rules or divine ordinances in the Craft, the underlying ethical framework has to be derived from the ways in which neopagans speak about their world. It is in the statements accepted by most witches that you will find the ethical basis of the neo-tribe.

An Ye Harm None, Do What Ye Will*

This phrase, also known as the Wiccan Rede (the witches' advice) is the closest thing that neopagan witchcraft has to a doctrinal statement. Doreen Valiente presents the Rede in its best-known form as part of a poem she wrote, entitled *The Witch's Creed*. The closing quatrain and couplet of this poem are

---

* Some of our eagle-eyed readers may have noticed that the name of this book reads "An Ye Harm None"—without the apostrophe following *An*. This is *not* a typo.

Most Wiccans today assume that the apostrophe should be there, perceiving that the apostrophe is replacing the letter *d* in *and*. In fact, this is actually not the case. Chas Clifton, Pagan author and English Professor at the University of Southern Colorado, points out that *an* is an archaic English word:

From the *American Heritage Dictionary*: An—archaic—And if; if. "An I may hide my face, let me play Thisby too." (Shakespeare, *A Midsummer Night's Dream*).

In actuality, the statement essentially reads:

"If ye harm none, do what ye will." This statement is discussed further in the text itself.

And Do What You Will be the challenge,
So be it in Love that harms none,

For this is the only commandment,
By Magic of Old, be it done!

Eight words this witches' rede fulfil,
An harm ye none, do what ye will.

Valiente here harkens back to ceremonial magician Aleister Crowley's
Law of Thelema—"Do As Thou Wilt Shall Be the Whole of the Law;
Love is the Law, Love Under Will"—but she changes its emphasis by
replacing "Love is the Law, Love under Will" with "An harm ye none."
Since this emphasis on preventing harm is not seen in Gardnerian pa-
pers before 1953, it is likely something that was added by Valiente during the time in which she participated in his group. Her Rede is
fundamentally social; it describes how people need to live in order to
have a harmonious society—a workable balance between individual
freedom and responsibility to others.

These eight words, while sometimes called the One Law, are not a
"law" in the sense that was discussed earlier. The Wiccan Rede is not
something that can be passively obeyed—one must actively negotiate it
in order to live responsibly. The Rede does not come with a list of what
constitutes harm and how to avoid it; these decisions about the best action in any given circumstance are left to the individual. Nor can the
Rede be fulfilled merely by avoiding certain actions. In Christianity,
there are two types of sin: sins of commission and sins of omission. Sins
of commission involve the things that one does; sins of omission involve the things that one fails to do. The Rede has these same dimen-
sions—a person can cause harm by acting, but s/he also can cause harm
by failing to act when action is possible. For example, a friend an-
nounces to you that she has a date with a particular man she met at a
party. You know the man's ex-wife, and know that she left him because
he was manipulative, controlling, sexually and verbally abusive. Do you
try to dissuade your friend from getting into a relationship with this
man? On the one hand, it is her life, and all you have to go on is

hearsay. On the other, she could sustain lasting psychological harm if a relationship were to develop and this man is actually bad news. If you choose to say nothing and your friend suffers through that bad relationship, you share in the responsibility for the outcome, given your decision not to disclose the information that you had at the time. Choosing not to act is still a choice.

In daily practice, interpretations of the Rede and applications of it to daily life distinguish between *hurt* and *harm*. *Hurt* is short-term pain, unfortunate, but also unavoidable in a great many situations. If a young child is in the kitchen with you and, from the corner of your eye, you see him reach out for a red-hot burner, you are likely to react not with a calm speech about the fact that burners are hot and we do not touch hot things. You are more likely to grasp the child's hand firmly and jerk it away from the stove, to slap his hand, or to push the child back. In any case, the child will be frightened and upset and will probably begin to cry. He may even be a little hurt if he fell on his bum onto a hard floor. You have possibly *hurt* the child, but you have not *harmed* him.

Harm is the term reserved for permanent or long-term damage. If, after you push the child away from the stove, you yell at him and tell him what a stupid and irresponsible child he is, how he should not be allowed in a kitchen, and how you don't understand how you ended up with such a useless, worthless offspring, you may inflict harm. If the child understands what you, his parent and protector, are saying to him, then he may internalize the message that he is worthless, irresponsible, stupid, and unwanted. People spend years working on these kinds of messages in therapy. They are *harmful*.

There will be times when avoiding harm is impossible. Witches then have to think in terms of greater and lesser harms. For example, we unquestionably harm plants and animals when we eat them; does that mean we should not eat? Not eating would be harming ourselves, since the human body does poorly without sustenance. The choice then becomes about *what* to eat, not about whether to eat at all. The greater harm supersedes the lesser harm. This is not to suggest that human life is intrinsically more important than plant life (in fact, it could be argued that, in some cases, plant life is more important than human life, particularly when one is discussing the importance of preserving biodiversity), but merely recognizes that individuals often have responsibilities that would produce a cascading chain of harm were they simply to remove themselves from society by failing to eat.

There is a "duty of care" for one's self implied in the Rede. Neopagan witchcraft does not glorify self-sacrifice and martyrdom. It is difficult to bring good into the world from a dry well. Ignoring one's own needs in favor of fulfilling the needs of others is not a balanced way to live. This does not mean that one has leave to adopt a totally self-centered attitude, but it does mean that meeting one's own needs must be factored into the "potential harm" equation. For example, if your partner is a social butterfly who likes to be out and about with people, and you force yourself to go out frequently because it makes your partner happy when you would prefer making a nice dinner at home, then it is possible that, over the long term, you are harming both your own well-being and your relationship. In that situation, resentments are bound to develop. The immediate hurt that is apt to come out of a relationship discussion might well be preferable to the harm that would be caused by not speaking out.

Harm leads to suffering. Prominent pagan author Judy Harrow divides human suffering into two categories: naturally caused suffering and humanly caused suffering. These concepts allow us to consider the existence of suffering in a way that illuminates how we, who live in wealthy, developed nations, are complicit in the existence of suffering, both in our own backyards and around the world.

Harrow defines naturally caused suffering as the outcome of natural events over which we, as human beings, have no control. Floods, volcanic eruptions, droughts . . . These things can cause tragic losses both in human and in cultural terms, and while we might labor to contain the damage, there is little that can be done about the actual event. Humanly caused suffering is different.

The ability to exploit and dominate relates to the illusion of separateness that persists even in pagan communities. Western cultures have developed a unique type of individualism, where self-contained personalities act primarily in isolation from others, so that the goal of a "good life" becomes individual self-improvement, be that financial, material, cultural, or spiritual. Seeing the world from this perspective distorts the whole notion of appropriate human relationships, both with each other and with our environment.

> As long as we hold to the consciousness that all life is not only Sacred, but fully interconnected, we know that to deprive others by taking more than our share is to hurt ourselves.... We suffer when we want more than our share from Nature. We cause suffering to others when we want more than our share from the human community. To want more than one's share, from humankind or from Nature, is the way of the dominator culture. Learning to live in balance, in partnership, as part of a greater Whole, is the way to reduce the needless suffering we cause to ourselves and to others.
>
> —Harrow 1996:21

This observation leads us naturally into the second ethical foundation of witchcraft.

The Law of Return (Karma)

The Law of Return in neopagan witchcraft is similar to the Eastern belief in karma. It states that every action you take, good or ill, has consequences, and that you will eventually experience the consequences of your own actions, whether it be in this life or in another. This does not mean, for instance, that if you push someone, then sometime later, someone is going to push you. It is not that literal. In general, it means that you yourself will experience, in some form, the amount of harm or good you have generated through your actions. The belief in the Law of Return is the strongest ideological deterrent to negative, harmful and/or antisocial behavior among many neopagans. The potential cost of harmful behavior to the individual is perceived to be very high. Many witchcraft traditions express this as the Threefold Law of Return, meaning that an individual will experience three times what s/he sends out. Others refer to the Ninefold Law of Return, whereby good karma returns three times, but bad karma returns nine times—three times three.

The notion that one is entirely responsible for the conditions of one's own life and one's own happiness, which is the logical endpoint of the notion of karma, is one of the things that distinguishes the neo-pagan worldview from that of the Abrahamic religions (Judaism, Christianity and Islam). It is also one of the things that can be mislead-ing and harmful in the Craft, despite its apparent moral neutrality. If one's present condition is the result of one's actions in this life or in a previous life, then everyone gets what s/he deserves, right? People are disadvantaged because they have something to learn from it, aren't they? Most often, this argument is invoked to blame the disadvantaged for their own situations, and to justify a reluctance to provide them ad-equately with the necessities of life.

While some neopagans believe that karma may influence the cir-cumstances of one's birth—and of course, there is no means by which this can be proven—the social environment is far more critical in shap-ing the circumstances of one's life. While the well-off person may feel a sense of personal superiority, believing that s/he is entitled to that standing entirely on the basis of his/her meritorious conduct and hard work, that particular ethic is of little comfort to the abused, the under-privileged, or the marginalized. In fact, that attitude contributes to the suffering that less well off individuals experience. In pagan terms, the disadvantaged experience harm due to societal features that act to per-petuate poor conditions and suffering. Such features include govern-ments that are more willing to dispense corporate welfare (tax breaks and subsidies for business) than social welfare. We can all be said to be complicit in that harm, to the extent to which we participate unques-tioningly in social institutions that create and maintain social inequalities.

As Above, So Below

This phrase expresses the neopagan belief that all things are inter-connected: material and non-material, physical, emotional and spiritual. It reflects the notion that there is both a microcosm and a macrocosm implicit in all things. The microcosm might be a single human life, the macrocosm the broad sweep of history. The microcosm might be a sin-gle coven ritual, the macrocosm might be all the diverse religious celebrations that are occurring at that moment, or all the rituals of that type ever done. It reminds pagans that everything they do is part of something broader, and that changing themselves is the first step in changing the world. Pagans do not believe that human beings stand uniquely apart from the rest of the natural world, or from divinity. The interrelatedness of all these spheres means that the personal is not only political—one of the hallmark phrases of modern feminism—but the personal is also environmental and spiritual.

"As above, so below" also suggests the sense of balance that many neopagans consider essential to living a "good life"—especially in its extended form: "As above, so below/as without, so within." Not only does this mean that, for example, material aspirations need to be in balance with spiritual aspirations, or that work life needs to be in balance with home life, but that, in a broader sense, the exploitation of the Earth as a resource for human needs and comforts must be balanced by preservation of the Earth for biodiversity and the needs of other species.

The Earth Is Sacred

Almost any neopagan, regardless of his/her particular tradition, will affirm that the Earth is sacred. By this, neopagans generally mean both the planet as a whole and the individual patches of dirt we encounter in our everyday lives. It is not just majestic forests, roaring seas and placid pristine lakes that are sacred, but also urban container gardens, public parks, and the occasional sad dandelion poking up through a crack in the sidewalk. Some neopagans use the terms "the Earth" and "nature" interchangeably, while for others, the connotations of the terms are very different.

The Earth is taken to be the macrocosm, the planet on which we live, the living, breathing, evolving ecosystem that James Lovelock called Gaia. Talk about the Earth tends to focus on loss of biodiversity, the threat of genetically modified organisms, sustainable development, global warming, and other "big picture" concerns. Discussion about nature in North America tends to focus on the wilderness—those places that exist as they have for thousands of years with minimal human intervention. "Nature" also can mean those places that are away from civilization, even if once inhabited. It means places where the imposition of human activity on the landscape is not obvious and overt.

In Europe and Great Britain, where a much longer history of agrarian and urban habitation has rendered pristine, untouched nature extremely rare, "nature" tends to refer to the pastoral and agricultural countryside—the village as opposed to the city. One can see this in the Gardnerian sabbat cycle, from which the seasonal cycles of most modern witchcraft traditions derive. These celebrations of nature are those of domestic agriculture: sowing, growing, harvesting, slaughtering, waiting out the winter in hope. These relate to the cycles of wild nature: germination/mating, flowering/birth of young, growth, seeding/maturation of young and preparation of winter stores, and dormancy/hibernation, but are not identical to them. While the sabbats portray human beings living in harmony with the inevitable cycle of the seasons, it remains true that nature celebrated in this context is domesticated nature—nature in service to human beings—rather than nature of and for itself.

So how, then, does neopaganism differ from mainstream Western modernity? In the Abrahamic religious traditions that dominate many ethical discussions in the West, many followers generally perceive that the inherent superiority of humanity to nonhuman "nature" is established in the words

> God said to them [the man and the woman] "Be fruitful and multiply, and fill the earth and subdue it; and have dominion over the fish of the sea and over the birds of the air and over every living thing that moves upon the earth." And God said, "Behold, I have given you every plant yielding seed which is upon the face of all the earth, and every tree with seed in its fruit; you shall have them for food."
>
> —Gen. 1:28–29 RSV

This passage is often interpreted to mean that humankind is justified in taking from nature what it desires in order to fulfill the divinely ordained requirement to multiply and subdue. Admittedly, this is only one of many possible interpretations of this passage; there are many more Jewish, Christian, and Islamic environmentalists than there are pagan ones, simply by virtue of the fact that there are many more Jews, Christians, and Muslims worldwide than there are pagans.

Max Weber, a noted sociologist of religion in the early part of the twentieth century, remarked that the process of moving from a village-based society to an urban society was one that "disenchanted" the world. By this he means that the drive to make things more efficient and more productive, to have "sensible" rules and processes, distances human beings from nature, because nature can never be entirely controlled and bureaucratized. Nature, therefore, loses its status as something that informs moral action, and becomes simply a commodity—something that can be used. Pagans, by and large, are unsatisfied with the disenchanted world they have inherited. Part of the fundamental goal of those who become involved in neopagan religions is to re-enchant the world around them—to imbue it with spirit, power, and moral potency. To do this, they reach back to Romantic thought, which was a prominent feature of the nineteenth century.

One of the Romantics' chief criticisms of urbanization, industrialization, and Empiricism was that these processes distance people from nature and the "natural" environment. Closeness to nature was centrally important to the Romantics because they believed that it inspired the imagination to new heights, thus deepening human insight and human emotions, thus enabling people to live in greater harmony with themselves and with their environment. The affinities between Romanticism and neopagan witchcraft in particular, can be seen in Doreen Valiente's comment, "In a sense, the rebirth of witchcraft is a rebellion. It is being carried out by those young and old . . . who are . . . profoundly disillusioned with the scientists who promised us Utopia and gave us the nuclear bomb" (1989:207).

Where Enlightenment thinkers privileged reason, knowledge, and progress, Romantics privileged emotion, intuition, beauty, and harmony. Among the best-known English Romantics were writers and poets William Wordsworth, Samuel Taylor Coleridge, Percy Bysshe Shelley, Elizabeth Barrett Browning, and Jane Austen, as well as the Pre-Raphaelite painters and their followers. For these artists, nature was where one finds eternal truths, ideal beauty, and models for a freer, less constrained way of living.

Like the Romantics, neopagans value a closeness and a feeling of connection to nature in the sense that nature teaches, inspires, and models. The Earth, with its cycles of birth, growth, death, and rebirth, provides the most central metaphor for "a life well and truly lived." The divine, in neopagan witchcraft, is not to be found in some distant theological space from which the Earth was somehow created and now exists as an artifact from which the divine has withdrawn (as in deism), but in life as it is enacted. Human life is understood by pagans as emulating the cycle of the seasons, which existed before humanity and which shall continue to exist long after humanity has become a dusty memory blown upon the winds. To neopagans, it is only through life that the Gods can be made manifest. The Earth, then, is sacred because it nourishes and sustains all life, and is seen by pagans to be the source of the only truths that are eternal.

Thou Art God/dess

This is the quintessential expression of the relationship between the human and the divine in most branches of neopaganism. "Thou Art God" was coined by science fiction author Robert A. Heinlein in his 1961 novel, *Stranger in a Strange Land*. The first significant term Heinlein introduces is "to grok," which is to understand deeply, in the fullness of all interconnection—with the heart and the being, rather than with the rational mind.

The divine is located within the individual, potentially within all individuals simultaneously. This is a more radical version of the Christian Anabaptist teaching, which says that there is a spark of the divine within everyone. It would be heretical, from an Anabaptist perspective, to suggest that an individual could "be" God. And yet, that is precisely what "Thou Art God/dess" suggests. Each individual is equally divine—this is not a power given to some that elevates them over others. Some people may be more in touch with their own divinity, but that does not make them intrinsically more valuable than other people.

Each individual has life experiences, beliefs, values, preferences, and foibles, but he or she also participates in the divine, which binds each person into the web of life—and which enables the individual to move outside his or her personal experiences through sympathy and empathy. It is through this understanding, referred to as immanent divinity, that pagans believe they are connected with the Earth and with nature. Nonhuman nature is believed by many to be "more fully divine" in that it does not possess the capacity to develop a "personality" that is capable of obscuring the divine.

This acknowledgment of their own divinity is often especially powerful for women who have grown up in Western religious traditions in which divinity has traditionally been spoken of in male terms. "Our Father." "The Son of God." "God of our fathers." While there is a Mother of God, at least in some branches of Christianity, she is a role model and not a symbol through which women can participate in the divine. In neopagan witchcraft and Goddess worship, women are able to experience themselves as a part of the divinity that is intrinsic to all things, from rocks and grasses to cats and chipmunks to women and men.

Implicit in the statements "Thou Art God/dess" and "The Earth is sacred" is the idea that neopagans must approach everything and everyone they encounter with the same level of respect that they show to other, more explicit, expressions of divinity. The covener is just as divine as the priestess. The student is just as divine as the teacher. The child is just as divine as the parent. And the checkout clerk who seems to prefer talking on the phone to ringing through your order is just as sacred as anyone else, if perhaps lacking in courtesy and etiquette. While neopagans do not generally subscribe directly to the Abrahamic admonition "Do unto others as you would have them do unto you," they set themselves a higher standard by making their goal of conduct to treat all natural things, both human and non-human, as sacred.

Goddess Is Alive, Magic Is Afoot

This phrase, sometimes used as a power-raising chant, expresses the relationship between divinity and magic. The existence of divinity, here expressed as Goddess, means that magic is actively present in daily life. One cannot have a world saturated with divinity without also having things that are not easily explainable through logical, rational means. A world where magic is present is a world with open-ended possibilities. It is a world that defies simple explanations. One Starhawk chant goes, "She changes everything She touches and everything She touches changes." Change is at the core of the neopagan experience of magic. Most definitions of magic given in neopaganism rest on those originally presented by two ceremonial magicians: Aleister Crowley and William Butler. Crowley's definition is "Magic is the Art and Science of causing change to occur in accordance with Will"; Butler's is "Magic is the art of effecting change in consciousness at will" (Bonewits 1971:28–30). Because the individual is divine, and because everything is connected through that divinity to everything else, neopagans believe that thought can affect matter, without the need for concrete intervention by the thinker. They view this interconnectedness as the mechanism through which the universal web of life maintains itself.

The neopagan universe consists of a macrocosm and a microcosm. Changes in one will be reflected in changes in the other through the mediation of the divine, which is the force within both that binds them together. The individual is a microcosm of the world in which he/she lives. Change is perceived as a reciprocal process, in which both the macrocosm and the microcosm are transformed.

CHAPTER 1

Environment

"An ye harm none, do what ye will" is applicable not only to the way we treat ourselves but also how we treat both the human and nonhuman world around us. Sometimes, it is not clear how a simple decision, such as what fabric to buy or what plants to put in your garden, can really cause harm, but every action we take has ramifications in life. Those who take the Craft seriously know that we are expected to think not only of the immediate effect of our actions, but also their long-term and third- or fourth-generation impact.

In witchcraft, there are two aspects of the environment: one's microenvironment and one's macroenvironment. "As above, so below; as without, so within." The microenvironment is one's inner environment; the macroenvironment is one's surroundings: home, clothing, the planet on which we live. We all want to live in a comfortable environment, but some of the things we do to make our environment "comfortable" quickly can cause someone else to live quite uncomfortably. There are questions to ask in making such choices; hopefully, asking these questions will enable you to weigh important options to make the best decision for your life—with minimal negative impact on others. Sometimes we overlook the fact that even seemingly minor decisions can have a long-term effect on others, yet these are all things which fall under "an ye harm none, do what ye will."

Fabrics

There is an old adage, "Clothing makes the man" (or woman); but what and who makes the clothing? Many pagans wear natural fibers in an effort

to be environmentally responsible, but it is not always the best choice
for the environment in general, or even one's personal environment. At
the simplest level, there are two classes of fibers used to make clothing:
natural and synthetic. Unfortunately, just because a fabric is "natural," it
is not necessarily without ethical issues for a neopagan consumer. The
benefits of natural fibers are comfort and connection to the Earth. Two
popular choices, cotton and silk, are detailed below. Additional natural
fibers include linen, wool, and hemp, which can be further researched
on the Web.

Natural Fibers

COTTON

To make cotton white, it is bleached with a chlorine-based bleaching process. Less brilliant, white "organic" cotton is lightened rather
than bleached, using hydrogen peroxide. While it is growing, cotton is
bombarded by synthetic fertilizers, herbicides, pesticides, and defoliants.
It may be a crop that is grown on only about 2.2 percent of the world's
cultivated land, but it uses over 10 percent of the world's pesticide, and
almost 25 percent of the insecticides. As well, many cotton garments are
cut and sewn at offshore factories where the pay and work conditions
of the seamstresses are far more reminiscent of Charles Dickens' time
than our own. The Worldwatch Institute suggests that consumers avoid
shopping at stores whose clothing brands are known to use sweatshops.
In the United States, these stores include Wal-Mart, Gap (Old Navy,
Banana Republic), and Target.

SILK

Silk is a luxury fabric, even in today's global market. There are two
major locations for silk manufacture: China and India. Chinese silk
tends to be smooth and satiny, while Indian silk tends to be softer but
more crinkly. Indian silk uses richer colors due to a different dyeing
process and order. For ethical-choice vegetarians and many others, wearing silk is often not an option, as the process of making silk includes the
killing of each silkworm while it is encased in its cocoon. The silk fiber

is the cocoon itself, which is boiled to destroy the "glue" holding it together. The fiber is then unwound from the cocoon. Rayon (see below) was originally formulated to be a silk substitute.

Synthetics

For those who are allergic to natural fibers and/or the dyes used in their manufacture, wearing synthetic clothing may well be the only option other than moving to a nudist colony. Most of the common synthetic fibres do have drawbacks to pagan-thinking consumers, however. Yet, as with all choices, financial ability and medical issues must be balanced against ethics and desires. Three common families of synthetic materials used as alternatives to natural-fiber clothing are considered here.

RAYON

Rayon was the first man-made fiber produced, achieving the look of silk at a fraction of the cost. Rayon is derived from cellulose, which is extracted from wood fiber; however, recycled paper or wood products cannot be used to manufacture it, as the fibers are too short once they have been turned into paper or related products. Rayon production consumes a large amount of water, and the fiber is highly flammable. Do not use rayon as your fabric of choice for robes: the "Burning Man" festival is NOT supposed to be your at-home ritual after your robe brushes against a lit quarter candle!

Do not be fooled! Some manufacturers try to sell rayon to the "green" market as a "natural" or "organic" fiber, but the process of changing inflexible wood into soft, silky fiber is long and involves some very toxic chemicals. The Occupational and Environmental Medicine web page from Harvard Medical School features a chart with examples of environmental causes of health problems, illustrating both short-term and latent, or long-term effects. The viscose rayon production industry is noted as a source of various ailments ranging from acute psychosis to such disturbing long-term illnesses as upper respiratory disease and kidney damage.

From a maintenance point of view, rayon fabrics often require sizing, (starches added to the fabric to stiffen it) as the fiber has little body of its own. When a sized rayon garment is touched by water, spots occur that may be difficult to remove. This also is the reason why, if you wash a rayon garment in a regular washing machine, it often emerges soggy and shapeless. Many rayons are marked DRY CLEAN ONLY, which brings up the side effects of toxic dry-cleaning chemicals such as formaldehyde. Despite the plethora of neopagans wearing cottonlike broomstick skirts made of rayon, these garments often cause more problems for both the wearer and the environment than garments made of other fibers.

POLYESTER

Polyester is a favorite for ropes, nets, and seatbelt webbing as well as filler for sleeping bags. Some polyesters contain chlorine, and those have become sources of illness and/or injury to humans during production, use, and end-product disposal. Polyester is made from polyethylene terephthalate (PET), a plastic derived from ethylene glycol (better known to northern residents as car antifreeze).

One very common use of polyester is in polar fleece warm wear. Used as a lightweight substitute for wool, polar fleece is a "special case" of polyester because it is made in a recycling process, not as virgin fiber. Polar fleece is made primarily from recycled PET soda bottles. It is by far the most environmentally friendly synthetic material. As is the case with many recycling processes, making polyester fleece out of an existing polyester material uses less energy than if the fabric was made as virgin polyester.

An interesting study was done in Denmark in collaboration with the Danish Environmental Protection Agency and the Federation of Danish Textile and Clothing Industries. Twenty textile fabrics were selected in order to test for various trace elements and chemical compounds. The selection of the fabrics was designed to cover as many different types of fibers and fabrics as possible. As well, supplementary studies using artificial saliva and perspiration (extractable antimony) were done for two of the fabrics containing polyester and four apparel textiles containing 100 percent polyester. The apparel textiles were purchased in three different shops around Copenhagen.

The study reported finding measurable amounts of various chemicals in the chosen fabrics, with a few surprises. There are poisons which are only an issue if taken orally (e.g., two glycols) showing up in measurable amounts in some polyester fabrics. This might not sound like a concern unless you are intending to eat your shirt or blouse for dinner, but we often forget to take into consideration the possible ramifications of this when the infant you are holding starts to gum the collar of that shirt. As most dog or cat owners know, antifreeze tastes "sweet" and is therefore an attractive poison to pets roaming around when left out or spilled in pools on the ground. It is worth wondering about this: if glycol is leaching out of polyester clothing, are our infants sucking and chewing on sweet-tasting poison?

ACRYLIC

This is the fuzzy fabric that took over much of the wool market in the latter half of the twentieth century. Acrylic is defined as a manufactured fiber in which the fiber-forming substance is any long-chain synthetic polymer that is produced from a petrochemical and then spun. Acrylic is a favorite fabric in sports clothing as it wicks sweat away from the wearer's body so that it can evaporate into the air. This makes acrylic a big hit with runners, cyclists, and other athletes, and no more environmentally friendly substitute has been found so far. There seem to be few health risks in wearing acrylic fibers; some people suffer some skin irritation such as eczema.

We must remember that both acrylic and polyester originate in the petrochemical industry, and our exploitation of fossil-based resources has a tremendous impact on the environment.

MAKING THE CHOICE

Overall, natural fibers seem most appropriate for clothing, where you have a choice. Depending on factors such as allergies (e.g., does linen "pick" at your skin? Does wool make you break out in rashes?) and safety issues, wearing natural fibers is sometimes not an option. Some natural fibers burn only briefly when lit and then sputter out, making them better choices for ritual clothing used around open flames.

Natural-fiber clothing often costs more than synthetic clothing, and that can be a financial disadvantage. As well, some natural fibers come from impoverished countries where forests are being felled to make room for cash crops, and the wages paid to farm workers harvesting crops such as cotton are often well below subsistence. So when you look at that sharp new top or pair of pants, some of the things you might wish to consider are

- What is the environmental impact of this material?

- Can I find out if the garment is made by union hands, or by an off-shore sweatshop? Has child labor gone into the harvesting of the raw material?

- Are there any alternative substances that wear the way I need this to wear, and function as required?

- Can I afford the unbleached cotton shirt, or can I only manage the chlorine-bleached item? Could I find this in a more environmentally friendly format at a secondhand store? Has good workmanship gone into this item, or will it fall apart in a year?

- Do I really need this piece of clothing, or am I just falling prey to the consumer "buy buy buy" message being hammered into North Americans via the media and peer pressure? Is there anything wrong with wearing last year's (three years ago's) fashions and/or colors?

Chemicals

Cleaning Solvents and Products

A great many commercial cleaning products contain toxic chemicals. This is why they are so consistently labeled KEEP OUT OF REACH OF CHILDREN. Look for alternatives. Before the days of specialized cleaners for all things and all uses, grandmother had old-fashioned cleaners that were not nearly as toxic to our lungs and the environment. One of the best all-around cleaners, which is also perfect for those with perfume or ammonia allergies, is a simple mix of baking soda and white vinegar. As long as you do not want a floral, sweet perfume invading your home and don't mind the area smelling vaguely of pickle juice, this mix takes off the most stubborn stains from sideboards, floors, toilet and sink areas, and almost anywhere else. It is embarrassingly inexpensive, and has a very light environmental footprint. On top of all that, you can wash it down the sink without poisoning the environment!

Numerous Web sites and books feature recipes for all sorts of cleaning alternatives that have less of an impact on all of us. Other common alternatives for household cleaning include: borax, baking soda, liquid or flake unscented soap, cornstarch, citrus solvent, and trisodium phosphate (TSP). One great Internet site for simple recipes is "EarthEasy" (eartheasy.com/live_nontoxic_solutions.htm).

Fluoridation

Exposure to fluoride during tooth development can result in fluorosis, a mottled discoloration of the tooth enamel. Fluorosis is increasingly common among people drinking fluoridated water, and the incidence of fluorosis increases as the concentration of fluoride in the water increases. At a standard concentration for fluoridated water, one person in eight shows fluorosis severe enough to be considered cosmetically displeasing. There appear to be no additional medical problems with fluoridated water, and children living where the water is treated consistently show fewer cavities (see Alan R. Gaby, M.D., at www. thebetterhealth store. com/News/WaterFluoridation1012.html).

If you are concerned about the level of fluoride to which you or your children are exposed, one thing you can do is switch to a non-fluoridated toothpaste. Children especially like to eat toothpaste, which is why most fluoridated brands suggest that you give a child no more than a pea-size amount.

Chloramine

Chloramine is used to treat drinking water in some areas of the United States, and it can be toxic to human blood cells undergoing kidney dialysis as well as to pet fish. Dialysis patients are usually advised to consult their doctors about how to remove it from water used in dialysis. In the 1990s, a long-awaited water project in Arizona called the Central Arizona Project (CAP) started to bring potable drinking water to large cities such as Tucson and Phoenix. From the beginning, CAP experienced a myriad of water problems. The chloramine-treated water was eating away much of the old infrastructure of Tucson's water pipes, leaving some pipes held together by little more than calcium and other chemical build-up (like scale in a tea kettle). Many people, particularly the elderly, complained not only about the bad taste of the CAP water, but some manifested symptoms such as headaches and upset stomachs. For quite a while, CAP water was relegated to irrigation use until the chloramine problems were ironed out through chemical changes, improved filtration, and mixing the CAP water with naturally occurring waters.

Off-Gassing and Sick-Office Syndrome

Off-gassing is the common term for the process through which volatile chemicals evaporate in nonmetallic materials. For example, building construction materials release chemicals into the air through evaporation for years after the products are initially installed. This means that you continue to breathe these chemicals as you work, sleep, and relax in your home or office. Off-gassing is the most common reason for what is commonly called "sick-office" syndrome, where large numbers of workers complain of chronic fatigue, headaches, and difficulty breathing. For many years a large government office skyscraper-complex near Ottawa, Canada, the "Place de la Chaudiere" was nicknamed the "Place de la Shoddy-Air" by workers because of sick-office syndrome.

Nasty airborne toxins, called volatile organic compounds (VOCs), originate in paint, flooring, stains, varnishes, plywood, carpeting, insulation and other building products used in your home or office's construction. In addition, today's airtight construction methods help seal these substances in the building, rather than allowing fresh air to dilute and ultimately dispel them. Once VOCs are in your system they are stored in body fat and, with ongoing exposure, can lead to serious health problems. Many of these commonly used building compounds are known carcinogens, but their use is not regulated by government bodies, and the construction industry seems to be in no rush to self-regulate their use. Indoor air quality is a significant health issue, and should be considered in every construction project.

Inside Finishes

Structural materials are not the only things that can off-gas. Important choices can be made about the finishing elements of your space. Particleboard, melamine, and synthetic carpets all off-gas, sometimes for a considerable while. Furniture glues off-gas, as do upholstery stain repelling treatments. Paint off-gasses—oil paint more noticeably than acrylics. For those with sensitive respiratory systems, all of these can pose difficulties. Choosing natural materials, however, can help to minimize the amount of volatile chemicals in your home environment.

Flooring

- *Natural stone*, such as slate, marble, and granite, is an attractive flooring material that suggests solidity and permanence. Stone is inert, long lasting, and will not cause disposal problems later. It will likely be difficult, however, to find out where and how your stone was quarried. Open-pit quarries are unsightly and usually alter the nature of the ecosystem around them during the process of clearing the area. Stone also tends to be a "high-end" finish, and so it is often more expensive than other alternatives.
- *Ceramic tile* is a less expensive alternative to natural stone. Also inert and biodegradable, ceramic tiles are usually glazed to protect their finish. Some tiles will stand up to harder wear than others. It is possible to get unglazed ceramic or clay tiles as well as those that have been painted or treated to look like something else (often natural stone). In general, as with most things, the less processed the tiles are, the more environmentally friendly they are. Ceramic tile is available in a wide

range of prices, so it is not as prohibitive as natural stone; however, a lot of ceramics are produced offshore, and so it is difficult to know what the labor conditions of workers might be like in the place they are produced.

• *Linoleum* is an older flooring material that has made a big comeback in the last few years. Linoleum is a man-made flooring with natural components: linseed oil, pine resin, wood or cork flour, limestone, and pigments. Linoleum is available in sheets or tiles, in a wide array of colors and patterns. Once very common, linoleum was replaced in many applications by vinyl sheet flooring. Linoleum off-gasses very little, is made of widely available renewable resources, and because its pattern goes all the way through rather than being stamped on top, will retain its beauty as it wears, sometimes lasting for decades. Linoleum will not melt or ignite except at very high temperatures, and the fact that linseed oil is inherently antimicrobial, makes it a particularly good choice for kitchens.

• *Natural wood* floors have always been a popular choice. While stains and varnishes will off-gas for a time, the wood itself is problematic only in how it might be harvested. Forestry companies often engage in unsightly and ecologically damaging clear-cutting, and replant rows of trees of a single species, giving forested areas the character of a farm rather than a natural ecosystem. There are niche companies that carry only hardwood that has passed certain forestry management standards (Forest Stewardship Council). It's advisable to do some online research before heading out to shop. There are also companies that specialize in "reclaimed" timber—wood salvaged from demolished buildings and logs pulled from the bottoms of rivers and lakes. These reused woods are often unique in character.

• *Cork* flooring is gaining popularity among renovators. Most cork is grown in Spain and Portugal. The bark of the cork oak (*Quercus suber*) can be harvested every nine to ten years without damaging the tree, which makes it a faster-renewing resource than hardwood. A cork oak tree can produce usable bark for 100 to 150 years. Cork flooring is available both in natural shades and in colors, is warm to the feet, and helps dampen the noise of foot traffic. In addition, the natural properties of cork tend to make it resistant to mold, mildrew, and insects.

Some companies use some "post consumer" cork—wine corks, for example—in the production of their floors. Properly maintained, cork floors are as durable as hardwood.

• *Bamboo* is a relatively new specialty flooring material to the North American marketplace. Timber bamboo grows mainly in China and Vietnam, so there are probably labor-standards issues involved in its production; however, it can be harvested every four years without harming the root system of the plant. Bamboo is a grass rather than a tree, and will therefore continuously send up shoots throughout its growing cycle. Chinese bamboo is grown on slopes unsuitable for other types of plants, and is managed in a traditional manner without irrigation, chemical fertilizers or pesticides. Bamboo is harder than most woods used for flooring, and is thus very durable. It is not, however, grown in the United States due to its negative impact on other plant life.

• *Carpet* varies widely in its environmental friendliness, since it is made from a huge variety of materials and undergoes various production processes. Most of the carpet available is made with synthetic materials—usually nylon—which may off-gas, and may have energy- or water-intensive production processes. Some producers now reclaim old carpets and recycle them into new carpeting. All-wool carpeting is available but expensive. There are also carpetlike offerings made of sisal or seagrass, which are renewable natural materials. As with most of the products listed here, companies vary in their environmental conscientiousness, so the best course of action is to do a little bit of online research before signing on the dotted line.

• *Laminate* floors are usually made to look like hardwood, stone, or tile. The material is made of wood and paper bonded together by resins—natural or synthetic, depending on the manufacturer. When choosing a laminate floor, try to look for a company that uses timber and sawmill by-products for its wood component, organic vegetable inks in its coloring process, and other applications of recycling technology.

MAKING THE CHOICE

Clearly, there are many health hazards lurking around our homes, from the water we drink to the building materials used to make our houses and furniture. There are many factors to take into consideration when choosing where to live, keeping in mind that as pagans, we choose to respect the Earth as our mother, and harm none. Some things to keep in mind regarding where and how you live are

- How old is the house? Can I find out whether asbestos has been used in the insulation? What about other toxins, such as lead-based paint?

- Does the community I am considering moving to fluoridate its water supply? How happy am I about this? Does it use other chemicals to which I might react? Do I have the option of using a well system? Can I afford to buy bottled or springwater?

- Can I walk more lightly upon the Earth by using green cleaning agents in my home and/or office? Will installing something such as a HEPA filter help improve the air quality in my home?

- What are the existing finishes in my home? Can we replace some with more environmentally friendly choices?

- Will anyone take me seriously at work if I start manifesting symptoms of "sick-office" syndrome?

Asbestos

Even when a substance is recognized as harmful, it can be extremely difficult to get it completely out of our lives. Most people remember some things about asbestos, but did you realize that it has shown up in children's crayons as recently as the turn of this century?

The Ancient Greeks named this mineral *asbestos*, meaning "inextinguishable." Its harmful biological effects were noted early on by both the Greek geographer Strabo and the Roman naturalist Pliny the Elder. They both mentioned a sickness of the lungs common to slaves who wove asbestos into cloth. Asbestos was considered magical to the Greeks and Romans, and was used for the wicks of the eternal flames of the vestal virgins, the funeral dress for the cremation of kings, and even as napkins. It is said that Romans cleaned their asbestos napkins by throwing them into a fire, for the asbestos cloth would come out of the fire whiter than when it went in. It was said that Charlemagne had asbestos tablecloths, and asbestos was used for insulating suits of armor. Marco Polo was shown items made from asbestos cloth on his travels.

It was not until 1934, however, that the first case of the lung disease asbestosis was diagnosed. Despite this, through the 1930s and 1940s most of the medical information was withheld from consumers and those who handled asbestos products. During the 1960s, evidence emerged indicating that asbestos fibers posed a dangerous medical risk. In response to the mounting evidence linking asbestos exposure to respiratory disease, the United States federal government began to regulate asbestos in the 1970s through the Environmental Protection Agency and the Occupational Safety and Health Administration. Historically, asbestos was a very popular insulating fiber, and as a result, thousands of home owners have had to hire specialists to remove the asbestos insulation from their homes. Asbestos was so ubiquitous in homes that most families had oven mitts with asbestos pads to shield the hands from hot pots and pans.

Despite the health risks of asbestos exposure, it is still used in many automobile brake pads, and some vermiculite (a gardening product) has had very high levels of asbestos detected. The U.S. government has ruled that exposure to six different types of asbestos (including chrysotile, amosite and crocidolite must be regulated because of their potential to cause disease, including cancers. Two of the six—tremolite and anthophyllite—were found in many crayons tested by a Seattle newspaper in 2000. The contamination allegedly originated from talc (a common ingredient in children's crayons) that came from the area near a closed asbestos mine in New York state. It may be legislated as a toxic substance, but people are still being poisoned by asbestos exposure today.

Toxic Chemicals in the Household

People tend to be sloppy when it comes to handling toxic materials in their homes. Businesses could be fined for handling toxic chemicals the way people often do at home. Items such as poisons, paints, oil, solvents, automotive fluids, cleaners, herbicides and many others must not be dumped into the household garbage, as these bags end up in land-fills. Water then seeps through the landfills and toxic chemicals end up in our water table. In areas that burn garbage, you may end up breathing in your own toxic chemicals!

Almost all municipalities have household chemical drop-off days and/or locations. Household toxins must never be dumped in storm drains; storm drains flow untreated into rivers, lakes and oceans! As well, do not dump stale-dated medicines into the water system, as they can have a profound effect on the fin and gill members of our world.

Recycled and Recycling Materials

Recycling can happen at the global and individual levels. Recycling is second nature to many pagans, for as we consume, we must also put back in order to maintain the balance between the human and the rest of the natural world. Some actions are simple in theory but require planning. When you go to the local grocery store, tell the clerk that you do not need a bag, and use your own reusable canvas bag or backpack. This of course, demands that you keep bags with you (if you drive a car of course, this is easy to do!) or at least remember to bring them when you go to the grocery store. Many secondhand stores have dozens of these inexpensive canvas bags for sale. It is a small step toward caring for our mother the Earth, but it is also a simple one.

Humans consume all sorts of things on a daily basis: food, water, medicines, vehicle-related items, and much more. Our waste products are myriad and varied: how we dispose of them and how much we need in order to meet our desires need to be considered if we are to live our lives as self-aware Wiccans and pagans.

Composting

Composting is a good method to deal with the organic waste generated by a household, particularly in parts of the world where it is warm enough to compost outside twelve months of the year. In the more northerly climes, one can compost outside part of the year at least, and may wish to consider indoor vermicomposting for the rest of the year.

Compost is the end product of a complex feeding pattern involving hundreds of different organisms, including bacteria, fungi, worms, and insects. What remains after these organisms break down organic materials is a rich, earthy substance your garden will love. Understanding how to make and use compost is in the public interest, as the problem of waste disposal is rapidly becoming an urban crisis. Landfills are brimming, and new sites are not easily found. For this reason there is an interest in conserving existing landfill space and in developing alternative methods of dealing with waste. As the old children's song says, "Don't throw your junk in my backyard, my backyard's full!"

Composting replicates nature's system of breaking down materials on the forest floor. Shed and discarded plant parts disappear into the brown crumbly forest floor, creating something called humus. This humus keeps the soil light and fluffy, and is what composting aims to create. Almost any organic vegetable material is suitable for a compost pile. The pile needs a proper ratio of carbon-rich materials, or "browns," and nitrogen-rich materials, or "greens." Among the brown materials are dried leaves, straw, and wood chips. Nitrogen materials are fresh or green, such as grass clippings and kitchen scraps.

Kitchen refuse can include broccoli stems, carrot or orange peelings, tea bags, apple cores, coffee grounds, banana peels—almost everything that cycles through your kitchen. The average household produces more than 200 pounds of kitchen waste every year. Eggshells are a wonderful, mineral-rich addition, but decompose slowly, so should be crushed. Eggshells from which the membrane has been removed can also be crushed and used as a barrier against slugs, which might be tempted to munch on ornamental garden plants like hostas. You can compost meat, but it is not generally recommended. Meat is slow to break down and smells horrible in the process, as well as being a tempting snack for wild critters such as porcupines and raccoons in the North, and javelinas or coyotes in the South. You should not compost vegetables that have had high-fat sauces on them for the same reason. In general, raw vegetables (without dressing) will compost better than cooked ones, because cooking changes the acid and enzyme balance of food.

The Garbage Disposal

The sink-mounted garbage disposal, is a handy way to get rid of some of the kitchen waste in a home, but there is a heavy price to the environment, both in terms of what you are using (vast quantities of water) and what you are not using (compost). Some municipalities discourage residential garbage disposers because of inadequate sewer systems or water supplies. Even if your community allows disposers, using one may cost you more than you think. They use about 2 gallons of water per minute for most sinks, or about 700 gallons per year! Not only can they potentially increase your water bill dramatically, a disposer's added consumption is a real concern in drought areas such as the southwestern United States.

Plastics

A great deal of the planet's used plastic can be recycled, but it faces one huge problem: plastic types must not be mixed for recycling. Great idea in theory, but it is nearly impossible to tell one type from another by sight or touch. Even a small amount of the wrong type of plastic can ruin an entire batch of melted plastic. The plastics industry has responded to this problem by developing a series of symbols, commonly seen on the bottom of plastic containers, to identify plastic types. Keep in mind that not all plastics are being recycled at this time, and not all municipalities offer recycling of all types of plastic. If your municipality does not, you may wish to consider starting a recycling campaign.

Glass, Steel, and Aluminum

Glass, steel, and aluminum are easy to recognize and recycle. Glass bottles must be recycled on their own and not mixed with other types of glass. Clear glass is the most valuable type, while mixed colored glass is nearly worthless to the recycler. Try not to place broken glass in with your recyclables, as it is dangerous and hard to sort.

Paper

Most types of paper can be recycled. Newspaper recycling has been going on profitably for decades, and the recycling of other paper is growing. Because the cost of virgin (never used) paper pulp has soared in the last few years, more plants have been built to use wastepaper. The key to successful recycling is to collect large quantities of clean, well-sorted, uncontaminated, dry paper.

Virtually all paper products are marked when they contain recycled products, but they should also feature the percentage and type of recycled content. The label "recycled paper" is not sufficient, as that label can mean anything from 100 percent recycled paper to 1 percent re-manufactured ends of large paper rolls. From a recycling point of view, the more "post consumer" paper the better, as this term is specific to paper that we, as consumers, have returned to the recycling center. As well, the use of soybean-based inks is increasing as a renewable alternative to harsh, toxic petrochemical inks.

Vehicle Refuse: Motor Oil, Tires, and Car Batteries

All three of these products are easily recycled, which is a good thing, since they are all quite toxic to the environment. Car batteries are usually picked up at certain locations and times: most health food stores and some municipalities have information on when the next pickup(s) for auto batteries will be. As well, many auto supply houses, like Pep Boys in the United States or Canadian Tire in Canada, will accept your dead battery when you purchase a new one (often for a nominal disposal fee).

Tires, whether from cars, motorcycles, or bicycles, should always be properly disposed of. At the beginning of the twenty-first century, about 70 percent of scrap tires were being recycled or exported, compared to a mere 11 percent a decade beforehand. Many old tires can be retreaded. Retreading requires only one third of the crude oil used to make a new tire, which is a real environmental plus. Additionally, almost 15 million scrap tires yearly are chopped, ground, or powdered for use in a wide variety of products such as floor mats, adhesives, gaskets, shoe soles, and electrical insulators.

Used motor oil contains heavy metals and other toxic substances, so it is considered hazardous waste. Recycling used motor oil is easy. Pour used oil into a plastic milk jug and clearly mark it USED MOTOR OIL. Various Internet sources and local phone directories have information on where and when to bring oil for recycling. Motor oil must never be dumped in storm drains; storm drains flow untreated into rivers, lakes and oceans! One quart of oil can kill fish in thousands of gallons of water. Unfortunately, each year, do-it-yourself oil changers improperly dump more oil than the tanker *Exxon Valdez* spilled in Alaska.

Overpackaging

How often have you purchased a CD-ROM game to find out that the large, flashy box contains little more than one thin CD-ROM (within a plastic case) and a booklet with additional information and guarantee card? Talk about overpackaging! Many foods do not need to be boxed and then wrapped inside the box (this is, however, not the same thing as tamper-proof seals on over-the-counter medicines). Each layer of cellophane or plastic increases our use of petroleum-derived substances. From frozen entrees to furniture, manufacturers are often guilty of gross overpackaging.

We have a certain amount of say in this as consumers, in the way that is most often called "voting with your dollar." We can choose to buy our food in bulk amounts and freeze or separate it into smaller packages ourselves. We can buy in bulk with friends ("grocery clubs" are discussed further in Chapter 2). We can choose a brand of item other than our usual one if it is a less-packaged product. We can write to manufacturers and complain about their packaging. In Delta, British Columbia, one cereal company packages their products in recyclable plastic bags. The product costs 20 percent less than its main competitor and uses substantially less packaging (no cardboard box). So less packaging can be both a boon for the consumer and for the producer, if researched properly. There are also legislative options, usually referred to as "producer pays" laws. Germany passed these sorts of laws ten years ago, forcing manufacturers to deal with the waste their packaging creates. European companies have cut down on their packaging now that they have to pay to get rid of the excess. This means there is no incentive to double-pack items or go needlessly glossy. The idea has also spread through Japan, but North American corporations are resisting it.

MAKING THE CHOICE

How do you select products to use for food, entertainment, and transportation? If karma means that what we send out is returned to us threefold, imagine how fast we will drown in our own toxic waste and overpackaging! Ask yourself the following questions:

- Can I purchase a particular item in a smaller package, if most of the bulk is indeed packing material? Is the packaging recycled post consumer paper?

- Can I put pressure on my town hall to increase the items they recycle?

- Is a garbage disposer appropriate in my geographic area? Is my septic tank big enough to handle the waste generated? Is my plumbing up to the task? Is the extra water use worth it?

- What level of impact does this disposer have on the environment around me? Can I dispose of the targeted waste in different ways that serve the Earth? Do I have the right to devote this much water to this process?

- Can I compost, rather than send table scraps into the sink with loads of clean water?

- If there are not suitable recycling services where I live, do I have friends who live where the recycling services are better?

No one is expected to do all these things all the time—only as much as a person's health and situation allow. However, it does behoove us all to think about these things before the Earth we will to our descendants becomes irreparably damaged.

Power Alternatives: Getting off the Grid

North Americans have become very comfortable and complacent with their sources of power, and give little thought to how much energy it takes to run an average American household in the twenty-first century. A mere hundred years ago, there were very few things that required electricity to power them. Imagine life today without your air conditioner and/or heater, computer(s), telephone, radios, clocks, refrigerators and freezers, stoves and dishwashers! We take all these things for granted, and we should not. The fragility of the power infrastructure of North America has been demonstrated twice recently, reminding us how spoiled we really are: the ice storm in the Northeast in 1998, and the massive power blackout in August 2003 across much of the northeastern United States and in the densely populated Canadian province of Ontario. Similarly, during 2003, massive blackouts were reported in England and Chile, and another which originated in Switzerland, affected much of Italy as well.

Many people are turning to alternative energy sources, and/or installing backup systems. After experiencing power loss, many families in the Northeast changed their attractive but not warm electric fireplaces to heat-producing natural gas fireplaces or woodstoves (which, of course, will work even when the electricity is off). Some families purchased gas-powered generators, which, unfortunately, produce higher levels of toxic gases per unit than power from the regular grid. There are numerous alternatives to commercially available electricity. Not all of them will run all the electric toys we are familiar with these days, but here are some viable alternatives that may, at a minimum, reduce a household's reliance on the existing electrical infrastructure.

Hydropower

If you have water flowing through your property, you might be able to set up a small hydroelectric power system to provide your home with electricity. A small or micro system can produce enough electricity for a home, farm, or ranch.

Wind Power

Windmills are a common sight in parts of Europe such as the Netherlands and Bulgaria. Wind power has been used for centuries to move water, sail boats, and grind grain. Only since the mid-1980s, however, has wind power contributed appreciably to North American electricity supplies. The largest generating capacity in the world at present is in Germany, although Denmark is targeting wind as the source of half of its electricity in the near future. The largest public opposition to the Danish plan has to do with the visual intrusion of the "windmill farms." Some of the largest "wind farms" in the world are in California. Major installations in the United States are located in mountain passes where wind is more concentrated. Without the concentration of wind through passes, the density of wind power is usually considered too low to generate electricity commercially.

Geothermal Energy

Geothermal energy is, literally, the heat (*thermal*) of the earth (*geo*). The heat derives from radioactive decay beneath the earth's surface and, in certain locations, it is concentrated enough and close enough to surface waters to be brought to the surface for a variety of purposes. When it is above 150° Celsius (302° F), it is usually considered hot enough to be used to generate electricity, as it is in Italy, El Salvador, Mexico, Japan, Iceland, and Indonesia, among other countries. Several such power plants are currently in operation in California's Imperial Valley. Resources less than 150° Celsius, have broad nonelectric applicability. Indeed, the worldwide potential of such temperatures is many times larger than that used to generate electricity. In Europe, these lower temperatures are used for greenhouses, bathhouses, onion dehydration, laundries, and even hotel space heating. Reykjavik, Iceland's capital, is heated almost entirely with geothermal water.

Solar Power

In 1958, solar electricity was first used within the space program, for satellites. Today, solar power is a source of electricity for houses, offices, and other buildings on a stand-alone basis; even more important, solar power generating systems also supply electricity to the power grid itself.

Solar electricity can be used in three basic forms:

Stand-alone, where no electric grid is available, or a connection to the grid is not made, for some reason. Solar panels produce electricity for lighting, TV and radio, water pumping, refrigeration and tools. Normally, electricity is also stored in batteries, which ensure a steady energy supply both at night and at other times when the solar panels cannot produce electricity, such as on cloudy days.

One example of the financial savings available through using solar power is the solar heating of water. A solar hot water system can save 50 percent or more on the energy bill for domestic hot-water preparation.

Grid-connected, where the source of solar power is connected to the existing infrastructure. Solar panels can be used to produce clean electricity by using daylight and roof space.

Backup, where the existing electric service is of poor or unreliable quality. In the case of a blackout, solar electricity is intended to cover the electricity demand.

MAKING THE CHOICE

Scientists are investigating many more experimental ways to generate power that are promising but not yet considered viable alternatives to the ones discussed here. We know that fossil fuels are exploitative of the environment in their extraction methods and that world reserves are rapidly diminishing. In addition, recently discovered deposits tend to require more intensive extraction procedures than did those deposits that were exploited a century ago. Therefore, can an ethical pagan really afford to keep using things such as oil heating? Fuel cell research is burgeoning but is still some years away from supplying households with their entire power needs. Currently, however, manufacturers are selling dual-power (hybrid) cars in limited numbers. These use both petroleum products and hydrogen fuel cells. If you can afford this cutting-edge technology, it certainly helps cut down on the exploitation of our natural resources. Some questions to ask:

- Do I live in a part of the world that gets enough sunshine per year to use solar power to supplement or replace my existing source?

- Can I at least cut back my use of traditional power by using wind power?

- How expensive is it to switch my heating infrastructure?

- If my electricity market is competitive, do companies disclose how much of their production is achieved through alternative power sources?

The "Green" Environment

We do not often think of lawns, septic systems, and plants, yet these are part of our environment just as certainly as our home and power source. If we own, or even rent, a house, we need to think about the ways in which we maintain the land around the home. Composting and septic tanks are related topics, as residents who use septic systems and are not on a municipal sewer system need to be vigilant about substances they flush into the septic system, hence the usefulness of a compost bin or two. The person who chooses to be a true *paganus,* or rural dweller, needs to think about septic tanks and microbes.

Septic Tanks

A basic septic tank system treats wastewater in a three-stage format. First, waste exits the house through a pipe and enters the septic tank.

There, solids settle downward while grease and scum float to the top. Next, the liquid waste (effluent) flows from the tank through a distribution box to the absorption area. Finally, the effluent arrives at the absorption field, where it is distributed into the soil for treatment. If things are working correctly, microorganisms on the surface of the soil around the absorption area consume the organic pollutants in the effluent before the effluent itself reaches the groundwater. Meanwhile, the solids that settled to the bottom of the tank form a sludge that ultimately decomposes. The solids, bacteria, and nutrients in the liquid waste are removed as they percolate through various levels of soil. This natural process safely treats the liquid before it reaches groundwater.

There are ways of increasing the efficiency of a septic tank system. Most septic tank distributors offer various additives that can be put into the tank to aid in breaking down the effluent. As well, there are hydrogen peroxide systems, which differ considerably from traditional systems, and various microorganisms, sold as "live" cells, which happily munch on wastewater, cleaning it before it reaches the soil level. Septic system users must take extra care as to what gets "flushed" or washed down the sink, as some household chemicals can damage the microorganisms within the septic system, while others will actually corrode the holding tank and/or other components. Pay attention to the owner's information for your particular septic system, and try to keep that microbial community healthy and happy, or you could find yourself facing a multi-thousand dollar septic system repair job.

The Grass Lawn

Many people love having a green, lush-looking front and/or back lawn on their property. Lawns can be beautiful and do have some positive functions. They retain water, which is helpful during rainy seasons, and they actually do lower the ambient temperature around the house by a few degrees, increasing comfort on hot days. They also keep dust down in dry areas, and filter out many of the nasty contaminants in rainwater (acid rain). However, that lush lawn often comes at a price to the environment.

According to the U.S. National Wildlife Federation, the following are some of the environmental costs of lawns:

- Water wastage: 30 percent of water consumed on the East Coast goes to watering lawns, while 60 percent of water used on the West Coast is lawn related.

- Emission pollution: Per hour of operation, a power lawn mower emits ten to twelve times as much hydrocarbon as a typical auto. A "weedeater" emits twenty-one times more and a leaf blower thirty-four times more.

- Pesticide effects: Where pesticides are used, 60 to 90 percent of earthworms are killed. Not only are earthworms important for soil health, but they are also food for many local birds.

WEEDS

An environmentally friendly and fairly new way to control weeds in your lawn is the result of a serendipitous discovery using a corn by-product. Corn gluten meal products offer a nontoxic, effective alternative to chemical-based weed products for weed control in gardens and lawns. Among the weeds controlled with corn gluten meal are common lawn nuisances such as crabgrass, dandelions, purslane, and lambsquarters. Additionally, maintaining lawn pH at the proper level discourages weed growth. Dandelions are particularly fond of poorly maintained grass, so simply keeping the lawn healthy will dramatically reduce the need to use pesticides. Some municipalities, concerned about public health and water quality, have enacted bylaws banning the residential use of pesticides. Many have also reduced or eliminated their use of chemical pesticides in public parks and grassy medians. If your municipality has done neither, you may wish to write a letter to your local town council.

It is wise to remember, also, that many of what we now call "weeds" on our lawns are actually useful herbs and plants. If "The Earth is our mother, we must take care of her" is true, we should not be pouring damaging pesticides onto her body. Rather, we should be utilizing her bounty: dandelions for dandelion wine, dandelion-root tea, and a fresh mixed salad in spring. Plantain is edible, particularly the leaves, and in a poultice is good for cuts. Milkweed is good for athlete's foot (and is also the main food for monarch butterflies!), and many more "weeds" actually help process poisonous chemicals, such as dioxins, out of the lawn itself. Perhaps a "truce" can be called, and a balance maintained between the pure lawn and the natural salad bowl.

LAWN SIZE

How much lawn do you *really* need and/or want? For the single person living alone, the responsibility of lawn maintenance falls on his/her shoulders. That could mean acres of grass cutting, fertilizing, planting, growing, harvesting, and all the other green-space-related jobs. Perhaps in some cases, smaller is better. You have options with regard to how you cut your grass. If you have a lawn, this has to be done by humans, unless there are sheep or goats to do the job!

People with large acreage often go the riding lawn mower route, but as noted above, they do emit polluting waste gases. Manual hand mowers are nonpolluting, but they are a lot more work; a balance will have to be found in your individual lifestyle between the burning of fossil fuels in your riding mower and the amount of time demanded by a rotary (push) mower. There are, however, much better designed manual lawn mowers on the market today; these are not as heavy and are much easier to push than the old steel mowers. New materials and technologies also allow them to retain their blade-edge sharpness far longer. Residents who must purchase a riding mower should consider a "mower-sharing group" with their neighbors to make optimum use of it.

PLANTINGS

Choosing vegetation for a green space is an important decision. Some plants and trees, such as lavender and pine, give off common allergens. Many people are very allergic to pollens. Alien plants—those not native to your region—are often not a good choice as many of these also irritate the respiratory system. Mulberry and grass are two high-allergen plants that are native to the Eastern parts of North America. They have been transported into the deserts of the Southwest by folks from back East who miss their trees and lawns, and by those wanting to emulate eastern styles. Consequently, the areas where asthma sufferers have moved since the 1950s to get away from allergens are now top allergy locations (particularly Phoenix and Tucson, Arizona). There are ways to minimize risk in choosing plants for a garden, provided you are willing to do a certain amount of research. Certain types of leaf patterns indicate a tree reproduces asexually through wind-borne pollen (that blows into your nose), while in some species, it is primarily either the male or female trees that are the pollen culprits. (The offenders sometimes having up to ten times more pollen than the opposite sex!)

Water is always an issue when discussing flowers and plants, whether you live in a green area or an arid one. For instance, deserts are arid regions and average less than ten inches of precipitation per year. In these areas, it is wise to use plants that are native to that area of the world. This is called *xeriscaping*.

There are various types of plants suitable for xeriscaping your lawn, as well as grass substitutes. Cacti, also called *xerophytes*, usually have their own unique means of storing and conserving water. They often have few or no leaves, as leaves demand more energy and water to be maintained. Some plants have adapted to arid environments by growing extremely long roots, which allow them to acquire moisture at or near the water table. These are called *phreatophytes*. Using a mix of these two types of desert plants can produce a lovely garden while respecting the need to conserve water in such areas.

A couple of other options are available for use in dry areas as alternatives to grass lawns. One of the more popular desert choices is the "pebble" garden and/or lawn. White- or green-painted pebbles are used to simulate a lawn, and can be raked into different patterns, much as is done in Japan at some Buddhist temples, as a meditation of sorts.

You can xeriscape in non-arid regions as well, by using plants native to the region. Indigenous plants often require less care, as they are already well adapted to the climate, meaning they will need fewer additional waterings and less winter protection in cold areas. There are many attractive and vigorous ground covers that can be used as grass replacements in all or part of a yard. These include lamiums, woolly thyme, low growing sedum, aguga (bugleweed), goutweed, periwinkle and low-growing phlox. All of these are perennials, and will tend to spread in surface area throughout the years.

MAKING THE CHOICE

Some of the questions to consider when planning an immediate "outside" environment are:

- How green do I need the environment around me to feel happy?

- Am I "up" to tending high-maintenance lawns, plants, and trees? Is a fancy, manicured lawn my "style"? Can I start a healing herb garden or a food herb garden? Could I plant herbs and trade cuttings with my neighbors? Most perennials will require periodic division—surplus plants can be traded or given as housewarming gifts.

- Have I imposed a personal preference for high-water greenery in a land better suited to arid land plants?

- Could I install a ritual circle in the backyard? Will this mean walling off the yard from the neighbors if I work skyclad?

- Instead of a lawn, would a pebble garden be a better choice and a warm place to meditate?

- Are plants "alive" to me, or are they just ornaments?

- Does being aware of plants' spirits change how I care for them and interact with them? Do I interact with them at all? Do I think I should?

Environmental Activism and Environmental Extremism

Environmentalism has a wide spectrum of levels of advocacy and activism. Those who pay lip service to "An ye harm none, do what ye will" must keep it in mind when acting socially toward the environment. Some organizations are radical and step beyond the boundaries of nonviolent action into violence in order to draw the media to their causes. We do not have the right to inflict even more harm on the environment, no matter how well-meaning we may be in our actions. Please make a point to research before joining an organization that claims to work on behalf of the environment and/or natural world.

Basic environmental conservation can be as simple as going to a local green space (park, side of highway) and picking up litter: perhaps you and/or your group would like to sponsor a mile of highway and keep it maintained. This little environmental action can become a sacred act by starting or ending it with a meditation or ritual. There are dozens of small ways that one can have a direct effect on the people who make decisions for you (e.g., various levels of government). They are open to everyone, not only neopagans: perhaps your coven or a group of your friends can take some positive action at the local or state/provincial level. For each bill that is passed, someone had to come up with the idea, do the research, and then lobby, petition, and lobby some more for the idea to make the long trek to legally enacted statute. Some of the things you can do as an individual or as a coven include

- Informing yourself about your local politicians' positions on environmental issues. How do they vote on such issues? Encourage your friends to vote—it is both right and responsibility, and as Starhawk has said, "You cannot change the world by just praying" (*The Burning Times*, videotape, Donna Read, producer, National Film Board of Canada).

- Attending public meetings on rezoning, placement of power wires, cuts to public utilities, etc. Attend and publicize "town hall" meetings with local politicians. As a witch, use the powers of the elements to strengthen your resolve and help you speak for the trees and animals who do not, or cannot, speak with the human world. If "the Earth is our mother," act like a responsible child, not a petulant, lazy one.

- Circulating petitions. Many types of petitions are nonbinding, but they do mobilize people and place issues before the public eye, which is very important. A petition is a request for elected officials to do something that you and your neighbors—their constituency—think is important.

- Volunteering your time for the other spiritual denizens of your community. Local SPCA or Humane Society shelters use volunteers to walk dogs, cuddle cats, and whatever else needs to be done to keep up the quality of life for unwanted and unloved nonhumans. Or offer your time at the local wild-bird or wild-animal sanctuary if there is one in your area. You could also volunteer time or resources to environmental action organizations such as the one mentioned below.

Dragon Environmental Network

From their website at www.dragonnetwork.org:

Based in the United Kingdom, Dragon is a decentralized network with a set of basic principles. For over ten years, Dragon has been very actively working with other environmental groups and individuals. Their basic premise is the blending of environmentalism and neopagan magical thought, and they have many novel ideas in how to incorporate both approaches into an ethical, self-aware neopagan lifestyle. They describe their basic worldview thusly:

- Dragon believes that the Earth is Sacred

- Dragon is a decentralized network—a web of people working together on local, national and international issues

- Dragon combines practical environmental work with ecomagic. Each is as important as the other, and it is through this synergy that they focus their vision for change.

- Dragon is committed to Non-Violent Direct Action

Anyone who shares these principles and aims is welcome to join, regardless of their Religion or Spiritual path.
Dragon aims to:

- Increase general awareness of the sacredness of the Earth

- Encourage Pagans to become involved in conservation work

- Encourage Pagans to become involved in environmental campaigns.

- Develop the principles and practice of magical and Spiritual action for the environment (which we call "eco-magic")

Eco-Paganism

Eco-paganism is a form of paganism that is rooted in acknowledging and respecting the natural world. *The Wild* as it is sometimes called by deep ecologists is the natural environment that has not been damaged by mankind. One of the prime tenets of eco-paganism is in taking an active stand to stop what Dragon and other eco-pagans call the rape of the planet.

At the heart of eco-magic is non-violence, with its practice limited only by the individual's imagination. It is likely that those forms of magic that are based in hierarchy, and/or work by controlling spirits are not suitable for eco-magic. Some of the forms that eco-magic can take include:

- *The Spirit of Place*: Some of the most effective eco-magic involves working with the Genius Loci of the place, the Devas or Faery Folk. Let them know you are there to be of aid, and offer your help. They can often use the energy you raise far better than humans can.

- *Mythic "Spirit of the Place"*: In the United Kingdom and other old countries, there is a very strong and tangible "spirit of the place" associated with every village, town, and even grassy meadow. Many families have been on the same land (ancestral lands) for hundreds, or even thousands, of years. They are the people who "know" the land, and have a blood-tie to the place—*their* place.

The Sense of Place

For North Americans not of aboriginal ancestry, there is not often a "sense of place" calling to their bones. Canadians and Americans are very mobile people (some studies indicate that we move every five years!), and we do not have nearly the same attachment to a physical place as many in Europe have. Even those whose families came over to the continent on the *Mayflower*, or with Jacques Cartier, are practically newcomers to the land itself. One prominent English pagan who worked in North America for a few years expressed her dismay at how an entire culture, an entire people, could be so divorced from any ties to their land. Having lived most of her life in England, it had never occurred to her that North American neopagans have stronger ties to "national" or "regional" identity than they do to the land itself.

Many North American neopagans do have a sense of place. It is, however, more symbolic and ideal than actual. It is a sense of "mythic" place: the "old country," the "lantzmann." People of Irish ancestry think of an idealized mythical Ireland (not the Ireland of sectarian violence and/or potato famines); Scandinavians fill their hearts and bones with mythic images of Nordic and Germanic gods, goddesses, and places as part of their identity. A mythic place fills the soul with a sense of belonging, replacing the rootlessness that so typifies North Americans of European ancestry and/or heritage. For some this goes as far as learning a "mother tongue"; others learn folk dances and/or folk songs, or own a "national" costume.

It is this sense of mythic place that also leads many neopagans in North America to pantheons of goddesses and gods from their mythic origin locations. Celtic reconstruction religion is not quite the same as Wicca— in Celtic reconstructionism, one tries to live religiously according to the values and practices of the Celtic peoples, while Wicca is an adaptation of Celtic religion. Others turn to Hellenic reconstructionism, Asatrur (Scandinavian/Nordic), or Romuva (Lithuanian reconstructionism). Some of these paths have been barely below the surface during the reign of other religions in their lands, while others are being rebuilt from small fragments of memory and recorded practice. They are all, however, part of a larger effort to reclaim one's mythic place in the universe.

Modern practitioners living in North America can try to make contact with the spirits of the place where they live in one of two ways: They can either turn to their ancestral "spirit of the place" and see if this resonates (e.g., if a certain species of tree was thought of as a tree of knowledge in your "old country," you might want to see if there is one growing in your area to consult), or they can use the concept of "spirit of this place" and see if they can contact the spirit of the place where they are doing their eco-magic.

As most North American pagan practice takes place on Native American ancestral land, it behooves a coven or individual to find out what was considered the right way to contact these spirits by the particular tribes from that area. Many Native spirits will respond to offerings of tobacco; others prefer sweetgrass, or sage. They key is to pay homage to the spirit of place, no matter where you are. When all else fails, offer fresh water to the spirits of the place. No one refuses an offer of a drink of water when it is offered in friendship.

The ecology of the physical and spiritual universe is beyond us, so before one does anything, it is probably a good idea to do divination. How far to go with this principle is up to the individual, who should bear in mind that Gaia will have a broader view of things than any one person, and that any action be informed of this. Cast the runes/tarot, scry, meditate or whatever, but try to ensure that your actions are in accordance with the "big picture."

Eco-Magic Issues

GEMSTONES AND CRYSTALS

Before buying stones, remember to ask where the piece comes from and how it was mined. Many crystals have been strip mined, which is very harmful to the land. When one handles them, they will often have a feeling of being psychically fractured or distressed.

> As pagans who care about the land we will not support strip mining. Open cast or strip mining excavates large chunks of land to extract precious minerals without needing to tunnel below the surface. It can cause short and long term environmental damage through accelerated soil erosion and through acid water damage.
> —David Rankine, at Dragon Environmental Network:
> www.dragonnetwork.org

Along with strip mining, there are numerous other negative effects that many of us do not take into consideration on third-world communities resulting directly from the jewelry trade. Small artisanal mines keep popping up in poorer countries such as Mali, Thailand, and Sri Lanka, drawing more and more people to them in the hope of a better quality of life. Unfortunately, the small mines often mean sexual exploitation, child labor abuses, and poor health and safety conditions for the miners.

SILVER

Along with gemstones, neopagans are very fond of silver jewelry. It is very hard to trace where the silver in your ring comes from, but most silver mining in poorer countries causes environmental problems. Waste management, pollution of groundwater supplies, acids entering the ground, and pollution caused by some of the other metals found around silver are issues to be considered when thinking about buying a new piece of ritual jewelry. One option is to purchase something old or antique. This way you are not patronizing the "new jewelry" business driving the demand for inexpensive gems and metals.

HERBS

Many of us plant gardens. Ornamental gardens aim to look lovely; others feature herbs and plants that have food and/or healing properties (sometimes called "witch gardens"). The cuttings and plants in the garden have to come from somewhere, and have to be harvested in some way. Collect only abundant species of native and non-native plants that grow wild in your area. "An ye harm none" means remembering certain things when gathering plants for the garden, and remembering the same adage when we harvest them with our thanks.

Do not upset the balance of nature when harvesting from nature. By treading gently and not tossing the area around while looking for plants, pagans respect the four-footed, scrabbling, winged, and slithering members of the environment. Never take all that is there, as the animals will need some food, and the plants themselves need some propagation stock. Do your research first and be sure that what you harvest is not endangered or protected in the jurisdiction within which you are harvesting. Most countries have nonprofit or government extension offices that can tell you if a given flower and/or plant is legal to harvest (and not endangered). Try to collect from stems and seeds, and whenever possible, do not dig up roots. Know your plants!

It is usually illegal to collect plants from federal, state, or provincial lands, and it is polite and ethical to obtain permission before harvesting from private property as well. Whether public or private area, put in more than you take out. Pick up trash that you find, and carry it off the property. Leave none of your own. (An ye harm none . . . !)

David Rankine of the Dragon Environmental Network offers some very fine tips on how to harvest herbs magically:

> Visualize a gap in the energy, so that the point at which you cut or break the plant is "dead", and the plant will not be hurt by the cut. Next, seal the wound by gently holding the cut part of the plant and channelling healing energy to the plant. If a whole plant is gathered, it is best to use a magical tool such as a consecrated knife to loosen the earth around the roots before pulling the plant out. An offering should immediately be made to the plant spirit (such as milk and honey poured onto the earth it has been pulled up from), and if the plant is in seed, return some of the seeds to the earth.

Be magically proactive while harvesting. Harvest with an attitude of respect and thankfulness to the plant world that gives us such useful herbs and flowers. Offer water when you sit down to refresh yourself, and visualize the area you are in as healthy, blooming, and fruitful. This is one way of offering some of your energies in return for the energy given by the forest to grow what you accept from it. Last, do not forget to give back from where you have harvested! If you have been successful and grown your own plants from wild seeds, return some of your plants to the wild in order to restore their population.

Incorporating Choices into Your Environment

Clearly there are many "hidden" things to consider when looking at an ethical, pagan way of life. Some have to be balanced with one's means (e.g., can you afford to buy the unbleached organic cotton shirt or do you have to go with the sweatshop-generated offering from the big box store?), others with one's lifestyle. For example, you may want a witch's garden in your backyard, but you work odd hours and do not have the time to invest in the care and maintenance of the plants. Perhaps growing some herbs in the house would be a fair compromise: you get some fresh herbs for cooking, and improve the air quality within your home.

However you choose to live your life, remember to walk lightly upon the earth, both directly (in how you harvest and plant), and indirectly (in how you shop and choose materials for projects). These are the sorts of decisions neopagans should be conscious of in order to live an ethical pagan lifestyle, rather than an ethical lifestyle defaulting to "majority" ways of making decisions about their responsibility to, and within, the environment.

Resources

City of Greeley, Colorado, Water Conservation site (how to lower water usage in office and commercial facilities), www.ci.greeley.co.us/2n/Page.asp?fkorgID=44&pageURL=office

The Septic System Owner's Manual, by Lloyd Kahn, Blair Allen, and Julie Jones, illustrated by Peter Aschwanden, ISBN 0-936070-20-X

Survey no. 23-2003. Survey of chemical compounds in textile fabrics, cosponsored by the Danish Environmental Protection Agency and the Federation of Danish Textile and Clothing Industries, online at www.mst.dk/chemi/01081800.htm

CHAPTER 2

Lifestyle and Health

As our spirits inhabit our bodies, "Thou Art God/dess" becomes an integral part of lifestyle and health choices. In essence, how we choose to live in the temple of our bodies is how we choose to worship the gods and goddesses: "The Body is a Temple for the Gods." It would be lovely to do away with the material in favor of the spiritual, but some people enjoy both and choose to have both in their lives. Where and how you consume, whether it is a material or food product, can make an enormous impact on the quality of your life.

Making Purchases

The media creates great peer pressure to acquire, to have, and to hold things. It is hard to live under the bombardment of consumer culture when one is trying to live a leaner life, a less encumbered life, or a life with a minimal income level.

Need versus want is something we take too little time to consider on a daily basis. How many of us remember going up to a parent and whining, "Oh, I NEEEEED this, because everyone has one," and being told, "I don't care what everyone else has, you aren't everyone else!" As hard as it is to hold the line as a parent, it is even harder to hold the line for oneself. Living within your lifestyle and means is a real challenge; some statistics show that the average American household carries over $8,000 in credit-card debt alone. This "buy now, pay later" syndrome does not reflect the wisdom that one might expect from a people who affirm to themselves "Thou art God/dess." If you are indeed powerful, and a reflection of the goddesses and gods, then surely one can wait for something, and not imperil your budget and/or lifestyle by indulging in "I want it now" thinking.

Most working people are no more than three paychecks from being on the street. This is a frightening fact. Three missed paychecks are enough to fall badly behind in credit-card payments, rent or mortgage, car payments, and utilities. More people could take a page from the Church of Jesus Christ of Latter-Day Saints (the Mormons), whose prophets urge the faithful to save, to can their own produce from their gardens, and get out of debt as quickly as possible. It is less immediately satisfying to those who are consumption-oriented, but it is a prudent way of handling things.

As a rule, neopagans seem to come in two financial brackets: very well-to-do and impoverished. Academic studies of neopagans have shown that their median income (the income at which half earn more, and half earn less) is below the median income for mainstream society. The financially comfortable in the neopagan community can be prone to impulse buying, sometimes having large collections of amber and/or silver jewelry, state-of-the-art computers, electronic gadgets, and artistic ritual tools. Individuals in this position often have large houses and carry substantial mortgages. Unfortunately, the collapse of the economy's tech sector in the late 1990s showed exactly how precarious the lifestyles of many of these well-to-do young Craft practitioners really were—within a year, approximately three quarters were unemployed and selling their homes. Many of them were still unemployed a year, or even two years, later.

Products can be extremely tempting to indulge in. For the well-heeled pagan, patience is a virtue. Do you *need* to purchase that new car or book? Is it that you *want* the item instead? If the purchase is not a sale item, can it wait? Could you borrow and/or lease rather than buy and own? Some things are lovely to own but costly to maintain, while leasing or renting the same item can often be more cost effective. As well, leasing or renting polluters, such as gas-powered automobiles and/or lawn mowers, is often a better environmental choice. (Consider pooling with four friends for that snow blower or lawnmower.)

If you want to save a little money while lessening your impact on the environment, why not consider buying used, rather than new, items? A brand-new car loses a huge percentage of its overall value the moment you drive it off the lot: maybe a year-old model (or clearance at the beginning of the next model year) would do just as well. How about used infant clothing and/or toys? Babies outgrow their clothing so quickly that it is almost criminal how much you pay for brand-name baby garments. If you extrapolated the cost per inch of fabric to adult clothing, we'd all be wearing solid gold dresses and pants! More of the ways you can save money and use your cash wisely are discussed in Chapter Five, which deals with money issues.

Shop for clothing and/or kitchen items at secondhand stores as well. Many of them are sponsored by charities as diverse as Big Brothers and Big Sisters, the Red Cross, cancer societies, diabetes societies, and so on. When choosing secondhand shops that are affiliated with charities, be aware that some, including the Salvation Army/Red Shield, are not simply charities caring for the poor, nor are they "just" secondhand stores. The Salvation Army is a religious institution, and all funds from their sales and donations go to Salvation Army church-sponsored causes *only*. The doctrines of some charities are extremely moralistic and agressive. Please be sure to know what kind of organization you're supporting, and consider the options!

Financial Balance

Balancing your budget and your ethics can be a tightrope act at the best of times. When you are too poor to have options, it can be a near-intolerable way to "live." It's all nice and good to discuss choices of secondhand shops, but what if the Salvation Army is the only second-hand shop in your community, and you cannot afford new clothes? Then buy at the "Sally Ann"! Their clothing is very reasonably priced. In this case you have to make the choice between survival and ethics. Sometimes you can make ethical decisions about how to survive— other times it simply is not an option. Do not feel guilty about your choices: if you make them with thought and intent, then they are the best choices for you. No one else lives in your house, in your shoes, or on your budget!

"Scratch and Dent" Products

Seconds and "slightly damaged" items can save the smart shopper a lot of money on everything from food to clothing. Most "factory outlet stores" are in fact just branches of the retail store that might feature a special or two. Real factory outlets are usually located at the back or side of the retail store or manufacturing location. Occasionally a manufacturer will hold a special clearance of factory "seconds" and other slightly flawed materials at a large area like a community center or sports arena. These are definitely worth going to, particularly when they do not charge an entrance fee. If they charge a fee, they are probably being run by a "jobber," or middleman, who buys up seconds and resells them at a profit. Talk to your friends: there may be a factory outlet in your area.

A major place to watch for "scratch and dent" items is the grocery store. Many national stores will often have two types of bargains on foods: soon-to-be stale and dated items, and those that are dented or bruised. The former applies to everything from meat cuts to canned sauces. Meats are usually marked down 24 to 48 hours before their "sell by" date; they can be eaten that day, or frozen for future use. Other, less perishable sale items such as sauces and condiments can be placed on your shelves for later use. You can plan an entire meal on "scratch and dent" food: for instance, four-packs of green peppers can be combined with a discounted teriyaki sauce, a dented marked-down can of sliced pineapple, and marked down beef. Add some rice from home, and you have the ingredients for stuffed peppers!

With proper refrigeration, eggs can keep for weeks, even a month or more. To be certain, crack the egg into a small bowl before you add it to your bread, cake, or meatloaf. If the egg has turned bad you will know immediately: the highly sulfurous smell of a rotten egg is impossible to miss, unless you have no olfactory sensory function. After smelling a rotten egg the first time you will never forget again what a "bad egg" smells like!

Listen to your common sense, rather than the "best if sold by" and "sell by" dates on your food. You will help the environment by not wasting food, and help your budget. Numerous websites address the approximate period a given type of food will be fresh, as well as how long different types of foods can remain in a freezer. Think creatively about how you buy common items and research the options!

Sales Opportunities

Certain retailers will choose to have sales that are for "special" customers," members only, or held around holidays. These are not always predictable, but some times of year are more likely to have unannounced sales than others. End of year is a good time for some sales, particularly for cars; other sales occur around Christmas and Easter in the Christian calendar. Even if you don't identify with the holiday, you can share in the goodwill being imparted at those times of year.

Watch out for "members only" warehouse clubs; they are not designed with your budget in mind! Yes, you do save somewhat by buying in bulk, but actually not that much. Most of these membership clubs expect you to pay a yearly fee that, although not overly pricey, does have to be factored into the "savings" you get for everything you subsequently purchase. Bulk prices are often lower than buying at full retail price, but a smart shopper already watches the weekly sales flyers for good discounts at the retailers. Buying six cans of brand-name soup at a bulk/membership club can be more expensive than buying the same six cans of the same brand on sale at your local grocery store. Also, a large percentage of the goods offered at the membership clubs are made offshore in sweatshops and/or at the hands of child laborers, another ethical consideration for the pagan consumer. Will the membership-store pair of pants last longer than the ones you buy secondhand at the thrift shop? As with so many other things in the world, what appears to be a bargain often is not.

Ethical Shopping

MAQUILADORAS

There are ethical issues in how an item is manufactured. There are numerous forms of unofficial "slave labor" still perpetuated around the world today, and in our increasingly global market, we may inadvertently support these by what we buy and/or where we buy it. Mexico is a source of many inexpensive consumer goods for North America, and the *maquiladora* system helps perpetuate their poverty and our supply of inexpensive goods.

There are over one million Mexicans working in over 3,800 maquiladora manufacturing plants in northern Mexico near the American border. Mexican labor is inexpensive, and courtesy of NAFTA (the North American Free Trade Agreement), taxes and customs fees are almost nonexistent. Maquiladoras are owned by American, Japanese, and European countries, and some could be considered sweatshops, employing young women (maquiladoristas) who labor for as little as 50 cents an hour, working for ten hours a day, six days a week.

Many of the maquiladoristas, most of whom are single, live in shantytowns lacking electricity and water. These shantytowns spring up around the factory cities, as the cost of living around the Mexico/US border is often more than 30 percent higher than that farther south in Mexico. It is difficult to know which brand names use the labor from maquiladora shops, as they often export parts (e.g., components for computers, unfinished clothing) and the finishing work is done in the States.

CHILD LABOR

UNICEF estimates that approximately 246 million children are engaged in child labor. Of those, almost three-quarters (171 million) work in hazardous situations or conditions, such as mine work, agricultural work (particularly around chemicals and pesticides), and working around dangerous machinery. Child labor is defined as children below twelve years of age working in any economic activity at all, plus those aged twelve to fourteen years who are engaged in harmful work. The United

Nations classifies the worst forms of child labor as those involving children being enslaved, forcibly recruited, prostituted, trafficked, forced into illegal activities, and exposed to hazardous work.

BIG-BOX STORES

What is a "big box" store? A good definition can be found at the Wordspy website (www.wordspy.com):"A large-format store, typically one that has a plain, box-like exterior and at least 100,000 square feet of retail space." Opposition to the big-box type of store is increasing, as their sales plan of selling everything under one roof is forcing smaller family-owned stores out of business. Big-box stores are blamed by some for the demise of America's small and mid-size towns. Small towns often lose their small businesses, finding themselves dominated by big-box retailers filled with employees scrambling to keep low-wage jobs.

In a 2004 opinion piece for the *Seattle Times*, journalism professor Floyd J. McKay of Western Washington University commented that Wal-Mart was being sued in some forty cases alleging various abuses of labor laws, and in 2003, the company was reported as employing numerous illegal aliens as janitors. Wal-Mart has successfully opposed unionization and frequently pays well below the wages of competing stores. The cumulative effects of low wages, high-pressure jobs, and the chronic battles against unionization mark Wal-Mart as one retailer that does not appear to work within any of the neopagan beliefs. Make your best effort to stay in balance with the natural world;"An ye harm none, do what ye will"; respect the Law of Return/Karma. Stores may offer the consumer low prices, but at what cost is this being generated?

MAKING THE CHOICE

How does one decide where to shop and what to purchase? Perhaps your budget does not let you make all your choices on ethical grounds, but at least you can be informed. Some questions to consider:

• Can I afford to choose to buy four items at a big-box store and buy one at a higher-priced, more ethical retailer?

- Can I do a little bit of Internet shopping before I go to purchase, and discover if certain brand names use maquiladoras?

- Can I research organizations with "hot lists" of manufacturers and/or brand names that use child labor?

- Can I, perhaps with friends, make some of the items I was going to buy at a store?

Living Well

There are many choices to make about how we care for ourselves, our personal "temple for the gods and goddesses." If cash flow is not an issue, health certainly is. While we want to be comfortable and indulge ourselves, there is a wide range of considerations about what we "nourish" our temples with.

Ethical Foods

Many people today behave as if they think their food comes shrink-wrapped in Styrofoam packages from the local grocery store. The hectic urban lifestyle has created a market for fast and easy food. Few urbanites have any "relationship" with where their food comes from, and many frozen foods are overpackaged. A cartoon by Gary Trudeau, creator of "Doonesbury," illustrates a young child leaning over the pot as his mother stirs, saying, "What's for dinner, Mom?" In the next panel he walks away smacking his lips saying "My favorite! Boil-in-bags!" Convience, but at what cost?

There are otions for local and organic foods. Many Craft practitioners choose to live vegetarian, or vegan, lifestyles primarily based on the credo "The Earth is sacred"(and by extrapolation, all things in and on it). There are many horror stories arising from factory farming practices, from bovine spongiform encephalopathy (and its human variant, Creutzfeldt-Jakob disease) to variations of avian flu and SARS (severe acute respiratory syndrome). Even individuals who choose not to be vegetarians for ethical reasons must pay attention to how mass-farming methods affect our food supply and our health.

Beef

A series of mergers and acquisitions over the last twenty-five years has resulted in more than 80 percent of the U.S. beef cattle industry being concentrated in the hands of four multinational corporations. This sort of mass farming causes suffering for the animals and has resulted in the introduction of antibiotics and other chemical agents into the animals through feed and other treatments. There are numerous questions as to how much this massive antibiotic dosing might contribute to the development of "super bugs" (bacteria that are resistant to current antibiotic treatments), and how growth hormone additives to animal feed may cause children to reach puberty much earlier than in past generations.

Factory farms also practice the feeding of ground-up cattle by-products to live cattle as a standard use of the "waste materials." This has been linked to bovine spongiform encephalopathy ("mad cow" disease), a horrific disease that destroys the central nervous system and brain of the affected animal. BSE does not disappear when the animal is slaughtered: it can be given to humans who eat certain organs from these cows, and can lie dormant for a very long time. In humans, this is called Creutzfeldt-Jakob disease.

Most beef cattle spend the last few months of their lives in feedlots, crowded into manure-laden holding pens, where the air is thick with bacteria and the animals are at risk for respiratory diseases. Feedlot cattle are routinely implanted with growth-promoting hormones, and they are fed unnaturally rich diets designed to fatten them quickly and profitably. Although cattle are supposed to be humanely rendered unconscious before the slaughtering process begins, this is not always the case, and some animals suffer horribly before they finally die at the abattoir.

Veal

Veal is a by-product of the dairy industry. Most urban people do not give a lot of thought as to where their fresh milk comes from, but a cow must be pregnant and give birth in order to produce milk. Half the calves are female, and these are used in part to replace the older members of the dairy herd. Unfortunately for the male calves, they have little use in a dairy business and are earmarked for beef and/or veal usage. Within days of birth, male cattle are taken from their mothers.

Calves are confined in crates measuring just two feet wide, often chained by the neck to restrict all movement so that they cannot turn around, stretch, or even lie down. This severe confinement makes the calves' meat "tender" since their muscles cannot develop. Along with having their movement restricted, the calves are fed a liquid milk-substitute diet deficient in both iron and fiber. It produces the pale flesh fancied by "gourmets" as veal. At approximately sixteen weeks of age, these animals are slaughtered for the kitchen table, sold with tags such as "milk-fed" or "white" veal.

Poultry

At factory farms, each chicken is given less than a half square foot of space, while turkeys are each given less than three square feet of room. Shortly after hatching, both chickens and turkeys are "debeaked," a procedure whereby the ends of their beaks are snipped off, ostensibly to stop them from pecking at themselves or each other out of boredom or during fights. The process is performed without anesthesia.

With more people turning to poultry products as part of a cholesterol-conscious diet, the number of animals being ranched is astonishing. Ten billion chickens and a half billion turkeys are hatched in the United States annually. In addition to having been genetically altered so that they grow quickly and unnaturally large, commercial turkeys have also been genetically manipulated to have extremely large breasts in order to meet consumer demand for white meat. With such unnaturally huge chests, domestic turkeys cannot mount and reproduce naturally. Pity the poor turkey whose sole means of reproduction is artificial insemination! This is a sad situation for the fowl that had been proposed as the national bird of the United States by Benjamin Franklin. As an aside, the wild turkey is not only a beautifully plumed animal, but one of the smarter birds in North America.

Eggs

Sixteen inches is the suggested amount of room to be shared by four chickens in a laying, or battery cage. There are approximately 300 million egg-laying hens in the United States living in these small wire cages, which are stacked in tiers and lined up in rows. In this tiny space, the hens are forced to rub against each other and the wire of their cages, causing feather loss as well as bruises and cuts. Packed in like sardines, they cannot stretch their wings or legs, and cannot interact in ways in which nature intended.

Ethical Alternatives

There are numerous foodstuffs for those neopagans who choose to eat meat and/or egg products. Some of them will indeed be more expensive than factory farm options, and again, budget as well as ethics must play a part in the making of such choices. For cattle products, there is organically raised beef. Organically produced beef must be certified free of antibiotics, added hormones and/or drugs, and genetically modified feed. Meat cannot be certified as organic if its genetic makeup has been in any way modified (for speed of fattening, hardiness, more rump muscle, or whatever else might be thought of as "desirable").

Poultry which are free-range raised do not suffer in the same manner as the factory egg-layers. True free-range eggs are those produced by hens raised outdoors or that have daily access to the outdoors, but due to weather issues, many free-range operations are indoor floor operations where the chickens do move around freely. Free-range eggs are generally more expensive, as they demand higher production costs and produce fewer eggs per hen due to less stress on the individual birds. The egg's nutrient content is not affected by whether hens are raised free range or in factory operations, but the yolks (yellow parts) are often a deeper color due to the presence of grasses and bugs in the bird's diet. Free-range-laid eggs are often referred to as "happy eggs."*

Ethical Meat and Cheese

How do you find ethical animal-based proteins? Many small farms still cater to the organic food crowd (their products are often available at local health-food stores). Two other alternatives that many people do not think of are kosher and halal butchers. In both Judaism and Islam, a very strong emphasis is placed on how an animal is raised, treated, and killed for food consumption. Jewish thought holds that the butcher must be the most pious and holy man in a community because he will be most sensitive to the fact that the animal gives its life for ours, and the knife used to kill the animal must be utterly sharp and without any blemish or nick so that the animal will not suffer. The rules of halal, the Islamic dietary laws, are so similar to kosher laws that Moslems are allowed to eat kosher meat if they cannot find halal meat. Both religions dictate that no additives may be added to the meat. This means you are not going to find toxic dyes in beef to make it look red and fresh, for instance. As with other small-market suppliers of course, the food is more expensive but the quality is higher and the meat is not given things such as growth hormones and massive doses of antibiotics.

Vegetarians may buy kosher cheese with security, as one of the basic food laws of kosher food is that milk and meat cannot be mixed together. This means that any cheese or milk product certified kosher has used only vegetable rennet to clabber the milk, as animal-based enzymes would be in violation of the dietary restrictions.

Non-Meat Alternatives

Choosing what to eat is a far more over-arching decision than just whether to cook it yourself or buy it prepared. The two adages, "The

---

* But as with any other industry, caveat emptor. Some free range operators have reportedly crowded their poultry as badly (or worse) than commercial farms.

Earth is sacred" and "An ye harm none, do what ye will" can be interpreted variously. For some pagans, it is fine to eat whatever is available for consumption at the local supermarket. For others, eating animal meat is fine, but they feel that, ethically, they must hunt and kill it themselves in order to truly honor the spirit of the animal that feeds them. Still other witches choose to avoid some or all members of the "creatures with faces" family.

VEGANS

How strict you keep your dietary choices is between you and your gods. The strictest choice in dietary paths is that of the vegan (pronounced VEE-gun). Vegans avoid using or consuming animal products and dairy and eggs. They also do not wear or use items such as fur, leather, wool, down, and cosmetics or chemical products tested on animals. Vegans make this choice for a number of reasons: some individuals cannot break down certain animal-based proteins, while others make an ethical choice that they do not want to help support industries that raise and slaughter animals for food.

VEGETARIANS

Some people choose to be vegetarian because they do not like the smell or taste of meats. Others choose to avoid flesh foods because they view all things as being equal in the world, and all equally imbued with spirit. Some choose a vegetarian lifestyle because of the wastage of cereal grains on feeding livestock.* Thirty-six percent of the world's grain harvest is fed to livestock; a mere 10 percent of this grain would be enough to sustain 225 million people. Many ethical vegetarians feel that feeding grain to animals, which returns only a fraction as meat, milk, and eggs, is a horrific waste of natural resources.

OVO-LACTO AND OMNIVORE

There are varying levels of vegetarianism, depending on why one chooses this lifestyle and depending on one's metabolism. Some people do not process carbohydrate-based proteins well (for example, rice and

---

* Still others choose to excise meat from their diets for health reasons.

beans served together make a complete protein) and so they choose to add some additional foods to their overall diet. Ovo-lacto vegetarians eat eggs and milk products such as cheese and yogurt, and some vegetarians add fish to the menu but will not eat four-footed or winged animals.

Despite the stereotyped image of Native Americans as great hunters and carnivores, increasing research shows that most Native communities relied heavily on grains, fruits, and vegetables for their regular daily fare. To the Choctaw peoples, melon is the most sweet and holy fruit, while the Iroquois value fresh spring strawberries over all other fruit, making a sacred drink by mashing them with water and a touch of honey or sugar. Not all traditional people were heavily carnivorous. Perhaps this is one reason why they did not deplete the supply of animals the way the Europeans did when they came to North America. Many neopagans feel a spiritual affinity to Native Americans; many of us could learn from studying their diets as well as their spiritual beliefs.

Most North Americans are omnivores, making us a predator in the animal kingdom. Carnivores eat meat as their standard foodstuff, and although some people joke about being carnivores, they are in fact not so. The Inuit of northern Canada and Alaska are some of the few human communities who can survive for months on diets which are nearly entirely meat-based, but this is in part because they get the vitamins most humans acquire from vegetables by eating some unique foods, such as blubber. If you include meats in your diet as well as milk products, eggs, fruits, and vegetables, you are an omnivore. There has been a raging battle throughout the vegetarian community against the moniker "omnivore" for human beings, but biologists, paleontologists, and physical anthropologists offer very compelling information to back this assertion.

Frozen Meals

Many frozen foods are overpackaged. There are a cardboard box, a plastic dish, and a cellophane-type top wrap before you even get to the food. In many cases, the portion is a single one, so a family of four will generate four times the amount of refuse from eating that one meal.

Human beings have two soft spots on their palate, so to speak: fats and sugars. When one is removed, the other must be present in higher quantities to satisfy the urban taste for sweet and rich (read fatty) foods. Most "fat free" dishes are very high in sugars (including high-fructose corn syrup, sugar, glucose, and fructose-glucose, as well as honey, molasses, and various "natural" fruit juices); by comparison, most low-sugar foods are very high in fats. It's a no-win situation when it comes to your health. Even if you can find a frozen meal that is low in both fats and sugars, it is probably loaded with various salts (sodium, nitrates, nitrites, etc.). It becomes very hard to find a prepared meal that is healthy and low in salts, sugars, and fats. Despite this, many of us view the prepared frozen meal as worth the trade-off when time is at a premium.

Cooking at Home

Cooking saves resources and can be good for your budget. These days, the practice of home cooking is nearly extinct. Many of our parents and/or grandparents were born before the TV dinner was invented, and so they had to cook at home. Even the drive-in or drive-through restaurant is a modern creation. Families used to be larger, and how did they cope? They cooked. They cooked huge batches of food at a time, and froze what they could, or traded portions with neighbors. Self-closing plastic bags were not the norm in those days either. Portion control was managed by a venerable brand, Tupperware, which has had its own issues due to its plastc composition. Marketing of the "burping" bowl started in the late 1940s and early 1950s. Today, there is a plethora of name-brand and no-name reusable containers for meal storage and preparation, many of them very inexpensive.

Sensible pagans can return to cooking in large amounts and freezing and/or trading portions with friends and neighbors. Most people have some venerable family recipes, whether for pot roast, roast turkey, or scalloped potatoes. You could dedicate one evening per week, for example, for that week's cooking. If you prepare one large batch of food per week and freeze some portions, before long you will be able to rotate what you eat every day or two. You can take a different dish to work as a lunch almost every day of the week; most workplaces have facilities to reheat a meal, which can really save some money.

By cooking your own meals, you have far more control over what goes into your mouth and body. Hidden food hazards such as trans-fatty acids (not itemized as a separate category in the nutritional contents lists on food packaging until recently) can be avoided with judicious choices in ingredients. You can also avoid some of the other hidden risks in commercially prepared food, such as sulphites, stabilizers, and so forth. If you choose to buy primarily organic produce and meats, you have less exposure to the antibiotic residues and chemicals present in mass-produced foods. It is more work to make your own food, but your health will benefit, and your pocketbook will be happier, as most frozen and prepared meals are far more expensive than a home-made dish.

Bulk: Buying and Trading Dishes

How much food you buy at one time has to do with your household's needs and what storage facilities you might have on hand. Rural living used to include a "root cellar" or "summer kitchen" where some of the late fall root-type vegetables and hard fruits like apples could be stored through the hot part of the year. These days, apartment dwellers often have no such cool rooms; instead, the freezer has partially taken their place.

Most state or provincial government agencies offer free booklets on how to can and/or freeze produce. Check around and pick these up: they often feature great recipes for things like freezer apple jams, instructions on how to blanche vegetables, and more. There are rules that must be followed, particularly when canning or putting preserves up in mason jars, because they can be the source of potentially fatal contamination, such as botulism. Invite some friends over and have a canning, pickling, or spaghetti-sauce-making day. Try to time this for when produce is inexpensive and fresh. If you have a local farmers' market, use this resource for food purchases. One can often get a discount on a bushel of eggplant or tomatoes over the cost of buying a few.

Bulk buying is only worthwhile if you will do something with what you buy. Buying a pound of strawberries and letting half of them go bad is not savings; it is poor food management. Talk to your friends: perhaps you'd like to start a food co-op, or shopping club? These take different forms. Sometimes a designated person finds out what items members are running low on, and then goes out to buy the groceries. Items are rebagged in smaller amounts and dropped off, and payment is collected. Members take turns on a monthly basis. Other clubs are more formal, with a small fee (to cover things like bags, gasoline, etc.) on top and a set list of items that members receive every month (usually kitchen staples like carrots, potatoes, onions, apples, etc.). Sometimes grocery clubs are run through local community centers (and if there isn't a co-op in your area, why not start one?).

Alternatively, why not hold a cooking party and/or food trading group? It's easy to get together with up to a half dozen friends and agree to get together on a given day of the week (or weekend) and swap portions of the dishes everyone is cooking that week? (Just check on members' food allergies first!) Perhaps you do not have a good hand for making main dishes, but you are legendary for your breads or pies. There is always a spot for good-tasting, healthy food even if it is not an entrée.

Before festivals or holidays, why not set up a baking group? Some folks do this before holidays like Christmas, for instance: if there are six members of the group, each bakes six dozen of his/her favorite treats. The group meets before the holiday, and each person gets one dozen of each of six different cookies, fudges, etc. The group members save cash by making food at home, and each gets to share in the variety of sweets. Friends might take this opportunity to exchange recipes as well.

Gardening

Growing your own fruits, vegetables, and other useful plants returned as a trend in North America during the 1980s, when inflation ran rampant. Echoing the "victory gardens" of the World War II era, many families gave over a small corner of their backyard to grow a couple of tomato plants, a bit of squash, or whatever grew well in their area. The idea has remained in favor since then.

One does not have to have a large garden to make it worth while to grow crops; sometimes a small, mixed-yield backyard garden is the best idea for the urbanite. There are often many places where city dwellers can grow and tend plants with their own hands, such as community gardens and the small allotment plots many cities allow around electric transformer towers (this land is unsuitable for homes). Some people complain that the air sounds or feels "funny" around the transformers, but there seems to be little research on whether any of this has an effect on the quality of vegetation.

Trade your produce with friends. As anyone who has ever owned a garden knows, Mother Nature will shower you with more bounty than you and your family can ever hope to consume. In the Southwest, boxes with grapefruit or oranges are often left sitting at the side of the curb with TAKE SOME written on them. In New York City, you can sometimes find the same thing happening with boxes of tomatoes, ripe from the vine. If you have fifteen zucchini and your friends have twenty tomatoes, you could both profit be getting a large batch of rata-touille out of a trade.

MAKING THE CHOICE

How do you choose what food path to take in life? Decisions around what one eats are very personal, and people can be very defensive about their choices. Think about how you view the natural world and the human world. Are these different, distinct realms, or are we part of an interconnected whole? Consider these options:

• Can I cut down on my meat intake and thereby help the animal world ethically without feeling compelled to move away from animal-based proteins?

• Do I feel compelled to follow a modified vegetarian diet that in-cludes fish, eggs, and milk products?

• Does the possibility of moving from commercially farmed meats to free-range and ranched meats work for me?

Whatever you decide to do, please respect the choices of others as well. For an omnivore going out to dinner with vegetarians, it can be polite to ask if it offends them to share a table, if you plan to eat meat.

Your Body as a Temple

"Thou art God/dess." This is a basic tenet of most branches of Wicca as well as much of neopaganism in general, recognizing the divine in the individual. We can be as gods and goddesses if we strive to learn and understand, by extrapolation, that the body is a temple for the divine. Certainly, if this is the case and you choose to live a pagan life based on what you say you believe, then the maintenance and health of your body is a very important basic lifestyle choice. We all make choices for different reasons. Some people choose to ignore physical health, while others simply do not have as many choices about their health for financial reasons.

In the United States, health insurance is a major factor when considering one's physical health and one's ability to proactively maintain it. As stated earlier, many in the Craft are at or below the poverty line and may have little or no medical coverage. This is reality, and sometimes that checkup or that prescription just has to wait. How you set priorities in lifestyle choices, use of money, and proactive health choices is between yourself and the divine as you envision it. In countries with universal health insurance, like Canada, you may be able to visit the doctor and unable to afford the medicine s/he prescribes. Whether acute or chronic, medical issues will often collide with the day-to-day life choices you have to make.

There are three pillars that support your temple: nurturance, respect, and the ability to create peace, harmony, and balance within your environment. Physical health without mental health is not balanced and harmonious. Physical and mental health without self-respect and self-trust leaves you with two thirds of a tripod, which is an unstable foundation. If "Thou art God/dess" and "As above, so below" is true, think about how you can keep the three pillars of your temple in the best possible condition and balance.

Nuturing Your Temple: Nutrition as Worship

We all get lectures on basic nutrition from childhood on, but we choose to eat fast food, unhealthy food, and fattening food. The more research is done on human food needs, the more we find out that we are eating too much animal-based protein and far too little plant matter and grains. Any diet or food regimen that puts too much stress on one of the basic food groups while ignoring the others is questionable. Yes, you can survive eating just grains, or just proteins, or just fruits and vegetables, but you will suffer nutrient deficiencies and resultant illnesses if you are not very careful indeed. Cutting fruits and vegetables out of your diet leads to folic acid deficiency and illnesses like scurvy (from lack of vitamin C). Omitting complex carbohydrates, such as those in whole-wheat bread or pasta, can ultimately raise your risk for colon cancer and other diseases. As you balance your life and lifestyle, so too must you balance your food intake.

Before you eat anything, reflect on where it comes from. If you take a moment to think on the spirit of the animal or plant giving you its energy, you are offering a small moment of meditation and thanks back to that spirit. This is one appropriate form of "pagan prayer."

Some basic guidelines to consider:

• *The bulk of your diet* should come from grains, including bread, cereal, rice and pasta; vegetables; and fruit. Sample portions of these are sized thusly: one slice of bread (preferably whole grain); one ounce of ready-to-eat cereal; one half cup of cooked cereal, rice, or pasta; one cup of raw leafy vegetables; one half cup of other cooked or chopped raw vegetables; three quarter cup of vegetable juice; one medium apple, banana, or orange; one half cup of chopped, cooked, or canned fruit (packed in water or fruit juice, not in heavy or light syrup); three quarter cup of fruit juice.

• *Most North Americans drink far too much cow's milk* for their own health, despite the slick advertising campaigns with which we are bombarded. Many adults cannot digest lactose, and so must either avoid it altogether or use milk with lactase added. Consider lowering the amount of milk products you ingest daily. Examples of a single serving of a milk-type food are one cup of milk or yogurt, one and a half ounces of cheese, or two ounces of "processed cheese food" (such as Velveeta).

• *Consider dramatically reducing the amount of meats and legumes you eat.* North Americans are chronic overeaters of animal-based proteins in particular. A single serving in this category would comprise two to three ounces of cooked lean meat, poultry, or fish; one half cup of cooked dry beans or one egg; two tablespoons of peanut butter or one third cup of nuts.

• *Limit your intake of foods that are high in fat and sugars* and low in nutrients.

Staying Informed

Watch for urban legends about what might or might not be dangerous to your health. Like the constant barrage of computer virus hoaxes that plague the Internet community, there are urban legends about things from our daily life that are said to be dangerous but in fact are not. Make your own assessments about these sorts of warnings, no matter how trustworthy the friend who gives you this information. One of the more pernicious rumors is one regarding a link between some types of plastic and cancer. In fact, most concerns regarding plastics and our health are focused on the possibility of them melting and burning the consumer, not on their cancer potential. Consider this issue when choosing a dish for your microwave.

Exercise

In all probability, every person walking the earth today knows that a moderate amount of exercise is the best thing they can do to keep their good health. This being said, the fact is that most North Americans are not fond of exercise, and many neopagans, like other North Americans, are unfit and/or overweight.

In order to think about exercise in a practical manner, assess what you want to achieve: Do you want to lose weight, sculpt your body, bulk up, or increase your cardio health? These will all demand different types of exercise regimens. Your health can be improved with as little effort as a good, brisk one half–hour walk three times a week, or can be heavily structured at a gym. The choice is up to you, but takes commitment, sweat, and some discomfort at first.

You might find it easier to stay focused and motivated if you choose an exercise that is interesting to you or one that can be done while keeping your mind otherwise occupied. Those who own equipment often install a television nearby so they can exercise and watch their favorite TV shows at the same time. Others make sure they have a discman or other audio system loaded with their favorite music before they start their walk or workout. Don't forget to shop around. If you have chosen to take out a membership in a gym or workout facility, know your options. If you are on a limited budget but would like some training, see if the local YMCA, community college, or university offers classes. School–based classes are often quite inexpensive.

Conventional Medicine

Western Practice

Of the myriad types of health care the most common and most familiar one is allopathic medicine; the traditional Western medicine with which most of us grew up. Allopathy discards the concept of spirits or other divine interveners in one's health, and primarily treats the person's symptoms. If one has a runny nose, sneezing, fevers and chills, and aching joints, he/she will probably be treated for a cold or flu. Allopathic medicine deals with germs, microbes, and diseases. Although psychiatry is a branch of standard Western medicine (one must become a medical doctor before one can then be qualified as a psychiatrist), most allopathic medicine deals with disease. Psychology, on the other hand, deals with the mind as compared to the brain.

As mentioned elsewhere, use of the allopathic medical approach can be curtailed severely by one's budget and living conditions. Many neo-pagans have trouble attending or using the advice of allopaths, as they are considered part of the "mainstream" community. In addition, medical doctors in North America are often slow to accept the validity of any alternative medical advice; it is a tension that will probably not dissipate any time soon. New Age practitioners are most often loathe to accept modern Western medical advice, and a chunk of the neopagan community likewise is slow to accept medical advice from an M.D., particularly if it entails medications.

There is a fine line between knowing when to accept advice from the allopathic practitioner and knowing when to go with an alternative. Most neopagans are willing to accept that there are simply times when a general practitioner or specialist can give valuable advice. The trick is to learn when medications are needed and when they might be extraneous. Try to choose a practitioner whose views on medication are similar to your own, and do not be afraid to ask "why?" when they suggest a medication.

Should you find yourself in a situation where you need medication in order to return to health, or if ongoing medication is prescribed in order for you to function with issues such as arthritis, manic-depression, or diabetes, do not hate your body because of it. The Goddess gives us the bodies we have, and some of them have unusual challenges, perhaps to encourage us to grow beyond them. If you are prescribed medication, do your homework and see what it does and why it is prescribed for you, and watch for side effects. As with other products, be an informed consumer.

Complementary Medicine

Complementary medicines are used in addition to conventional treatments. The family of complementary medicine is basically a family of medical practices which, while not fully accepted by the allopathic community, are recognized as supportive therapies for certain types of medical problems. Many health plans will cover complementary treatments to a degree, while they rarely cover alternative or non-Western practices. Some of the most common forms of complementary medicines, which have a strong track record of success, are funded by many benefits packages.

CHIROPRACTIC TREATMENT

The nervous system is the information-carrying network of the body, and many of the major cables of the nervous system run through the spine. The relationship between spine and nerves is the focus of the practice of chiropractic medicine. The spine allows for freedom of movement and also houses and protects the spinal cord. When vertebrae become misaligned through trauma or repetitive injury, the patient's range of motion becomes limited and the nerves emerging from the spinal cord are affected. The resulting disruption of information that normally should pass between nerves and the rest of the body is called a subluxation. The interruption of nerve messages often leads to pain, disability, and an overall decrease in the quality of life. In addition, a misaligned spine will cause sub-optimal posture, which can lead to soft tissue (muscle, tendon, and ligament) problems in the surrounding areas. The removal of that interference has been shown to have significant and lasting health benefits. By adjusting the body to eliminate the subluxation, the doctor of chiropractic works toward restoring normal nerve control and message flow. The body is then able to relieve the symptoms and return to health.

ACCUPRESSURE

Accupressure is a science dealing with the human body and the flow of natural energy therein. There is nothing supernatural or magical about acupressure, despite the fact that magical practice also tends to talk about energy flows.

The underlying theory behind acupressure states that the human body has fourteen "imaginary meridians" that carry energy throughout the body. These meridians start at the fingertips, connect to the brain, and from there connect to the organ associated with that specific meridian. Obstructions in meridians cause the energy to flow slower through the affected area and organs, which results in a malfunction in one or more organs associated with the meridian. Pressure is applied to various "pressure points" on the body with the practitioner's thumb, stimulating the corresponding organs and glands of the body. The technique of applying and releasing pressure in a meridian is used to remove obstructions. Once an obstruction is removed, energy can then flow with regularity and the affected organs can resume its normal function.

MASSAGE THERAPY

A massage therapist is a regulated health professional in most jurisdictions throughout North America, and has completed a diploma program from a recognized massage therapy school. Massage therapy comprises hands-on manipulation of the soft tissue and joints of the body. Soft tissues include muscle, skin, tendons, ligaments, and joint capsules. Massage has been proven to have many physiological effects, primarily due to the therapist's hands moving over and manipulating the client's body. These different movements can physically stretch muscles, ligaments, and tendons, encourage the circulation through the tissue, inhibit muscular spasms and either calm or stimulate the nervous system. The therapeutic use of massage by a registered therapist affects all the systems of the body.

Alternative Medicine

Alternative (non-allopathic) medicines are rarely covered under medical benefit plans and cover a very wide range of practices, from the ancient Greek theories of the humors to widely-accepted alternative practices such as aromatherapy, naturopathy, homeopathy and reiki. Neo-pagans are often quite open to alternative forms of medicine.

AROMATHERAPY

Aromatherapy uses naturally extracted aromatic essences from plants to balance, harmonize, and promote the health of body, mind, and spirit. Aromatherapy, which explores the physiological, psychological, and spiritual responses of the client to various essential extracts is part art and part science. This alternative approach strives to observe and enhance the client's own innate healing process. Aromatherapy is holistic, meaning that it is intended as both a preventive and active treatment system. Natural and noninvasive, aromatherapy treatments with essential oils are designed to affect the whole body and assist its natural ability to balance, regulate, heal, and maintain itself.

NATUROPATHY

Naturopathy started during the 1800s in Europe where it was first known as "the nature cure." Naturopaths believe that healing occurs naturally in the human body if it is given what it craves—fresh air, sunlight, exercise, rest, proper diet, and pure water. The emphasis of naturopathy is on helping the body establish its own state of good health.

In determining the root cause of a client's problems, naturopaths do not actually diagnose or treat disease. Rather, they focus on health and education. They teach clients how to create an internal and an external environment that is conducive to good health.

REIKI

Although somewhat obscure, the origination of reiki is believed to have taken place in Tibet several thousand years ago. It is a well-known form of "energy healing." Energy healing involves the direct application of something called the *Chi*, the term used by Chinese mystics and martial artists for the underlying force from which the universe is made. Reiki is the direct application of the Chi to strengthen the client's energy system, or aura.

The reiki practitioner places his/her hands upon the person to be healed and focuses his/her intent toward healing, so that the Chi begins to flow. This energy manages its own flow and draws through the healer exactly the amount of energy needed by the client. The healer essentially keeps the healing space open and watches and/or listens for signs of progress.

NON-EUROPEAN-BASED MEDICINES

There are hundreds of forms of healing and medicine practiced around the world with native plants and herbs, traditional religious-based rituals and more. Many of these practices have not yet been imported into the English language and North American culture, so practitioners are few and far between. For instance, the Chinese have had a scientific system of using herbs and plant matter for curing ills and increasing health for nearly two thousand years, yet most of this knowledge is only slowly entering the English-speaking world. It is questionable for pagans to use rare and endangered animal parts as restoratives and/or medicines because of the obvious impact on the environment.

AYURVEDIC MEDICINE

Ayurvedic medicine is a holistic medical system that evolved among the Brahmins of ancient India about five thousand years ago. Ayurveda focuses on balancing the life energies within each of us. It recognizes that individuals are different from one another and therefore require different treatments. As a result, even though two people may appear to have the same symptoms, they may well require different remedies due to their different energy makeup.

Ayurvedic medicine is based on the belief that there are three fundamental universal energies, called the Tridosha, that regulate all natural processes throughout the universe. Ayurvedic practitioners strive to maintain and realign the alliance and balance between the mind and body. It seeks to heal illness and "unwellness" by restoring wholeness to clients from the fragmentation and disorder of the mind and body.

CUPPING

Cupping refers to an ancient Chinese practice in which a cup is applied to the skin of a client, and the pressure within the cup is reduced by changing the level of heat inside the cup or by suctioning out the air within, so that the skin and superficial muscle layer is drawn up and into the cup. In some cases, the cup may be moved while the skin is still held by the cup, causing some localized and therapeutic pulling of the skin and muscle. This technique is called *gliding cupping.*

Cupping is mainly recommended for the treatment of generalized pain, gastrointestinal disorders, and chronic cough and asthma, but is used for other disorders as well.

Celebrating the Feminine

Being a woman includes dealing with the monthly menses, which has historically been called nicknames like "the curse" or "that time of month." In fact, anthropological studies seem to indicate that in tribal societies where menstruation is celebrated (or at a minimum, not considered dirty or a burden), women do not seem to report either premenstrual syndrome or menstrual cramps! Menses are a sign of a fully blossomed woman and should be embraced and celebrated rather than hidden. Consider handling discharge with a minimum impact on the environment, through use of washable pads, menstrual cups, and natural sea sponges.

Respect Your Temple

"Thou art God/dess," "As above, so below," and "An ye harm none, do what ye will" all exhort neopagans to recognize the divinity within themselves and to act in a way that avoids harming themselves or others. Living off welfare when you are able to work harms the social safety nets designed to care for those who cannot care for themselves. Avoiding any responsibility for your own actions harms those who are targeted for what you have done (or not done, in many cases). Not living up to your full potential, or self-sabotaging your job or your health, does not honor the God/dess within your own soul. It is easy to sink into a vague depression if you are not working, if you are chronically under-rested, if you live in a situation with active or tacit abuse. This kind of situation does no good to the strong, beautiful, Child of the God/dess that lives within each and every thing on Her Earth.

There are huge pressures on people these days in North America to be a certain way: to have certain material possessions, to eat certain "cool" food products, to try certain mind-altering substances, to look a certain way. The media and our peers put pressure on us, whether intentionally or otherwise. It is very hard to go against the trends of modern life, but by choosing to self-identify as a pagan, a "paganus," or person with a rural-dwelling heart, you have already chosen to go against the mainstream trends of religion and culture in North America.

Starhawk, in her book *Truth or Dare*, classifies the concept of power in three different ways: power with, power over, and power from within. Self-esteem and learning to love oneself is the best example of power from within, the keystone to neopagan philosophy. Finding the fount of power within oneself is certainly the key to finding one's magical power: every person must learn how to tap into the magic of the self before he or she can use the magic that exists around each living thing. Because so many of us are from abusive or neglectful backgrounds, it is easy to get involved in Wicca in order to become a priest/ess to have power over others and power-trip on the position of authority. The real mystery of neopagan worship is to find the power from within, and realize that "Thou art God/dess."

Big Beautiful Women and Big Handsome Men

"If they really wanted to, they could lose weight"; "It's not healthy to be fat"; "Fat people are ugly." It is illegal to discriminate against people based on their sex, their race, or physical disability, but it is still perfectly safe to ridicule people based on their weight. It is one of the few discrimination areas still considered "politically correct," but it is not always treated evenhandedly by the courts.

This discrimination is particularly disconcerting when it comes from neopagans and witches (as it does from all sectors of society), for if "Thou art God/dess," then large men and women are the embodiment of the larger faces of the divine, just as the small population represents the smaller gods and goddesses. We may be as much a product of the twenty-first century as anyone else we interact with, but "An ye harm none, do what ye will" means to avoid hurting people by making thoughtless jokes because of their weight.

There are many venues within neopaganism that liberate large people from society's prejudices: ritual body-painting class, discussions and explorations of ritual sex magic, and positive figurines of large bodies as items to be venerated rather than spurned. If every person cannot find his/her own equilibrium of respect for his/her own body and soul, then it is impossible to live up to "Thou art God/dess." One can be healthy and fat or one can be healthy and thin. What one needs support for in this day and age is the ability to love oneself no matter what size and form one's body comes in.

All Spirit Is Equal

Judaism is one religion frequently criticized for its historic view-point that the disabled could not serve in any way in the priesthood. By comparison, Wicca and the Craft in general have no such restrictions, and thankfully so. There is no credo in neopaganism that says, "Some of thou art God/dess." It is a statement of completeness; all are divine, and/or have an aspect of the divine within them. Women are core play-ers in modern Wicca, "first among equals" in some traditions, and equal as priestesses with their priests in other traditions. Neopaganism is, as a rule, a highly inclusive religious system, where those in wheelchairs, with visual and/or auditory impairments may participate as fully as those who are "of sound mind and body." Many a Seeing-eye dog or other service dog has sat quietly within a circle as ritual progressed, and some larger covens and/or traditions often have sign interpreters for the hearing impaired.

MAKING THE CHOICE

It behooves us to keep these questions in mind as we choose a venue for public rituals:

- Can someone in a scooter or wheelchair make it to the ritual circle?

- If the ritual is at night, are there designated helpers for those who might have trouble seeing in reduced light?

- Some of the disabilities needing accommodation are hidden, but equally important. Does anyone have allergies that need to be taken into account?

- If there are recovering alcoholics, has someone made sure that the chalice contains ambrosia (a mix of milk, honey, and spices), grape juice, or other nonalcoholic drink?

- How about scent? Can we burn lavender (a very common cleansing herb) or does someone in the coven have a lavender allergy? What about essential oils and/or perfumes? Many people are allergic to the perfume stabilizers and/or the toluene used to extract scents from many herbs and flowers—these sorts of allergies can land participants in the hospital in anaphylactic shock.

Create Peace in Your Temple

Neopagans rarely have formal locations that are dedicated entirely as sanctuaries, yet the concept remains a valid one. For the Craft, this sanctuary is found within rather than outside of the individual.

In this world of hustle and bustle, stress and deadlines, it can become difficult to remember that we must stay grounded and centered in order to function usefully despite the distractions. Stress is a killer: high blood pressure, certain cancers, strokes, and heart attacks are all in some way linked to high stress levels in many people. Your well-being is more than just a way to be comfortable in your lifestyle; it can literally be a life-or-death decision. It is said that the secret of happiness is having someone to love, something to do, and something to look forward to. Your happiness is key to your emotional health and the maintenance of a healthy inner temple space.

Learn how to evaluate your lifestyle stresses in a realistic manner. If we have unrealistic, unattainable beliefs, then how we size up and appraise a given situation may not lead us to the most appropriate actions in that situation. Irrational beliefs often include "musts" and "shoulds" and insist on perfection—they're difficult, if not impossible, to achieve. It is more challenging to feel good about yourself and your life if you constantly set yourself up for failure. Try to turn negativity into empowering thoughts about yourself.

Emotional Well-Being

There are times when, no matter what anyone says or does, life just feels hopeless. Living hurts: this is a truth that no one can change. However, it is easy to accept that hurting is part of being human, and that we learn from both joy and grief. If we did not hurt, would we even recognize the joys of happiness? Self-esteem keeps away the dogs of despair and worthlessness, but not everyone learns how to enjoy a healthy level of self-esteem. Learning to love oneself and keep a healthy frame of mind is not easy for many in the Craft, who have suffered at the hands of others. What are the tools we have to practice love and self-respect?

Strategies for Coping

PUT YOURSELF IN THEIR SHOES

Have you jumped to conclusions in deciding someone thinks you are worthless? Could you put a different spin, or interpretation, where you may have made an irrational judgment? Suppose someone treats you badly, or makes what you interpret as a hurtful remark. Your first instinct may be to think that "So-and-so is a horrible person!" or perhaps "Everyone hates me." Think before jumping to a negative conclusion, which may also undermine your own self-worth. You can choose how you interpret things that happen in your life so that they are *them* issues rather than *me* issues. The key is to develop a realistic assessment of the situation, and to try to get beyond seeing situations entirely through the lens of possible feelings of powerlessness and worthlessness.

COMMUNICATE

Bottling up feelings of sadness or anger takes up energy you could be using in positive ways, and can cause problems in relationships and at work. Let people close to you know when something is bothering you and how you are feeling. If they are true friends they will care and want to help in any way they can. Expressing our feelings openly helps release tension, and also helps us recover from hurtful experiences. Hiding or holding back your feelings can cause stress that affects both our physical and mental health. Remember to express your feelings appropriately, however; there are times when displays of emotion are not helpful, such as at work, where you are expected to be "in control."

Arguments are healthy, too, as long as they do not become unpleasant and if both sides have an idea of "how to fight fairly." Learning to disagree without making each other unhappy is an important part of any relationship. Just remember to argue and discuss fairly: if you bottle it up and then let all your small concerns go at once, you will overwhelm the other person involved. As well, do not rehash old disputes over and over. Historical fights are just that; history. They are not ammunition to be thrown out over and over at the other person. Losing your temper is never a good solution to a problem; it may provide temporary relief, but ultimately will lead to more anger.

TAKE TIME TO THINK AND REFLECT

Emotions are powerful, and it is easy to be carried away by their intensity. Consider the possible positive and negative consequences of your actions rather than flying off the handle. Anger needs to be expressed, because it does not store well inside your body. Unchecked and unexpressed, anger can boil over into rage, which is a very destructive emotion. The key to expressing your anger in a healthy manner includes expressing it assertively and not aggressively. Take time to think about what you want to say, and express your anger by speaking in a strong, steady voice, rather than by shouting. Be reflective and open; do not attack.

DETERMINE WHICH END OF THE BINOCULARS YOU ARE ON

It is so easy to obsess about things we have done wrong, ways we could have fixed things, and how badly we acted. Considering and reflecting is one thing; obsessing about what cannot be fixed is not useful. Learn from your mistakes and then move on. Focus on positive things in your life. Make time for things you enjoy. If you have low self-esteem, it is easy to listen to each minute criticism of what you do or who you are and embrace these as huge truths in your life. If everything others say looks huge in your eyes, you are on the wrong end of the binoculars.

Most of us value the opinions of others without "considering the source," as it were. Sometimes what others tell or advise us is aimed at making them feel better, even when it in turn, does us harm. Remember that your own opinion is valuable, and also remember that you may well be your harshest critic. Make sure you are using those binoculars correctly. It is far more useful to look through the binoculars the correct way, bringing in the things from far away so you can see all the small and wonderful triumphs in your life clearly, and in focus. Try expressing one positive affirmation each day about yourself, such as "I have the skills to do this job well," or "This is second nature to me." They may feel odd at first, but they do help turn around your self-esteem and support your own sense of self-worth.

TAKE CARE OF YOUR BODY AND MIND

Your physical and mental health are two sides of the same coin. Care for your body by exercising regularly, eating healthy foods, and getting enough sleep. Don't abuse drugs or alcohol—sacred substances should be handled with reverence and used in a sacred manner. Try self-relaxation and/or meditation, both when you are in a stressful time in your life and when you feel calm.

Psychic Care

The psyche is both the easiest and hardest thing to care for. To this day, one of the best books on keeping your psychic self cared for is *Psychic Self-Defense* by Dion Fortune, first published back in the 1940s. She classifies the types of astral attacks one might deal with, and tells how to repulse them. Astral attacks are incidents where highly charged emotions are focused on the intended victim in order to amplify the negativity already existing in that person. The most common effect of this sort of attack is a drop in the victim's energy levels. Fortune describes etheric projection attacks, where etheric matter is sent from the attacker to the victim in a form that appears as a pale creature to drain or frighten the victim. Psychic attacks can involve artificial beings, which are etheric thought-forms that look like creatures (either real or imaginary).

There are other forms of attack that can affect the unsuspecting and unprotected mind: psychic vampires, discarnate spirits, and the sort of spontaneous entity created by nature herself.

PSYCHIC VAMPIRES

Insecure people often cling to stronger personalities. Psychic vampires are like energy leeches, sucking the emotional and/or physical strength out of the person they attach themselves to until the "victim" is essentially "sucked dry." Psychic vampires sometimes leave their victims so exhausted emotionally, and physically that they may have trouble controlling their emotions, and manifest symptoms similar to chronic fatigue syndrome.

At the practical and non-magical level, the best defense against psychic vampires is a firm, unwavering NO. If you feel that you are being crowded, stifled, and sucked dry by an acquaintance, find yourself some physical and emotional distance. Make yourself unavailable and find some "me" time to recharge. If you are exhausted, you cannot do your tasks and cannot be of help to those who honestly need and deserve your support! Before long, the vampire will drift away to look for another unshielded person to latch onto. Remember, if you feel you are being psychically devoured, be sure to raise your shields and reflect the "black hole" energy being used on you.

DISCARNATE SPIRITS

These are spirits that do not rest. They can be locked into a place for several reasons: perhaps they are from people who died due to trauma, are malicious by nature (remember the tales of the gods and goddesses have figures like Loki as well as Odin!), or are young spirits who intend to play with you. Discarnate means they do not currently have bodies, although they may have had physical forms in the past. These sorts of spirits are more likely to try and physically inhabit your body (much as orishas do in Yoruba religious practice, or lwas in Voudon) and use you as their "transportation" while they are in residence. Often the target person does not even remember being possessed, as many forms of possession force the host-spirit into a sort of dormant state, so that they remember nothing they do while used as the spirit's "horse." Not all possessing discarnate spirits are malicious, for we often talk about being "possessed by the Muses," or inspiration. Often these are discarnate spirits working through us to create good things and express creativity in the world.

There are a few good ways to dispel a possessing entity if it is not de-sired. One of the most efficient ways to rid a person of a discarnate en-tity is to spray a fine mist of alcohol in the face of the "horse." Ideally this would be neutral grain spirits or vodka (high-proof drinking alco-hol, not rubbing alcohol!). In western Africa this is done by putting the alcohol in your mouth and spitting, spraying it much as our grand-mothers used to spray water on clothing while ironing it. If the entity is not malicious, they will often leave when an external voice asks them nicely to vacate the vehicle.

SPONTANEOUS ENTITIES

These are not created by any sort of human action, but are the by-product of nature herself. Wild forces of nature such as hurricanes, thunderstorms, and earthquakes stir up incredible amounts of natural energy, and sometimes this swirling energy will coalesce into a form of sorts, not unlike an etheric projection. This sort of entity swirls around the area where it formed, causing havoc, migraines, breathing difficul-ties, and a palpable sense of anxiety among those who are close enough to perceive the entity itself. These have no will of their own, and as a rule they do not move in any organized or intentional manner. Spon-taneous entities dissipate as the natural occurrence that created them dissipates. These entities can also form in locations that have been the site of a high level of negative emotions for a very long period of time. In this case, the manifestation will tend to dissipate when it is no longer being fed.

PROTECTING YOURSELF

The best defense against any of the psychic threats out there is a good psychic shield. Many popular books on magic and witchcraft have how-to sections on shielding and grounding yourself: use these. Don't just create a generalized "protect me" type of spell: create specific shields to protect yourself from the negative energies around us, from the intentional attack to the spontaneously created storm-entity. Con-struct shields that are multipurpose. They should protect you against physical, etheric, emotional, and occult attacks on the human or astral planes. Pay attention as you build your shields, so they cannot be destroyed by anyone or anything that might bear you ill will. Visualize your shields as powerful and impermeable, and visualize them daily.

As well, if you think you are under psychic attack, assess your general health and well-being before you conclude that you are being violated on the astral plane! Ask yourself: Did I eat enough today? Did I get enough sleep? Am I under undue stress? Can I imagine anyone or anything that might want to do me harm? Could there be a conventional source for my discomfort and/or illness?

If you visualize your psychic shield as an aura of mirrorlike reflective light all around your body and nothing happens, you may be misreading a physical symptom as having a psychic origin. If you erect a good psychic shield, you should feel a "pinging" off your shields when something is trying to get in but is being repelled. If you fire up the shields and get nothing at all, maybe you need to check if you took your morning pills, your orange juice, or that first cup of coffee rather than accusing others of being up to psychic no good.

Guns and Military Service

Because of the strong emotions military service and gun use invoke in many Pagans, they are excellent examples of how one's internalized values as a neopagan must determine how one chooses to live one's life. There are various traditions within neopaganism. Some traditions are pacifist in nature, while others embrace the concept of the Warrior Way. Within North America, the bulk of the Craft was formed and shaped by the U.S. antiwar movement of the 1970s as the Vietnam war was brought into the home by modern television coverage.

The debate about the ownership of handguns within the neopagan community encompasses many of the same concerns as the debate about Wiccans going into their country's military services. For some, military service is as sacred a calling as being a vegetarian is to others.

Neopaganism is a diverse family of religions, with diverging worldviews. The pacifist, hippie roots are still very close to the surface, but there is a new breed of neopagan arising: the ethical warrior.

The Craft demands a high level of self-awareness from its practitioners, and this includes the ability to formulate a cosmology, or worldview, and then make ethical decisions based on that worldview, called axiology. For many pagans, it is difficult to balance the concept "An ye harm none, do what ye will" with active military duty. Still others embrace the concept of karma insofar as they are the instruments of the God/dess, and bring the wrath of Kali, Anath, or Shiva upon those who deserve it. Many of the gods and goddesses of our ancestors were not divinities of "bunnies and light" or "strawberries and elves," as it were. Death and destruction, although painful to humans, clears the way for new growth and birth to occur. Some of the oldest Wiccan texts talk about knowing how to hex and blast, as well as how to bless and cure. If Neopaganism is a religious family of balance, then the peaceful practitioners must also accept that for some, the other side of that balance is the path of the Warrior.

> Our very survival as a people and the continuance of our way of life requires that we sometimes fight to defend it. It should be remembered that the [Wiccan] Rede does not preclude our acting in self-defense when threatened. The modern Pagan soldier who places himself in harm's way to protect his countrymen is no less than the Warrior of ancient times. He does not kill uncaringly, he does not wage war for glory or thrill, he prefers the way of the peacekeeper over that of the soldier. He does not blindly follow orders, rather he weighs what is asked of him against the ethical framework of his religion. But he also understands that until the world becomes a different place, he or she will be called upon in time of crisis to place their life on the line.
>
> —Carol Kirk, "The Warrior's Path"

If you are a pagan following the path of the warrior gods and heroes, a gun is a logical tool, just as any other warrior's weapon is. If you are a pagan following the path of nurturer gods and/or balance, does the use and ownership of guns put things *out* of balance, or *in* balance? There are numerous reasons to own a gun, even though owning guns does not sit well with many neopagans. As so many urbanites know, the security of one's home, possessions, and loved ones is not always achieved by protection spells alone. The Craft is quite split on this issue, as some believe that a path of balance demands no tools that could be viewed as "aggressive" as it were; tools could in theory throw off the natural balance.

Gun users point out that there are diverse reasons for owning firearms, and most of them are legitimate social reasons. Guns can be used for: recreation, four-footed pest control, self-defense, and supplementing the food supply. Some authors point out that gun ownership is much like learning how to handle magic. Both are dangerous when misused, and indeed, some authors describe untrained persons trying to utilize magic as much like "handing a child a loaded gun." A gun can be merely a sport tool; a magical spell can be performed as "idle sport" to some practitioners. Much like the misuse of a gun however, a poorly executed magical spell can also cause harm. The issue is the use of the tool, not the tool itself. One can use the same explanation with a less-touchy subject: power tools. Would you hand a power drill or high-speed electric stapler to someone who knew nothing about tools? Would you hand a book of spells to someone who had had no training at all? Power tools evoke a less emotional response from many pagans than gun ownership does, but both have the same basic elements: use something powerful without training and you run the risk of hurting someone.

Lifestyle and healthy choices are personal decisions. Most important, remember that even when another member of the Craft chooses a lifestyle you might not choose for yourself, you must respect their right to make those choices while supporting ethical conduct.

Resource

"The Warrior's Path—Pagans in the Military," by Carol Kirk, ©1999, at
   Military Pagan Network, Inc., www.milpagan.org/PC/
   the_warriors_path.html, © 2001

CHAPTER 3

Relationships and Sexuality

Relationships are a constant in all of our lives. While we have a physical body from the moment we are born, many seminal thinkers in the fields of cognitive development argue that we have a "Self" only because we interact with others. According to these theories, children deprived of care and interaction in their earliest years do not learn to communicate symbolically by language or gesture, and do not learn strategies for coping with their worlds other than those that are provided by instinct. Each interaction in which a person engages creates him/her as a being in relation to another person or group of people. Interaction is how one learns who one is, what the world is like, and how to go about living in it. All art, all music, all language comes out of a need to "be in relation." If one were alone in this world, there would be no need to communicate, except perhaps with the divine. If one were utterly alone in the world, there would probably be no reason to conceptualize a divinity as anything other than one's own self.

Relationships are a central part of what defines us as human beings. They are essential not only to our physical survival, but also to our psychological and spiritual health. Yet most of us find that much of the stress and the worry and the trouble in our lives originates in the relationships we have with other people. This is perhaps not surprising. Since our relationships with others are crucial to our well-being, they are often points at which we are particularly vulnerable. "Being in relation" involves communication, which can often be difficult and frustrating. It involves trying to understand the expectations that might be built into, but not explicitly stated in, each and every particular situation. It involves balancing our vision of ourselves with the views others have of us. Most of all, it involves thousands of daily interactions, many of which are done totally unthinkingly, in accordance with a cultural script or a family script or an occupational script that we have internalized over time and which has become a part of our "taken for granted" reality.

We go through our lives assuming that other people share this taken for granted reality, and many of the difficulties we encounter come out of interacting with those who either do not share in it, or share in it only incompletely. All of us have expectations about reality and about social interaction. We may not be able to articulate what they are, exactly, but we know that they exist, because people display marked discomfort, anxiety, and sometimes hostility when these expectations are breached.

The pagan worldview is one that focuses on personal responsibility for one's own actions, through the widespread belief in karma, and in the divinity of all people (at minimum, this is often expanded to cover all living things, or even simply all things!). These two notions have profound implications for the way in which we conduct our "being in relation." The first suggests that we are ultimately responsible for what we do or fail to do, regardless of why we did it or failed to do it. How many times were we told as children, "I don't care who started it, that's no reason to hit someone!" The second suggests that we have a moral obligation to treat other people as fundamentally equal to ourselves. That does not mean the *same* as us, but simply as equally worthy, as children of the gods, to receive respectful treatment. Does this mean that you have to be nice to everybody, all the time, no matter what? No. After all, how many times have you said to yourself that if a person is upset with you you wish they would just say so? Treating people with honesty and respect is not always compatible with being nice or friendly. It means that we ought to be conscious of how we treat people: if we are accountable for our behavior, it should be a choice, and it should be a choice made for reasons with which we are comfortable.

Relationships are not only something in which we engage with other humans. Neopaganism recognizes that there is a nonhuman world that has equal status with the human world, and to which human beings relate. This comprises both the nonmaterial world of spirits and the material world of the other than human, of animals and of the body of the Earth. Each action we take puts us in some kind of relationship with these other elements of the universe in a way that may be more or less respectful. Just as we need to be conscious of the implications of our actions for other people, under the ethical guideline of "harm none," we need to be aware of the implications of our actions on the nonhuman world.

Some people say that there are different kinds of relationships. Certainly, different relationships—different interactions—invoke different rules and expectations. While this chapter examines many different categories of relationships it does so with the notion that there is only one "quality" of relationship, of relationality, and those factors that vary are circumstances and intensity. At their heart, all relationships are fundamentally founded on trust, honesty, and respect; it is the degree to which these are expected that varies. Thinking about relationships in this way is a useful device for understanding how consistent you are over the range of the relationships and interactions in which you find yourself.

Family

The earliest relationships in which we find ourselves are those within our family of origin. Family of origin are those people with whom one grows to adulthood. For many, this is the *nuclear family*—one conjugal couple and their biological children. This family model is a very North American standard that increasingly does not reflect the reality of many people's families of origin, even in the Western world. The composition of households changes more often now than it did in the 1950s and 1960s—when the nuclear family model was the standard—as divorce and remarriage are more common, adult children may rejoin their parents' household with their own children, and unrelated adults may spend many years sharing household space.

Relationships experienced as a child are the ones in which one has the least choice and the least ability to extricate oneself. They also occur at the time when one learns the interaction style that s/he will carry for the rest of his/her life. In childhood, one learns learn what kind of place the world is, how much to trust those around one to meet one's needs, and what to expect from adults.

Some of us are fortunate enough to have positive experiences inside our families of origin, and to be provided with solid templates for subsequent relationships with our own partners, children, and friends. Research conducted in the neopagan community, however, suggests that the majority of neopagans experienced their childhoods as problematic, either because of physical or sexual abuse, emotional or physical neglect, or the substance abuse problems of adult caretakers (Rabinovitch 1992, Reid 2001). In these cases, the models of relationships that they learned as children are unlikely to be the ones that they would wish to carry into adulthood and reproduce with their own children. Many people in this situation must take some conscious measures in order to counteract these destructive relationship models. They combine therapy with reading about parenting, talking to other parents, utilizing online resources, and possibly attending parenting classes or face-to-face support groups. The important thing for anyone raising children, regardless of his or her own personal background, is to remember that it is our responsibility as parents to equip our children with the tools and models they require to make healthy lives for themselves. If this was not done for us, then we have catch-up and healing work to do on our own psyches.

Casual Interactions

The majority of the interactions in which we engage on a daily basis are impersonal ones, interactions we do not usually think of as constituting relationships. Even these, however, are parts of our "being in relation." Standing with others at a bus stop, buying milk at the convenience store, ordering a pizza—all of these activities bring us into a sphere of interaction with other people. Much has been written about the decline of civility in society, the abandonment of standards of "common courtesy" or "manners." It is in these impersonal interactions that this is often felt the most.

Because the majority of us live in sprawling suburban areas where we know comparatively few people, and frequent fairly anonymous institutions like shopping malls, mega-groceries, and big-box stores, we rarely have regular and sustained contact with the same people in the course of our day-to-day lives. We tend to encounter people in specific roles—cashier, bus driver, waitress—rather than as whole people. Much of the time, we cannot situate the people we encounter other than in the role through which we encounter them.

"Thou art God/dess," however, means that those "strangers" are children of the gods, just as we ourselves are, even if we would prefer not to think of them that way—such as when they are chatting on the phone rather than ringing through our order! While there may be an excuse to be irritated or upset, there are few excuses for treating people badly. Successful "being in relation" boils down to treating other people with consideration and respect. If no one ever treated anyone else in a way that they themselves did not want to be treated, it is likely that a good deal of civility would make its way back into day-to-day life.

Sometimes, increasing the ambient level of civility involves nothing more than paying better attention to our surroundings as we move through our day. Busy schedules, deadlines, and a near constant feeling of having too much to do often mean that we are thinking of something other than what we are actually doing a good deal of the time. We miss the opportunity to do small things for others because we are simply unaware of them. Sometimes, civility involves speaking in situations where we are accustomed to being silent. It takes very little to not only be civil, but also to be a "bright spot" in someone's day. For instance:

- Smile at the cashier, waitress or other service person. Odds are that their day has been at least as long as yours.

- If someone is wearing something you find appealing or attractive, tell them so. Most people like to hear that they look good and that others admire their taste. Sincere compliments are always welcome.

- Rather than fuming that someone is taking up two seats on a crowded bus, say something polite. While you may get a belligerent response, you may get a seat. Perhaps the individual didn't notice that the bus got crowded since they sat down.

- If you are in a hurry, let people know. "We are a bit pressed for time, so if you could bring us the bill with the food, we'd really appreciate it."

- If you are not in a hurry, be generous. I routinely give up my place in the women's bathroom line to pregnant women, who are invariably effusively grateful. You may get to the head of the line a couple of minutes later, but how important is that?

- Ask for assistance before you are completely frustrated. Frustration tends to blunt one's listening and communication skills.

- Say something rather than just pushing past people, and apologize if you bump them. A person may not have noticed you, or perhaps it has not occurred to them that you would like to get by.

Communication

What may be obvious to you may not be obvious to others. This is probably the crux of what lies at the heart of many troubled relationships, both superficial ones and our deepest relations. When we choose silence over communication we are not taking care of ourselves and others. Communication builds connections between ourselves and others—connections that are important in a universe where everything is sacred, where everything is wholly itself and part of a greater whole. Communication, like everything we do, is a skill; it has to be learned and practiced. And like most things, it is easier to do well when there is less at stake, whether in physical or emotional terms. No one is expected to communicate the innermost secrets of his/her soul to complete strangers; these relationships do not require that level of trust and disclosure. Casual or impersonal relationships are based on a trust that people will act in a manner appropriate to the situation, and that people will display at least the level of forthrightness required to move the interaction along.

Sometimes communication necessitates doing things that are socially awkward, like sending back a meal, or reporting poor customer service to a manager. While giving people the benefit of the doubt and excusing bad behavior are not the "wrong" thing to do, speaking out also has its place, especially when not to do so will diminish your entire experience of something you should have found relaxing or enjoyable. A feeling of having been treated badly or inappropriately, however, does not entitle you to be rude. In general, a non-confrontational statement of your problem combined with a suggestion of what could be done about it is usually the most effective way of getting your issue addressed. Remember too, that, especially in a retail situation, the cashier may not have the authority to help you. Rather than becoming upset with them, ask to have the situation escalated to someone with more corporate discretion.

Honesty does not mean you are obliged to answer socially inappropriate questions. Most socially inappropriate questions do nothing to facilitate an interaction, and should be met with a puzzled look and a firm "Excuse me?" This will cause most people to back off. In the persistent case of someone who will not drop the question, looking them in the eyes and saying "I cannot imagine a single circumstance in which that might be your business," will often suffice. Some questions are simply part of a routine of interaction, and are not expected to be answered with complete honesty. On the other hand, when your doctor asks how you have been feeling, he or she honestly needs to know the details. This is *not* a place where reverting to the standard "fine, and you?" is appropriate.

Friends

Friendships differ from casual interactions in several important ways. Friendships have some continuity; one sees or speaks with friends on a regular or semi-regular basis. There is a sense that the relationship continues to exist between encounters. Friends encounter us in more than a single isolated role. One of the ways to think about how close a friendship is involves thinking about how role-tied it is. Do you see one another in more than one context? For example, if the friend is a work colleague, do you see them outside of work? Would you consider inviting them to a backyard barbecue at your house?

Your closest friends will tend to be the people who are present in more than one area of your life. Because of this, friends will be privy to information about your life that outsiders are not, and you will be privy to information about their lives. The amount of information you feel comfortable giving a friend will usually depend on how close you feel to that person, and also on how free you are with information about your life in general. Some people need more privacy than others, and some are more comfortable talking about themselves than others. The uniqueness of each friendship, because of the personalities of the people involved, can often cause difficulties and misunderstandings. The assumptions that you have about the nature of friendship are likely to be different from those made by others in your life. If left unarticulated, assumptions can lead you to feel hurt by others, and to hurt their feelings in turn. Communicate your ideas and expectations with your friends.

Relation is a word derived from the same Latin root as religion—*religare*, which means "to bind together" or "to reconnect." We are each of us responsible for maintaining the ties that connect us to our important others, including making decisions about when and what kinds of ties are appropriate. Remember, you are part of each of your relationships, and just as you have a duty to endeavour not to harm others in your relationships with them, you have a duty not to allow a situation to harm you. Culturally, many of us, especially women, have been taught that our chief duty is to see to the happiness of others, even when that means sacrificing our own happiness and well-being. Ultimately, when we undervalue ourselves, we send the message to others around us that it is all right to undervalue us. Paganism does not valorize self-sacrifice, nor does it stigmatize activities done simply for our own pleasure or the gratification of our own desires, so long as in the attainment of these things, we do not subject others to harm.

It is all right to "get something" out of friendships. In fact, it is important that you get something out of your friendships. Why engage in them otherwise? Friendships represent an investment of time and emotional energy for both parties, and it is important to the health of a friendship that these investments be mutually beneficial. Sometimes, what we get from our friendships is not healthy, either for us or for the other party—when that happens, both parties need to work toward making changes in the relationship. A better balance needs to be found. Friendships often take work; the friendships you are willing to work the hardest to keep are those that are the most important to you.

Not all friendships are deep and profound relationships that are going to last forever. Some arise in a particular circumstance—a college class, a new parents group, a book club—and taper off gradually when you are no longer involved in this activity together. People change throughout their lives, and it is expected that friends will change as well. There is nothing intrinsically the matter with drifting away from old friends, so long as it is not done in a way that leaves the other party hurt and confused. Often, if our lives change again, we will find ourselves revisiting some of those old friendships, and that is difficult to do if we have gotten into the habit of burning our bridges behind us with emotionally messy leave-takings.

Cohabiting

Cohabiting relationships are a special kind of friendship. While we often think of cohabiting in the sense of people living together in a conjugal arrangement that has not been legally formalized, this is only one of the various forms cohabitation takes. In the somewhat tighter economic circumstances we have experienced in the last decade or so, people are living with a wider variety of people, later into their lives. You may find yourself living in a college residence, or with a number of housemates. You may take boarders when you buy your first house. You may live with someone before, or instead of, getting married. You may move back into your parents' home after a divorce or financial upset, or may take in your elderly parents when they cease to be able to live independently.

In a cohabiting situation, you not only have to share some of your life, but you also have to share your space. This means an ongoing process of negotiation about what is and is not permissible, what is and is not acceptable to all of the various parties involved. It is a delicate balance between freedom to do as you choose and respect for the comfort levels of others. In all cases, regardless of whether you are moving in with the love of your life, with a best friend, or with a couple of near strangers, it is good to have a formal set of house rules early on. These rules should not be able to be changed arbitrarily, but should require the agreement of everyone in the household. Periodically, rules will have to be changed; something someone thought they would be fine with is now bothering them, or the situation has changed. House meetings are a good way to address this. They can be held on a regular basis, to keep tabs on how people are finding things and what is coming up in their lives, or on an as-needed basis, when someone feels there is something that needs to be discussed.

One of the things that needs to be established from the outset is how much power, authority and responsibility each member of the household has. While "all household members are equal" works in some cases, it is not always appropriate. Some of the household members may be children. While it is appropriate to allow them to have some degree of input in how the household is run, it is probably not appropriate to allow them to block a consensus decision among the adults. There also may be issues having to do with people's legal relation to the home. Below are some questions to consider:

- If we total three people, none of whom are romantically involved, living in a house that only one of us owns, what are the responsibilities of the non-owners with regard to its upkeep? Are they expected to take a turn mowing the lawn or shoveling the driveway? How about cleaning the kitchen or the bathroom? If the roof needs repair, does each pay part of the cost? What about damage they cause, for example, to the hardwood floor of a bedroom? How much freedom do non-owners have to change the living space? Can they paint the walls? Change the carpet? Put locks on their doors?

- Whether living with parents, lovers or friends, there needs to be some advance discussion of what is held in common. What areas are considered common spaces. What areas are private? What is the standard of cleanliness expected in common spaces? How is the work to maintain that standard of cleanliness to be apportioned? What are the consequences if someone is not doing their fair share of the household labor? What about towels, pots, pans, cutlery, and dishes? Small appliances like a coffeemaker, popcorn popper, microwave, or waffle iron? What about food? Does everyone contribute a certain amount of money toward a general stock of groceries? Are some staples purchased by the household, with everyone buying their own "goodies"?

- How much privacy is each person accustomed to? When is it all right to enter another person's private space?

- How are utility bills going to be handled? Does everyone pay an equal share? What about Internet and telephone service? Cable television? If you have a couple and a single sharing a two-bedroom apartment, does the couple pay one half, or two thirds of the household expenses?

- What is the policy on visitors? Can anyone have people over? Are there limits on how many? What about overnights? Out-of-town guests who need a place to stay for a few days? Can visitors be left alone in the house if no household member is home? Is it okay to bring sexual partners home? Are some sexual partners okay and others not?

- Is magical practice going to be an issue? What about coven meetings?

- If I am living with a romantic partner or partners, and not everyone is earning similar amounts, how will contributions to general expenses be handled? What does that mean in terms of the ownership of the house or items in the house, should the partnership later dissolve? While these things are spelled out by law in a legal marriage situation, this is often not the case in common law, same-sex, and other forms of romantic liaison.

- How much accountability is desired in the household? Do I call if I am not going to be home for dinner, or home later than I expected? Do I let people know when I will be away for the weekend? Do I leave contact numbers?

Sexual Partners

Paganism does not surround sexual expression with special sets of prescriptions and proscriptions in the way some other religious traditions do. Pagans treat sex as a natural part of human life; like all other aspects of human life, it is a way in which one can reach out to the gods. Human sexual activity is the microcosmic representation of the generative power of the universe. While some pagan traditions have a heterosexual bias in their mythology and in their symbolic language, many others do not. The Charge of the Goddess says specifically, "All acts of love and pleasure are my worship." That is not, however, an invitation to indiscriminate sexual license—it means that sexual relationships, like other relationships, must have a basis in trust, honesty, and respect. They must involve treating one's partner or partners in the relationship as full, worthy human beings and children of the Gods. All of the moral principles that apply in other areas of life apply equally in sexual life.

This is particularly important because our society has made sex a fetish, in the sense of it being something to which an excessive amount of attention is directed, and as a charm that is believed to have supernatural, almost magical, powers. Having sex is supposed to make a person more masculine or feminine (whichever is more appropriate), improve one's mood, build one's confidence, enable a person to attract more sexual partners, and make one more powerful and more important. The implicit promise that buying products will get you more sex is used in advertisements for everything from beer to cars to household cleaning products. Fashion, especially women's fashion, often presents us as highly sexualized creatures. Sex is routinely confused with romance, love, and commitment. It is an activity upon which many people hinge large parts of their self-esteem and treat as a proxy for their attractiveness and their worth as a human being. It is no wonder that it is an especially emotionally charged aspect of our lives, one capable of producing intense highs and miserable depressions. Sexual relationships, if they are to be happy and fulfilling, require a particularly high level of self-awareness, self-respect, and awareness of one's partners.

Sex with Yourself

The most important sexual relationship you have is with yourself. "Among all acts of love and pleasure" are those for which you do not require a partner. Relating to your own sexuality in a positive manner is an important component of the ability to relate to someone else's sexuality positively. Exploring your own body without the distraction of someone else is enjoyable and also gives you insight into what arouses you—what you like, and what does not work quite so well for you. Paying attention to your own body will help you evaluate your responses to visual, tactile, olfactory, and auditory stimuli—what kind of setting you like for intimate encounters.

Everybody has sexual fantasies. It is only when sexual fantasy obscures the real person in a sexual encounter that it becomes a problem. People deserve to be treated as unique, not as the raw material onto which a fantasy is projected. Many people feel uncomfortable with the content of their sexual fantasies for a number of reasons. We can find ourselves fantasizing about things we find profoundly unacceptable in real life, such as rape or coercion. Some of this discomfort is produced by our socialization, which, even today, has a fairly prescriptive set of standards for what "nice" girls and boys should enjoy. Sexual fantasies can be a way out of the socialized box in which we have trapped our sexuality. If you are uncomfortable with some of your sexual fantasies or preferences, it's important to try to confront and deal with your discomfort, rather than trying to ignore or bury either a piece of your sexuality or a piece of your feelings.

First, remember that not all—maybe not even most—of the fantasies you have are things you actually plan or even wish to do, at least not in the form you see in your imagination. In the sphere of sexual fantasy, it is important to remember that the cultural status of sexuality as a "special case" may lead us to worry about sexual fantasy in ways that we do not worry about fantasy in general. Instead of becoming distressed over the dissonance between fantasy and our real wishes, we can, in a general way, calmly draw boundaries and find compromises that allow us to enjoy and benefit from our fantasy life without allowing it to lead us into harm. When fantasy is working well in your life, it is a rich source of information about who you are and what you want.

Sex with Others

All sexual activities with others need to be safe, sane, and consensual. Consensual sex is particularly important. The fact that Roman and Greek gods seem to have had sex with anyone who caught their fancy, regardless of their feelings on the matter, is not a model for healthy sexual activities. Consent to sexual activities is given in an unambiguous way, after a certain level of honest communication has taken place. Without communication, there is no informed consent.

- Young children cannot give consent to sexual activities with adults. Every jurisdiction has a statutory age of consent law, and the laws should not be breached under any circumstance.

- People who are drunk or high cannot reliably give informed consent. Alcohol and drugs impair and alter normal reasoning processes sometimes resulting in consent that would not have been given in sobriety.

- People with some kinds of developmental disabilities may not be able to give informed consent to sexual activities—they may not be intellectually mature enough, or they may lack an understanding of the implications of sexual activities. This must be considered on a case-by-case basis; many developmentally disabled people can have rich emotional and sexual lives.

- People in extreme emotional distress cannot reliably give consent. Like those who have had too much to drink, their judgment is impaired and they may not be able to determine what is in their best interests. Some people do find sex comforting and life-affirming, and will turn to it as a way to cope with emotional difficulties. A person should never feel *obligated* to have sex.

- People with whom you are in an asymmetrical power relationship (boss/employee, teacher/student, doctor/patient) cannot reliably give consent. It is best to terminate the power relationship first, before exploring the potential for sexual activity. In some cases, such as that of psychotherapist/client, the ethical codes of the profession may indicate that a sexual relationship is simply not appropriate.

- Coercion is not consent. If there is great pressure to engage in sexual activities, or if sexual activities are the condition for a desired reward, any agreement that might be reached is not true consent. In sexual encounters that incorporate domination and submission activities clear limits need to be negotiated in advance, and each party must be able to terminate the situation at any time.

If you are not certain that someone can give you properly informed consent, *do not have sex with them.* Ignoring proper consent will leave you open to a charge of rape or sexual assault, or you will acquire a reputation of being manipulative and predatory.

What is involved in informed consent? First, there has to be a certain level of disclosure, if nothing else, about one's current relationship status and any sexually transmitted diseases (STDs) one may have been exposed to or be carrying. Some people do not wish to become sexually involved with people who are involved with others, regardless of whether the relationship is open or closed.

Second, there must be some kind of agreement about the context in which the sexual activity is taking place. Is this a casual encounter, undertaken for the mutual physical pleasure of both parties? Is it understood as part of an ongoing relationship that is at least partially sexual in nature? Is it understood as part of a romantically oriented relationship? Sex, regardless of how culturally laden we may have made it, is still an activity. By itself, it does not imply any particular relationship. That is why the relationship around it needs to be discussed and not assumed; it is never safe to assume that everyone engaging in the activity shares the same understanding about the relationship.

Every individual has two fundamental rights in a sexual encounter, and the obligation to respect others, who have these same rights. The first right is to set boundaries. You are responsible, under the "harm none" guidelines, to make every effort to preserve your own health, safety, and sanity in sexual encounters. If you do not wish to engage in a particular sort of activity, if you wish the activity to stop, or if you want the activity to occur only under particular conditions (for example, with condoms), then you are entitled to set these boundaries and to insist that others respect them. Anyone who tries to violate these boundaries after they have been clearly explained, or who puts pressure on you to compromise on issues of your perceived safety, is not someone with whom you would wish to be involved.

The second fundamental right is mutuality, or reciprocity. That is, a person is entitled to "get something" out of a sexual encounter. This something can be physical, it can be emotional, it can be spiritual, or it can be magical—the key is that it be something you desire. Sexual encounters in which only one party consistently satisfies his/her needs and desires are exploitative. This pattern holds a strong chance that the partners are heading toward an abusive relationship. There is nothing wrong with giving sex to someone as a gift; however, it is wrong for someone to demand or expect another to do so, and do so consistently. This expectation does not fall under the description "all acts of love and pleasure."

On the other hand, expecting partners to know boundaries without having communicated them, even inside a magical community, is unreasonable and unfair. If you are not getting what you would like out of a sexual relationship, you need to speak up. Like any other human activity, sex requires practice, patience, and communication. Strive to communicate effectively with your partner.

Some people will interpret any commentary on their sexual "performance" as criticism. Because these things can be very difficult to discuss, you may want to try a first foray in a letter or e-mail. The advantage of this is that it allows you to take some time with the message, to revise it, edit it, and ensure it says exactly what you want it to say. Letters tend to convey gravity, seriousness, and care. The disadvantage is that written communication simply does not convey the same amount of information that in-person communication does. E-mail and letters lack body language, tone of voice, eye contact, touch, and all of the many other things that help us convey our meaning to people face to face. What works for you and your partner can change over time, as you become more and more acquainted with each other's lives.

Sexual activity is energetic—it is a potent way to raise power. Some religious and magical traditions treat sexual activity as a particular sort of discipline, to be studied, learned, and respected. Because sex can involve a lot of vital energy, it is important to realize that some people come out of a sexual encounter feeling very much as though they have come out of a high-powered ritual—energized and "in tune" with the world around them if the power has been properly released, or agitated and drained if it has not. It is important to be aware of the energy that surrounds your sexual encounters, and deal with it appropriately. You should be prepared to engage in the same kind of care after a sexual encounter as you might after a ritual: ensure that there is healthy, protein-rich food and plenty of water available, and leave enough time between the encounter and other commitments to ensure a gentle transition from one to the other.

Sex with More Than One

A polyamorous relationship is one in which one, usually both, of the partners is free to pursue other sexual and emotional relationships with the explicit consent and encouragement of the other partner(s). In some cases, these will be discrete relationships, carried on at a distance from one another, and sometimes they will result in extended, interconnected, "amoeba like" groupings where many of those involved know one another. The additional complexity of polyamory comes out of the number of people whom you have to consider and consult, and the number of needs and desires to respect. Islam allows a man to take more than one wife, but only to the extent that he can treat them all justly. One probably does not have the same expectations of every person with whom s/he is involved; nevertheless, it is still necessary to negotiate expectations with which all involved are happy and comfortable. A relationship in which one party does not feel his/her needs are being met is going to be a problematic relationship. There may be an infinite amount of love in the universe, but each of us has a finite amount of time, energy, and money. The more intimate relationships in which one is involved, the more his/her personal resources are spread out. This can lead to hard and often painful choices about priorities.

If you choose a polyamorous sexuality, it will mean discussing the nuts and bolts of your sexual practices a lot more often, and with more people, than in a monogamous setting. Your partners will want to know what kinds of sexual activities are going on and what level of precaution each person is taking to prevent sexually transmissible infections. In the age of AIDS, this is reasonable information to expect from all of your sexual partners, and all of their sexual partners.

Once more than one person is involved, there is not, and never has been, any such thing as completely "safe" sex; like most human activities, sex carries risks. At the same time, it is important to view the messages we so often receive about the special inherent dangers of sex and sexuality with some suspicion. If we reject the alarmist messages we receive, we must take care not to fall headlong into uncritically accepting the romantic, glamourizing ones. The most difficult part of maintaining sexual health for most people is not in learning the facts and techniques they need to know, but in cutting though the mixed messages and poor communication that prevent them from putting techniques into practice.

Sex is, on average, more dangerous than gardening and safer than riding a motorcycle. Starting from that point, we can examine ways to stay as safe and healthy as possible while honoring our interests and desires. If you can find a sex-positive health care professional with whom you can be open about your sexual practices, he or she will be your best ally in protecting yourself and your partners. Even so, you will need to take primary responsibility for your own health and safety.

The two primary resources for safer-sex information are books and web pages. Well-written books on sexuality and safer sex can be expensive, are often difficult to obtain, and become out of date relatively quickly. Web pages are free and relatively easy to access for most of us, but can disappear or become obsolete and are somewhat more difficult to assess for credibility. Although references on human sexuality and safer sex, especially online, come and go and are updated frequently, here are a few online resources that we have found to be both useful and long-lived.

Society for Human Sexuality, at www.sexuality.org/index.html

Scarleteen: Sex Education for the Real World, at www.scarleteen.com

San Francisco Sex Information, at www.sfsi.org

Sexuality and U, administered by the Society of Obstetricians and Gynaecologists of Canada, at www.sexualityandu.ca

The Body, an AIDS and HIV Information Resource, engineered by Body Health Resources Corporation, at www.thebody.org

MAKING THE CHOICE

Relationships can be rich sources of happiness and well-being. They can enrich our emotional and spiritual lives, as well as renew and reinforce our feelings of connection with the divine and with the universe. They can also become a drain on our emotional, physical, and psychic resources.

It is important to be clear about why you are engaging in a relationship; what you aspire to get out of it; how closely your needs and desires are being met; and what you are willing to do to transform it into a relationship that is healthier for you. The solution to a problem relationship could be in better communication, but sometimes it lies in ending the relationship. Try asking yourself the following three questions:

- Am I happy in this relationship?

- Can I imagine ever being happy again in this relationship?

- Can I see a way of getting from here to there?

If you answer no to two or more of these questions, then it may be time to end the relationship—and this applies to all relationships. There is a limit to how much you can change on your own. If the other person is not willing to work with you toward change, you cannot accomplish it alone.

Magical Relationships

By virtue of your involvement in paganism, there may be several categories of relationships in which you engage that your non-pagan friends do not. In each of these, all of the ordinary guidelines regarding relationships apply. There are unique considerations that arise from the fact that these relationships centrally incorporate a magical element, which is rarely found in "mundane" relationships. The involvement of magical elements heightens the responsibilities of all the individuals involved in three ways: to communicate effectively, to negotiate expectations and interactions, and to set appropriate boundaries.

Relationship with the Divine

One's most important magical relationship is between oneself and the gods. Unlike some other religious traditions, one of the hallmarks of neopagan traditions is that they are based on the idea of a direct, unmediated relationship with a divine that is simultaneously immanent and transcendent. This is the fundamental insight expressed in the phrase "Thou art God/dess." The gods exist both inside and outside the individual, and link the two inseparably. This is what is meant by "As without, so within." It is not the case in neopaganism that all that is good and admirable in the universe is attributed to the divine, and all that is evil and unlovely is attributed to human nature. Neopagans recognize that people are not perfect, and neither are the gods. Every human emotion and human failing is reflected in the universe of the divine. One need only look at mythologies, both ancient and modern, to see that. The gods are wise and benevolent and nurturing, but they are also angry, hot-tempered, and sometimes gullible.

Each of us nurtures our relationship with the divine in different ways. Some people express it through art or music, some through gardens, some through the work that they choose to do. Most important, we nurture our relationship with the divine by taking care of ourselves and our lives, by ensuring there is space in our lives through which the Gods can move and act, and enough peace and quiet for us to hear them. We do a disservice to both ourselves and our gods when we allow ourselves to become so wrapped up in the details of life that we lose sight of the whole picture, the web of life of which we are a part.

If you are finding that you feel a sense of disconnection from the gods, some of the things you may wish to ask yourself are:

- When do I find I feel closest to the gods? How much time am I making in my life for these activities right now?

- When was the last time I did something for me, just because I wanted to? Did I enjoy it, or did I feel guilty for not doing other, "important" things?

- How do I feel about myself right now? What is my self-image like? What sorts of things might I do to improve it?

- How much time am I spending with the people who are important to me? What are my relationships with them like?

You may find that when you work on your relationship with yourself, your relationship with the divine will also improve. Similarly, if you work on your relationship with the divine, you may also find that you feel better about yourself.

Covens and Other Working Groups

A coven is a group of individuals who have decided to celebrate the pagan holidays and do magical work with one another. Working with others can have many benefits for all involved. Working as a solitary pagan can be a lonely, frustrating business. Without fresh perspectives, feedback and occasional guidance, it is sometimes difficult to tell if you are making progress on your spiritual journey. Having the resources of a group of people to draw upon brings new talents and opportunities to everyone's practice. A supportive environment of like-minded people can make you feel less isolated in a world where being pagan is still far from mainstream. Celebrations often feel more celebratory when they are shared.

Not all pagan traditions refer to these as covens—some will use terms such as *circle, grove, ring,* or *troth.* Generally, these are closed groups, so participation is limited to members and those specifically invited. In order to preserve the intimacy and small-group dynamic of these gatherings, regular membership rarely exceeds thirteen people. Some groups contain both men and women, while some are restricted to one sex. A group may be headed by a priestess and/or priest, or they may be non-hierarchical, with leadership responsibilities rotating among members in turn.

Whatever the structure, it is important that all members understand the guidelines and expectations of the coven. A coven is traditionally a space in which the principle of "perfect love and perfect trust" holds sway, and it is difficult for people to feel trust in a situation they do not fully understand. It is also more likely for someone to come to believe that their trust has been betrayed if membership conditions and expectations are not made clear from the beginning. When beginning a magical working group or coven, some of the questions one might wish to clarify with everyone involved include:

- What is the purpose of this group? Is it primarily a ritual group? A study group? A teaching group? A celebratory group? How does each of us understand the group's purpose?

- Will the group's purpose be best served by a time- or outcome-limited structure or an open-ended structure? For example, is the goal to enable each of the group members to attain the level of competence required to run his or her own group? Are group members working toward a new understanding of the wheel of the year, which could take them one or two years to accomplish?

- What responsibilities need to be undertaken in this group? If there are classes, who will prepare them? If there are rituals, who will write them? Who will lead them? It is important that the responsibilities in a group be shared among members. This helps to prevent people from feeling marginalized, and it helps to prevent those people who tend to take on responsibilities from feeling taken advantage of and burning out.

- How are new members admitted to the group? Are they sponsored by an existing member? Must they apply? How do other members meet them? Are new members admitted by consensus or by some other mechanism? Will there be an "inner" and "outer" group? What happens if someone joins and then becomes disruptive?

• To what extent are group members allowed to discuss things that happen inside the group with those who are not members? Can some things be discussed and others not?

This last question is often particularly important, because groups vary tremendously in their attitudes towards secrecy. In most traditions of neopaganism, while it is acceptable to identify yourself as a practitioner, it is never polite to identify anyone else, unless they are very public about their affiliation or you have specific permission. You may be allowed to refer to your coparticipants by their "magical names" outside of the group. Many groups expect that its membership will remain a secret. Some groups restrict access to their teachings and ritual forms to members of their own group or tradition. Many of these groups require members to take some form of oath of secrecy at some point during their training. In groups that emphasize secrecy, all members should be alert to the fact that secrecy can be used in manipulative and exploitative ways, and should commit themselves to preventing this. Secrecy, when improperly deployed, can destroy relationships built on trust within the group. For example, if one member of the group is receiving extra, "secret" instruction from group leaders, and other members discover this, their trust in both the group leaders and in that particular member may be compromised.

Working together magically causes people to be more open and vulnerable to one another than they are in daily life. It is for that reason that the space within a coven's circle is supposed to embody an atmosphere of perfect love and perfect trust. This will not happen right away, and it will not happen automatically. Perfect love and perfect trust are goals—they are to be striven toward—but there should be no feelings of inadequacy or blame if they are not. This kind of intimacy takes time, patience, hope, and communication. Ultimately, if there is not a willingness to open oneself fully to the other members of the group, this will reflect in the energy within the circle, where small tensions will be magnified through the ritual work that is being done.

All small groups are crucibles for conflict, and coven groups are no exception. If there is some conflict among members of a group, this is not a sign of failure. It is natural and normal to experience conflict when bringing different individual personalities with different histories together to work cooperatively. In many of the older British Traditions, it is strongly suggested that people not enter a circle with those with whom they are in conflict. This is a wise suggestion; however, it is not going to strengthen your group if, in situations of minor conflict, the only recourse is to withdraw from participation in the group. Certainly, if the conflict cannot be resolved, this is a likely possibility, but do not undermine the resilience and the vitality of your group by allowing things to get to this point prematurely.

It is good for members of the group to discuss how they might like a conflict handled while it is still hypothetical. You may wish to ask people what kinds of conflict resolution techniques they are familiar with, what has worked for them in the past, and what sorts of experiences they have had with conflict, power, and authority. Individuals should be encouraged to try to work out a conflict on their own first. Managing conflict is an important part of one's own personal development, and the process should not be short-circuited by having all interpersonal conflicts appropriated by the group as soon as they occur. Some of the things you may wish to consider if you are experiencing conflict with another group member are:

- How do I define this conflict? What do I think it is about? When do I think it started? How is it that this situation is causing me to feel? Am I angry? Afraid? Annoyed? Feeling unsafe? What would I like to see happen, ideally?

- How much of this conflict is about the other person, and how much might be my own issues? Is it possible that the behavior of the other person reminds you of behavior you have experienced from other people in the past? If you feel excluded or overlooked, could that reflect, in part, your own feelings of insecurity? Sometimes it is the behavior of the other person that needs changing, but sometimes we can try to change our own responses to the behavior.

- How can I effectively communicate what is bothering me? It is not reasonable to expect change in response to a need that you have not verbalized. Some sources on conflict resolution stress the importance of "I-statements." For example, "You never include me in your social gatherings" can become "I do not feel included/welcome at your social gatherings." If the person is not immediately put on the defensive, you may find that it is a simple miscommunication or oversight that has produced the tension.

- If there is a behavior that needs to be changed, can I provide the other person with an alternative that is acceptable to me? Often a person will not be aware that what they are doing is a problem for others until it is mentioned.

If a situation cannot be resolved by the individuals involved, or if the conflict has escalated or spread to other members of the group, causing divided loyalties, then a neutral third party might be needed to facilitate discussions. This person can then talk to everyone involved about how they define the problem and what they believe the solution should be. A facilitator cannot solve the problem, but he or she can try to help those involved come to an understanding of one another's positions. A solution imposed from the outside may displace tension, but it will not eliminate the conflict unless it is accepted wholeheartedly and in good faith by all those involved.

Over time, your coven will change. This is a natural part of growth. Some people may find another spiritual path or leave because of a conflict that stubbornly resists resolution. An individual may find that she no longer has the time to fulfill membership responsibilities of the group. Everything that grows will change; this is part of the wisdom we have inherited from the Earth. Some changes will be happy changes, and some will be grieved. Where possible, try to bring a sense of closure to all involved. A ritual of departure, with or without the departing member, will allow remaining members a space in which to explicitly acknowledge and accept the feelings they have.

Working Partners

You will probably work with a number of different people in different contexts throughout your pagan career. At some point, you may wish to take one of these people as a magical working partner. While working partnerships are often thought of in connection with the leadership of groups, this is not the only situation in which one might wish to take a working partner. A working partnership is to magic as a marriage is to love. It can be more or less exclusive by mutual agreement, and it can entail a commitment to do some amount of magical work together, a commitment to watch out for each other, and a commitment to a deeper level of trust and intimacy than either partner ordinarily finds elsewhere.

Like a handfasting, a working partnership can be time limited or open ended, but it is usually formalized through some kind of ritual that involves an oath or an undertaking before the gods as to the nature of the partnership. Partnerships may be marked with some exchange of tokens, but need not be. As with anything formalized with a ritual, the dissolution of a working partnership should also be marked with a ritual that will unbind the particular ties between the partners, leaving them free and unpartnered once more. Any tokens previously exchanged to mark the partnership should be returned to their original owners.

While working partners are ordinarily of opposite genders, reflecting the movements of polarity and duality found in much magical work, this does not have to be the case. Most important is the polarity in the energy each person brings to the partnership. Energy is not constrained by physical sex. Working partners are often romantically involved, although this does not have to be the case. It is entirely possible to become a working partner to someone with whom you have never been romantically or sexually involved; it is also possible for a working partnership to outlast the sexual or romantic element of a relationship.

This is why the "sacred marriage" between the God and the Goddess that is celebrated as a mystery in many traditions is more often enacted symbolically between partners. Some questions for you and a potential partner to consider are:

- What do I bring to this partnership? What do I hope to gain from it?

- What do I consider the three most important elements of a magical working relationship? How do these compare to what my potential partner considers important?

- What do our magical universes look like? How do we each conceptualize the elements? Which faces of the Goddess and God am I most comfortable working with? What mythologies do I prefer to draw upon for my metaphors?

- How do I learn? By reading? Talking? Listening? Smell? Through my body? From dreams? Trance? Divination? Visions?

- How do I prefer to work? Full, formal ritual? Informal ritual? Spontaneously, with little preparation?

- In what ways do I hope that this magical partnership will enrich my spiritual practice? My mundane life?

- Where are my magical and spiritual practices in terms of the other priorities in my life?

At minimum, you must share some agreement on core values and goals for a magical partnership to be viable. You must have a profound and deep respect for your partner, who will see you at emotionally and psychically vulnerable points. There should be an abiding affection between you, and a complementarity in your strengths and styles. Two partners who are strong in the same areas have less to contribute to each other's growth than partners who are each strong in the other's area of weakness—so long as this does not lead to a division of labor in which you begin to rely on the other person doing the things you find "hard." Working partners should be like two sides of a coin—different and yet indisputably part of the same fundamental whole.

If you are unsure about entering into a working partnership, it is better to wait. The right person is not going to suddenly vanish from your life if this is the way that things are meant to go. A feeling of "rightness" is important to any sort of magical commitment. In many forms of initiation, the candidate is told, "Better to fall upon thy knife than enter here with fear in thy heart." Entering into a working partnership is similar to an initiation in this way. Preparedness cannot be rushed, and attempts to hurry things along should be viewed with suspicion.

Teacher/Student Relationships

There are many different kinds of teacher/student relationships found in paganism, because teaching and learning go on in many different ways. When we work with our peers, people at about the same level of training as ourselves, we are all teachers and all learners, puzzling things out together. When we are working with those less experienced than ourselves, we may be guides or role models. When we work with those more experienced and more senior than ourselves, we seek to augment our own knowledge through getting guidance from those more experienced.

Sometimes, learning within a magical context occurs tacitly—that is, from being around when things are being done. This form of learning is problematic; because it is not accomplished consciously, misunderstandings and misinformation about the process or practice in question can make their way into one's subconscious, leaving the learner with a vague sense that he or she knows more and is more competent in a particular area than in fact he or she is.

Some groups offer public or semipublic classes, in which the requirements of teachers are to present the material to the best of their ability, to answer student questions, and sometimes, to evaluate students' knowledge through written assignments. This situation is most like the conventional classroom setting, in which students of varying degrees of ability are exposed to the same material, at the same time, by a single teacher. While this is how a great many people get their start in neopagan practice, it is not what is usually thought of when the teacher/student relationship is discussed. This is because many traditions of neopaganism are organized along a "mentorship" model, in which an individual works closely, in a hands-on fashion, with a more experienced person for an extended period of time.

There are many different reasons to seek out a teacher. People new to paganism, having done some reading, often want more concrete direction than that which is found in books. They want feedback, and to know that they are doing it "right." If they wish to be part of an established initiatory tradition, then they will require instruction from someone within that tradition in order to be granted legitimacy in their later practice. More established pagans may wish to enhance a certain area of their practice, and will seek out someone known for a particular type of expertise—herb lore, trance work, or ritual writing, for example.

In general, the teacher/student relationship in paganism should be the main role in which two people find themselves. Because this relationship necessitates a recognition that one person has some degree of authority over the other, it is difficult to layer over other, more equal preexisting relationships. A teacher is necessarily going to be in the position of having to sometimes correct and criticize, and this can be much more difficult if there are existing emotional entanglements. It also becomes more difficult to define when the student/teacher relationship is "on" if there is interaction between the teacher and the student in a variety of different roles.

Like all other relationships, the teacher/student relationship will be most successful if both parties understand the goals and expectations of the relationship. This will require prior negotiation as well as possible renegotiation over time.

MAKING THE CHOICE

Before embarking on a search for a teacher, students might wish to answer the following questions for themselves:

- What kind of instruction am I looking for? What am I interested in learning? Can I learn this better under someone else's guidance than I could on my own? Why?

- How much of my life am I willing to give my teacher authority over? Is there a place where I believe his or her legitimate authority ends? Where is that? For example, would I be willing to heed an instruction to work on my physical body (get more exercise, go to the gym) before working on my magical life? Would I change my eating habits? Would I refrain from romantically pursuing someone my teacher did not view as suitable? What are my boundaries?

- In what settings do I learn best? How much oversight and guidance do I want?

- How much time can I reasonably expect to commit to my program of study?

- Are the significant people in my life supportive of my desire to do this? Do they understand the commitment of time and energy it may involve?

- What is my end goal? Do I wish to become a member of a coven? Do I want to start my own group someday? Am I preparing myself to eventually take students of my own? Do I want to become involved in more public work, in pagan chaplaincy or advocacy work, for example?

Choosing a Teacher

Once you are clear on what you wish to accomplish and why, you are prepared to venture forth and consider individual people. This may be much easier for those living in urban areas with a number of known and established groups than it is for those living in smaller communities, or those where the pagan scene is much more underground. "Because he or she was the only person I could find" is not sufficient reason to work with someone. You would be better advised to work on your own than to work in an incompatible relationship. Underage students should be prepared to have prospective teachers tell them that they will need full parental knowledge and consent. Minors are legally subject to parental authority, and a responsible teacher will not undermine that.

Having found seemingly a suitable teacher, there are more things to consider:

- What is this person's reputation in the community? How much is known about him/her? How long have they been in this community? Are there any unsavory rumors circulating about them? Can these rumors be verified or dispelled? If the individual is asked about the rumors, how does s/he respond?

- Is this individual a member of an established group or tradition? As his/her student, how much contact would I have with other members of the group? Is this a group I might eventually wish to join? Is it a tradition in which I would be comfortable?

- Does this person have other students? How many? Can I talk to him/her about how s/he feels about the training they are receiving? Does the person have former students in the community? What do they say about the training they received with this person?

- If the individual does have other students, will I be receiving one-on-one or group instruction, or a mix of both? How well do I think I will work with this person's other students? Does this teacher do the bulk of the instruction, or is much left to his/her senior students?

Becoming a Teacher

Being approached as a potential teacher is flattering. We all appreciate being thought of as knowledgeable and competent, especially in areas that are important to us. By itself, however, flattery is not a good or ethical reason to take on students. While you probably know of people who seem to collect students solely for the prestige of having them, this is a situation that is unlikely to last long, as these people fast develop reputations for being incompetent or indifferent teachers. As a teacher, you are responsible for the knowledge and skills you equip your students with, and partially responsible for the results of how these are used. You can indeed bear the karmic weight of having enabled an action. If you equip someone with magical credentials which they use in a manipulative, unethical manner in the community, you bear some responsibility for their conduct.

MAKING THE CHOICE

If you are considering taking someone on as a student, some of the things you may want to consider are:

- Given this prospective student's goals and aspirations, will I be able to provide the appropriate guidance and expertise? Do I have access to resources that will supplement areas in which I may be less strong?

- Am I the first person this student has approached? If not, for what reasons is s/he now approaching me? Has this person trained with anyone else in the community I can speak to about him/her?

- Does this person strike me as committed and hardworking, or does s/he seem like the kind of person who will be disappointed and disillusioned by the tedium and decided lack of glamour that is much of magical training? Is the student overly focused on the "status" aspects of pagan tradition, for example the "exact" requirements for an initiation or elevation?

- Do I have the time and energy to engage with a student (or another student!) right now? Is "teacher" a role that fits in with my own development and my own goals? Is the amount of time I can make available consonant with what this person wants or needs?

- How "together" is this student's mundane life? By involving myself with him/her in a magical mentorship role, how much might I come to be relied upon to "fix" other areas of his/her life? Do I believe that this sort of intervention is part of the mandate of a teacher?

- Given my assessment of this person, their temperament and style, do I think s/he will listen to me and respect my authority in the areas in which I teach?

If all of these issues can be settled to the satisfaction of both parties, the teacher/student relationship can go ahead. Some people like to negotiate a kind of formal contract that sets out the rights and responsibilities of each party. This is a useful exercise, because it provides a written record of those things about which you believe you are both in agreement, and a standard against which subsequent conduct can be judged.

Payment

In general, mentorship-style teaching in most pagan traditions is not reimbursed with cash. While you may expect to pay fees to attend workshops given by pagan notables, or for courses offered through an institutional framework such as a college or university, private and personal teaching is usually given free of charge. A teacher who charges a fixed fee per lesson should be regarded with suspicion. This is not to say that a student should not be expected to pay any of the costs associated with his/her training. It is customary for students to provide their own robes and tools, and to make contributions to the general ritual supplies that are depleted by their training. A student may, out of respect and appreciation for the time and efforts of their teacher, offer to provide non-magical services in return for teaching. This is common practice in many non-Western spiritual traditions. For example, a student might offer to help with yard work, small repairs, or transportation to and from awkward locations. If this is expected it should be stated up front. For example, "Because I spend a lot of time and energy preparing to teach and working with my students, one of the things I require is that they be willing to babysit my children one night a month so that I can have some time to devote to self-care." Like those who charge money for classes, teachers whose willingness to teach seems contingent upon the performance of personal services that were not specified in advance as part of the original negotiations should be viewed with suspicion.

The performance of sexual acts or the provision of sexual favors as a condition of training is never an appropriate request! If you receive such as request, you should not only refuse it, but you should also make other pagan elders in your community aware of it. Most pagan communities are very intolerant of this kind of predatory behavior. Do be aware, some covens originating out of a British Traditional framework require the Great Rite to be done in actuality rather than in token as part of the third-degree initiation. Other Traditions do not. Ascertain a coven's policy well before accepting an offer to initiate.

Magical relationships should be characterized by all of the same qualities that make other relationships healthy and rewarding. They should involve consideration, honesty and respect. Even when (such as in teacher-student relationships) one party is under the authority of another to a certain extent, there must be a way in which each party can express his/her feelings and concerns and expect to be heard by the other.

Respect and trust must be mutual for any relationship to be successful.

Resources

Courage to Heal: A Guide for Women Survivors of Child Sexual Abuse, by Ellen Bass and Laura Davis (New York: Perennial, 1988).

The Ethical Slut: A Guide to Infinite Sexual Possibilities, by Dossie Easton and Catherine A. Liszt (San Francisco: Greenery Press, 1988).

Wicca Covens, by Judy Harrow (Secaucus, N.J.: Citadel Press, 1999).

Miss Manners' Basic Training, by Judith Martin (New York: Random House, 1998).

Health Care Without Shame: A Handbook for the Sexually Diverse and Their Caregivers, by Charles Moser (San Francisco: Greenery Press, 1999).

Truth or Dare, by Starhawk (San Francisco: Harper and Row, 1987).

You Just Don't Understand: Women and Men in Conversation, by Deborah Tannen (New York: Ballantine Books, 1990).

SM 101: A Realistic Introduction, by Jay Wiseman (San Francisco: Greenery Press, 1998).

CHAPTER 4

Children

One of the most value-laden "choice" spheres in the world is the constellation of issues that coalesce around children. Will you have children, or not? Does not wanting children make you a selfish person? Is it somehow more pagan to have children and continue the circle of life and of care? Is having children globally irresponsible, particularly when developed countries use far more than their share of natural resources?

And if *you* have children, what will you do with them once you have them?

Whether they choose to have children or not, many people come to feel as though they have to defend themselves to others. Sometimes, the most effective way to head this off is to stonewall the conversation. When someone begins to criticize your reproductive choices, you can simply say something to the effect of, "While I am sure you have opinions on this matter, I don't particularly care to hear them. Shall we move on to another topic?" While this is blunt almost to the point of being offensive, it is also difficult to misinterpret. You are under an obligation to make a reasoned and informed choice about your reproductive trajectory; you are not, in fact, under any obligation to explain or defend that choice to anyone not immediately involved.

Choosing Not to Have Children

If you have made the choice not to have children and you cannot anticipate any situation under which you would change your mind, you might consider a permanent sterilization option—vasectomy for men,

tubal ligation for women. Although both of these procedures are theo-
retically reversible, there is no guarantee of success, so sterilization is a
poor short-term option. A woman in her 20s, may find that doctors are
reluctant to perform a sterilization, especially if she is unpartnered. She
can try shopping around, but there is a good chance that she might
have to resign herself to waiting until she is older or partnered.

Keep in mind that opting for sterilization, does not negate the need
for vigilance in sexual activities. Both vasectomies and tubals have been
known to fail, or to spontaneously reverse themselves, and neither offers any protection against sexually transmissible diseases. As a friend
once commented, "When I asked him to use a condom, he replied that
he was fixed. I asked if he was sterilized and shrink-wrapped too." From
a safer sex perspective, condoms are always advisable in any situation
where the goals of the sexual activity do not include procreation. One
cannot avoid the reality that vaginal/penile intercourse always carries
with it the possibility of a pregnancy. If one is truly set against a pregnancy occurring, there are many other sexual activities in which one
can engage that do not carry this risk.

Women who do not want children at the moment but may wish to
have them later should consider other contraceptive measures in addition to condoms, which can break and slip. Birth control pills are very
effective when taken properly, which means at the same time every day,
but they are not recommended for all women. Other "continuous protection" options include Depo-Provera injections, Norplant contraceptive implants, IUDs and transdermal patches. For an assessment of what
kind of birth control is right for you, visit your doctor or a Planned
Parenthood clinic. Remember, other forms of birth control do not replace condoms for protection from disease.

There is more to the decision not to have children than simply a list
of technical pregnancy avoidance procedures. Whether or not you want
to have children in your life will also affect whom you date. Getting involved with someone who wants children in his/her life someday
means letting him/her know fairly early on that you do not share that
aspiration. Developing a deep love relationship with an individual while
hoping all the while that s/he will change his/her mind about something so important is not respectful of either partner's life goals. Put

bluntly, it can potentially generate a lot of negative karma. It is difficult to maintain a healthy, supportive intimate relationship if one party feels as though they have had to make a huge sacrifice to keep the other.

If you meet someone amazing who has kids from a previous marriage, try to keep in mind that while s/he may not have custody at the moment, you may still have to deal with the kids in the future. As a veteran stepmother once said, "Being a step-parent is like being the vice president. Sure, you signed on for one job description, but you have to know in the back of your mind that you could be catapulted into a totally different role on a moment's notice." Step-parenting carries a lot of the same obligations as parenting, but does not always come with the same rewards. You will also end up having to deal with this amazing person's previous partner, if only at one remove. This constant reminder of a partner's previous life and previous love is something that many people have difficulty with in a romantic relationship, particularly when the presence of children means that "current family" priorities frequently have to take a backseat to "previous family" priorities—whether that means a lower standard of living due to child support obligations or restrictions on activities: for example, not being able to take extended vacations or immerse yourself in adult-oriented activities with your partner because of visitation agreements.

Accidental Pregnancy

Accidents can happen. Condoms break, diaphragms shift, the Pill can become useless when a woman takes certain antibiotics like tetracycline. What will happen to your relationship if there is an accidental pregnancy? How do you feel about abortion? How does your partner feel? On one hand, it could be argued that terminating a pregnancy is no different from what happens in nature—not all seedlings survive. It is also possible to argue that, if we live in a meaningful universe in which things happen to us for a reason, the pregnancy is meant to happen and it should be allowed to continue to term. Ultimately, it is a deeply personal decision that has to be made within a personal, emotional and practical context. What does neopaganism say about abortion? Neopaganism does not say *anything* about abortion. Neopaganism's situational morality means that there are no "one size fits all" answers. Pagans must decide what they think about abortion on their own, within the context of what they believe to be true about the world.

One of the most immediately obvious considerations for many pagans about abortion is "harm." This is partially about whether or not abortion harms a fetus, and whether a fetus can be harmed in the sense that is meant by the Rede; it is an individual's responsibility to discern the potential harms entailed in having the abortion vs. not having the abortion. Either decision has the potential to be life changing—but which is the most likely to minimize harm in the circumstance? Men often feel held hostage by the woman's power to choose. While it may also be his potential child, she is the one ultimately empowered to decide whether she will carry to term. It is her body. If a man does not want a woman to continue with the pregnancy, and she decides to do so anyway, the potential scope of the man's choice changes. Because we are all ultimately responsible for the consequences of our own actions, the man has responsibilities toward the child. By law, he must, at minimum, provide financial support for the child's upkeep. He may choose to parent actively or not, but he will not be able to escape the reality of now *being* a parent.

Respecting Choices

Individuals who are childless by choice often face criticism from others who are not themselves intending to live that lifestyle. Such criticism can be viewed as deeply inappropriate from a pagan standpoint, where a lot of emphasis is put on being respectful and tolerant of others' choices, so long as those choices are not harming people. Since there is not much one can do to compel others to be respectful, one of the more appropriate ways to deal with it is to refuse to allow the situation to escalate. Each instance will be different. Some people will ask about the motivations behind your choices because they are trying to understand them—and this is true of almost any choice, be it your particular form of spirituality, your occupation, or your musical preferences. Many times, these people are not being judgmental as much as they are confessing their ignorance, and need to be treated differently from those who want to hear your reasons so that they can start an argument about why they are not good enough. While the first might deserve a thoughtful, honest answer, the second might be better stonewalled. "I don't care to discuss this with you" or "I can think of no reason why that would be any of your business" come to mind as useful conversation stoppers. Just as you have the right to make the choice, you also have the right to elect not to defend it to all comers.

If you want respect for your own choices, it is always wise to endeavor to respect the choices of others. Invariably, their choices will impinge upon you much more than your choice to be childless will impinge upon them. Contrary to popular belief, it is as difficult to control a child as it is to control an adult. When a harried parent with a screaming toddler in the grocery cart is behind you in line, it might be a better response to allow them to go in front of you rather than to glare at them with a "can't you do anything about that child" look. Giving them your place in line furthers both your goals and theirs. When we look for solutions based in kindness, we can bring more good feeling into the world.

Choosing to Have Children

Women who want children, especially as they get older, often do not want to invest a lot of time and emotional energy in relationships in which that important life goal would not be met. Female fertility, according to recent studies, begins to decline much earlier than previously believed, beginning a downward slide at 28 that gains momentum very quickly as a woman moves through her 30s.

Pagans often discuss their decision to have children in terms of their participation in the web of life. Children are one of the gifts that we can give to the world. It is important to remember though, that they are only one of the gifts. Raising a child requires a huge commitment of time, energy, and resources, and those people who choose not to have children use those resources to different ends just as creative and valuable. When we say that women experience all of the aspects of the Goddess—maiden, mother, and crone—it is important to keep in mind that the defining feature of the mother aspect is not physical maternity; it is a combination of creativity, nurturance, and commitment. These can be expressed many ways other than the physical. It is sadly all too common for childless women to come out of rituals intended to celebrate and empower the feminine feeling alienated because of the perceived emphasis on motherhood in regard to children.

For those people who choose to have children, only one experience is almost universal. Having a child will change your life. Your whole life, not just the bits that seem obvious, like having to get a babysitter to go to a movie with your partner, or having a lot more to carry when you go out. Having a child changes everything—your relationship with your partner, your priorities, your career plans, your sex life, even your relationship with your body. Some of those changes can be anticipated, many others simply have to be dealt with as they are encountered, and while the broad contours of the experience may be the same for many couples, the details are always unique.

Preparing to Have a Baby

Having a child will change your life, no matter where you are in your life course. The best time to have a child will be when you feel ready to have the ongoing day-to-day reality of a child in your world. Exactly what this entails and when it happens will vary in each family.

FINANCIAL PREPARATIONS

Take a hard look at your current financial situation and try to anticipate what would change about that situation were you to have a child. Some things you may want to consider are:

• Do I have adequate medical insurance, and if not, what is the average cost of prenatal care and childbirth in my community? While in Canada, the majority of the cost of having a baby is borne by the universal health insurance plans provided by the provinces, in most parts of the United States, these costs are borne either by the parents or their private insurers.

- Will one family member need to be off work for a time to care for the child? Can I do without that income? If so, for how long?

- How stable is the employment of the parent who will remain in the workforce? Is it likely that they will be downsized before or soon after the baby is born? How large is our emergency fund?

- If we both return to work eventually, what sorts of child-care arrangements can we make? What are the costs of institutional day care centers and private home care in our community? Is there a trustworthy family member who could care for our child?

- What about day-to-day costs? Clothes, diapers, car seat ... the stuff we really cannot do without no matter how simple our lifestyle? Will relatives or friends pass things down to us, or will we be faced with either having to buy these things new or watching the "for sale" listings?

- Is my space going to be adequate for an infant? A toddler? Am I content with the neighborhood? If I decide to move, will I be paying more or less for my living space?

EMOTIONAL PREPARATIONS

While there may be no "'good time" to have a child, there are certainly bad times. One of the worst is probably when the couple or family relationship is already under a lot of stress. Some people want to have a baby because they believe it will somehow "fix" what is wrong with an existing situation. This strategy usually backfires. Here are some of the questions you may wish to consider when you think about emotional readiness:

- How strong is our relationship right now? Are we under a lot of stress? What are the sources of this stress? Are the situations causing the stress likely to change in the next year? Are we fighting? What sorts of things are we fighting about? Do the fights actually get resolved, or do they just get abandoned and show up again later?

- How much have we talked about what we think life would be like with a child? Do we have the same sorts of expectations? Have we talked about parenting philosophy, what we think is important for a child to learn from his/her parents and home environment? Do we agree in principle on child-care issues? Do we have the same reasons for agreeing, or are we getting to the same practical ends by totally different philosophical means? Does it matter?

- How much have we talked about the kinds of lifestyle changes that will happen once we have a child? Will the division of labor be the same? How do we value paid work versus unpaid domestic work?

- What happens to ongoing activities? (Does she stay in the softball league? Does he still go out one night a week with the boys?) How are we going to balance parenting time, couple time, and individual time?

- Am I prepared to raise a child alone? While it is comforting to imagine that we will never be in this situation, the reality is that many of us will face it at one time or another, whether it is due to separation, divorce, or the death of a partner. If you do not honestly believe that you would have the emotional or physical resources to care for a child on your own, it would probably be prudent to meditate upon both the Rede and the threefold law before you commit to a pregnancy.

Available Support

It is often said: "It takes a village to raise a child." Unfortunately, in the urban environment in which most people live, a "village" is hard to find. Parenthood can be isolating, frustrating and demoralizing. As one new parent put it, "Ten years of university, and I spend my days performing tasks that could just as easily be done by a lobotomized monkey!" For people used to working in a group environment or those who have always endeavored to spend a lot of time with others, the day-to-day routine of parenting can be a very lonely experience. In addition, the needs of the child—who cannot meet them on his or her own—often come to supersede the needs of the parents. Parenting can be an extremely stressful activity.

When parents allow their own needs to drop to the bottom of the list, it can breed depression and resentment. In general, depressed, resentful parents are less effective than those who have managed to achieve some kind of better balance. Depression and resentment can cause parents to miss much of the joy and excitement of a child's early years—the ones spent discovering the world.

As mentioned in chapter 1, the Rede implies a duty of care for oneself. Remember, "Thou art God/dess." Sure, you are going to need to put the baby's needs first *a lot* of the time, but it doesn't have to be all the time. This is where support systems come in.

FAMILY

How are your relationships with your family? Your partner's family? Do family members live close by? How constrained are they by their own lives? Do they have infirmities, demanding jobs, school commitments or such that would prevent them from being able to give you an occasional break? Will your family respect your childrearing decisions and practices in your absence? Family can be both a boon and a curse for parents. While they represent a potentially enormous avenue of support, they can also be critical of your approach to parenting.

FRIENDS

Think about your friends. Are they mostly "doing" friends or "being" friends?

"Doing" friends are those with whom the focus is primarily on shared activities. You may be thick as thieves while you are engaging in the activity, but not see or talk to them much outside of that context. "Doing" friendships often become less intense or may vanish altogether during your child's early years, as there is simply less time available for activities. "Doing" friends are a great source of reassurance and reaffirmation that you are still an interesting and valuable person, despite being a parent. They remind you of the aspects of your life that are not totally invested in parenthood. They may not be the people who are going to help you fold your laundry or watch the baby while you go to get your hair cut.

"Being" friends are those with whom the focus is primarily on each other as people. It is a more personal kind of relationship. "Being" friends are the people with whom you can just hang out. They are the ones you can call to keep you company while you regrout the bathroom tiles.

How do your friends feel about children? Are they likely to be as willing to spend time with you even when you have a baby in tow? Do any of your friends have children of their own? Would it be possible to set up a "babysitting swap" with them? These small things can make a huge difference to one's parenting experience.

OTHER SUPPORT SYSTEMS

How family friendly is your workplace? Do they have parental-leave days, or are you going to have to use vacation or sick time to take care of a sick child or go to preschool graduation? Do they have flex-time policies? What is the corporate culture like? Is the workplace task oriented or time oriented? Is there an option to work part-time? To work at home? Despite greater awareness of this the issue, the worklife/homelife balance continues to be very difficult for people to negotiate.

How mobile are you going to be? Do you have your own car? Do you and your partner share a car? Do you live in an area with a good public transportation system? Would you be able to manage public transit with a small child and all the child's gear? Do you have an extra car seat in case someone drops by and offers to take you somewhere?

If you are working with a coven, how child friendly are they? Would they permit a young child in ritual? Do any of the other coveners have children? What do they do about ritual? Would they be willing to meet at your house while your child is small so that the child could be put to bed before ritual begins?

What services are there for parents in your community? Many communities offer playgroups, daycare, health clinics, or library preschool programs. If you choose to nurse, is there a La Leche League chapter? Is there a park within walking distance?

Do you have a pediatrician who supports your choice of parenting methods? How good is your relationship with your family doctor? A good relationship with a family doctor is particularly important, because it increases the likelihood that any postpartum depression will be detected and treated early.

There is no single known cause of postpartum depression. Women who previously have had an episode of clinical depression are more likely to suffer from postpartum depression than women who have not. Most studies suggest that it is a combination of biological, psychological, and social factors. This form of depression is often most successfully treated with a combination of medication and talk therapy. Your medical professional will be able to outline the pros and cons of the available pharmacological treatments.

Baby Debates

Once you have a baby, you will likely be sucked into at least some of the "baby debates." The more common ones to discuss here are: breast vs. bottle, crib or co-sleeping, cloth diapers vs. disposable, back to work vs. stay at home, and child discipline.

Breast vs. Bottle

The question of whether to breast-feed, bottle-feed, formula-feed or do some combination of all of these has become a very value-laden one in contemporary society. It is one of those issues that inspires "good mother/bad mother" labeling, and can act to demoralize mothers regardless of their choice.

It is widely agreed in the medical profession that breast milk is good for babies. Breast milk is a complex, changeable organic fluid. Early milk (colostrum) is different from milk produced after the first week postpartum. The composition of breast milk changes even during the course of one feeding, from the thin, lactose-loaded foremilk to the creamy, higher fat hindmilk. Breast milk contains antibodies that help to jump-start an infant's immune system. Exclusive nursing (no supplementation) also delays an infant's exposure to potential allergens, which can be an important consideration for families with a history of severe allergies. Babies who are breast-fed have fewer medical visits for ear infections and respiratory illnesses than their formula-fed counterparts. Because breast milk is more completely digested by babies than is formula, breast-fed babies have fewer, less smelly bowel movements. On the other hand, because no heavy residue remains in the baby's gastrointestinal system, breast-fed babies are hungry more often than many baby books suggest.

Exclusive breast-feeding tends to delay the return of the mother's menstrual cycles for six to nine months postpartum; this decreases her risk of both anemia and becoming pregnant again. Because nursing burns between 200 and 900 calories per day, nursing mothers tend to return to their pre-pregnancy weights more quickly than non-nursing mothers. This can be especially relevant for women who have had gestational diabetes during their pregnancy. Last, many women find nursing more convenient than bottle feeding. With breast milk, you always have it with you, there is nothing to sterilize, it is always the right temperature, and it is free! While many physicians will recommend exclusive breast-feeding for the first three to six months, and while many women in developing countries with unsafe water supplies will nurse until their child is four or five years of age, it is important to remember that *some* breast-feeding is better than *no* breast-feeding, and no one should feel guilty or like a failure for discontinuing breast-feeding or adding supplements before these times.

That being said, however, some women experience physical difficulties breastfeeding. If these cannot be corrected by a lactation consultant, nurse practitioner or La Leche league leader, these women will need to formula feed. In addition, some women will experience intense negative emotions around breastfeeding, particularly if they have a past history of sexual abuse. Nursing on demand can make a woman feel as though she has lost control and ownership of her own body. Some women take medications or have illnesses that make their breast milk problematic, and some families simply decide that formula feeding makes the best sense for their lifestyle.

One of the advantages of bottle-feeding, whether you use expressed breast milk or formula, is that it allows other members of the family to participate in the feeding process. This can result in considerable liberation for the mother, who will be able to leave her child in the care of others while she takes a "time out" from baby. It also means that night feedings can be handled by the father or another member of the extended family.

Crib vs. Co-Sleeping

The crib vs. co-sleeping debate has to do with a family's particular style of parenting. Co-sleeping simply means that the baby sleeps in a bed with someone else rather than alone in a crib. For this reason, co-sleeping is also known as the "family bed." Co-sleeping is particularly associated with *attachment parenting*, a style articulated in the many books of Dr. William Sears. Attachment parenting also tends to include child wearing (baby in a sling most of the time) and prolonged breast-feeding. The environment of trust, advocates believe, is best built up by offering even the youngest child a "child-centered environment" in which their needs are met quickly and consistently, hence the focus on having someone with the baby almost at all times.

Some people find that having the baby in the family bed means that the baby falls asleep more quickly and wakes less often. If the mother is nursing, she can nurse in the bed without having to fully wake up, get up, and fetch the baby. On the other hand, babies often take up more room in a bed than their small size would suggest. One parent may be a very light sleeper and not want the baby fussing in the same room. The baby may be a light sleeper as well, and wake when a parent rolls over or gets up to use the bathroom. While many people worry about rolling over on top of their babies, this appears to be an unfounded fear. After all, how often do you roll on top of your partner, or your cat?

There are many alternatives to the family bed that do not move to the opposite extreme of having the baby in a crib in another room. For example, some people remove one side of the crib and snug it up to the bed, so that the baby is within reach, but not in the bed itself. Others put a mattress on the floor in another room. The baby is put down there first. When the baby fusses, one parent goes in and lies down with the baby. The parent may then either fall asleep there or return to the room where his/her partner is.

While some people find that co-sleeping is the only way that they get any rest, others report that their child always slept fine on their own. Some parents believe that it is centrally important that a child learn to "self-soothe," that is, to calm him/herself down with minimal or no intervention from adults or other children.

How the bedtime routine gets handled is something that will vary from child to child, and needs to be revisited for each baby. Just as both "Thou art God/dess" and "An' ye Harm None" direct you to look after your own needs, they also establish your child as a unique individual and equally divine. Just as you would not necessarily use the same prewritten ritual to worship, say, Kali and Demeter, you should try not to allow yourself to be lured into the trap of thinking that all of your children must be raised exactly the same.

Cloth Diapers vs. Disposable

You would not think that what you cover a baby's leaky bottom with would be a terribly contentious issue, but disposable diapers have come to be seen in some quarters as emblematic of everything that is wrong with our consumer-driven society.

Proponents of disposable diapers point to their convenience—there is no need to soak, rinse or wash a disposable diaper (although, as with cloth, infant fecal matter should be scraped or shaken into the toilet before the diaper is put into the trash). Disposable diapers leak less frequently, especially on active toddlers, and disposable diapers are widely believed to keep babies drier than their cloth counterparts, thus reducing diaper rash. Studies have shown, however, that some of the dryness benefits of disposable diapers are deceptive, since parents tend to change a baby diapered in disposables less often than a baby in cloth. This results in the formation of bacteria in urine that is exposed to air being against a child's skin for longer periods of time, also contributing to diaper rash. There is no appreciable difference, overall, in the diaper rash rates of babies in cloth and babies in disposables; however, each individual baby will have their own reaction.

Advocates of reusable cloth diapers assert that there is a substantial environmental benefit to using cloth diapers, and suggest that using cloth is less expensive than using disposables over the long term. It is incontrovertibly true that the use of cloth diapers prevents a large quantity of waste from entering our landfill sites. Disposable diapers, it is estimated, can take up to five hundred years to decompose, and most children will go through approximately 8000 diapers during their earliest years.

As to cost benefits, these will depend on how you approach cloth diapering. If you elect to use a diaper service, where your bag of dirty diapers is picked up every week by the service and a new, clean bag is left in its place, you will generally be charged by the number of diapers in your regular order. Five or six dozen, especially when the child is young, is not unreasonable. You will tend to use fewer diapers as the child gets older and his/her bladder gets bigger.

Washing your own cloth diapers involves an initial investment in diapers and diaper covers, which can vary widely in price. Plain folded diapers of the type the diaper services use are often $10 to $15 per dozen, while shaped, fitted, or organic cotton diapers can run between $60 and $100 per dozen. Again, you will need between three and five dozen diapers per child, depending on how often you plan to wash them. While the startup cost can be high, the ongoing costs of washing your own diapers is quite low—usually an extra two loads of laundry per week. Even when you factor in the costs of the water, the power to heat the water, the power to run the washer (and the dryer if you do not live in an area where a clothesline is appropriate), and the soap, it is clearly much less expensive than either of the other two options. The disadvantage it has is that it is considerably more work, and does involve rinsing and soaking dirty diapers, a task that many people find distasteful.

Advocates of disposable diapers will frequently argue that cloth diapers are not without their own environmental impact. Cotton crops generally involve a lot of chemical pesticides. There is the matter of the power and the water required to wash them, and the amount of detergent this puts into lakes and rivers. Diaper services also tend to bleach diapers to remove stains and keep them as white as possible. On the other hand, one major disposable diaper manufacturer lists the ingredients in their diapers as: wood cellulose fiber (the fluffy, paperlike stuff, which itself, has gone through a bleaching process), sodium polyacrylate (the super-absorbent material that is in the diaper), polypropylene, polyester, and polyethylene (synthetic materials that help the diaper keep its shape and leak less).

Proponents of cloth diapers suggest that toilet training is facilitated by cloth diapers because the child can feel when they are wet, and it is a generally uncomfortable feeling that children would rather avoid, thus giving them motivation to go in the potty. Disposable diapers lessen that feeling of being wet, although children also tend not to like the feeling of a soggy mass of paper between their legs either. Manufacturers of disposable diapers have started to add "incentive features" to the design of their larger sizes, such as patterns that are visible when dry but fade when wet.

There is no dispute about the convenience of disposable diapers. To what extent you are willing to be inconvenienced by your environmental principles is a call that only you can make, but there are a wide variety of scenarios in which both types of diapering can be used depending on the circumstance. For example, you could start your child out in cloth and move him/her to disposables when s/he becomes an active walker. You could use cloth at home, but use disposables when you are out, so that you do not have to haul dirty diapers home in the diaper bag—although large sealable plastic bags make this less of a chore than you might think! You can use cloth during the day and disposables at night. While it might be better to completely remove disposable diapers from the waste stream, taking steps to *reduce* the number of disposables you use is also beneficial.

Back to Work vs. Stay at Home

This is probably the single most divisive issue among mothers, and it is beginning to become more of an issue for fathers as well, as the world of parental leave has now opened up to them. Will both parents work after the child is born, or is one parent going to stay home in the role of full-time caretaker? For many families, this question is settled by financial considerations—the lower-income parent's earnings are more than the cost of daycare, *and* those earnings are needed to sustain the family. In this case, the element of choice that presents itself is that of what kind of child care will be both appropriate and affordable?

There are upsides and downsides to both choices. Parents who choose to stay at home have their work devalued, and lose a lot of the positive feedback and adult interaction that can be found in the workplace. The stay-at-home parent is often expected to shoulder more of the domestic duties than was the case before, and not just those related to childcare. The upside of the decision to stay at home is the higher level of interaction you have when your child is young.

Women who stay home often find it easier to continue the breast-feeding relationship with their child than women who go back to work and are faced with the task of expressing or pumping, an exercise their employers may not support. Stay-at-home parents get to witness their child's "firsts" in person, rather than hearing about them from someone else. They do, however, need to make an effort to create adult social opportunities for themselves. Maintaining some "non-baby" interests, even if they are limited to participation in online groups, is important for the at-home parent's self-esteem and sense of self.

Working parents are bombarded by the media with information that children who have been placed in day care have poorer outcomes than children who stay home with a parent. Day care has been blamed for everything from bad grades to rowdiness to an inability to form adult attachments. What the popular media often chooses *not* to report, however are the contextual variables beyond "in day care" or "not in day care." For example, it is widely known that children from disadvantaged backgrounds do more poorly in school than those from middle and upper-class backgrounds. This has nothing to do with whether or not both parents were working, since it remains the case if one or even *both* parents are at home. The poor school performance has to do with the level of "school readiness" that children display when they enter the school system. The parents of children from lower-income families may not have been able to afford a high quality day-care setting. Who gives the child their earliest care is not as important as the quality of the care the child receives, and the environment within which the child receives it.

For parents returning to work, the issue of finding quality child care is paramount. For pagan parents, the issue can be complex. You want a setting that will nurture the divine within your child and bring that divinity out into the world. There are three basic options: a nanny (a child-care provider who works in your home); a home-based day care (you take your child to someone else's home), or a day care center. There is not one option that is automatically the best. You can find examples of good care and poor care in all of these categories. Parents are well-advised to start their research as soon as there is a positive pregnancy test, or even before, as many facilities and day-care owners have a waiting list, especially for infant care.

MAKING THE CHOICE

Some of the questions you might want to consider if you are looking at a *home day-care setting* are:

- How many children are being cared for? Most provinces and states have established legal limits to the number of children who may be taken in by a single caregiver.

- How close in age are they to my own child? An infant or toddler, for example, requires a different environment from older children coming for before- and after-school care.

- Does the caregiver have children? These children are often excluded in the legal counts. How might the number and ages of these children affect the care my child will receive? Do the caregiver's children look clean and healthy?

- Is the caregiver an independent, or is she affiliated with some agency that does periodic check-ins to help ensure the quality of care?

- Does the caregiver have any formal qualifications? How long have they been doing this kind of work? Are they willing to give me references?

- What happens when the caregiver is sick or on vacation? Does the caregiver charge two weeks of vacation time per year? What if we are on vacation? Do I still pay the caregiver for my spot?

- How close to my parenting philosophy is that of the caregiver? What is his/her approach to discipline? To toilet training? How does s/he handle food? Do I bring snacks for my child, or does the caregiver provide them? If the latter, how healthy are the snacks?

- How flexible is the caregiver about drop-off and pickup times? Is s/he willing to do evening work at all?

- If there is a television, how much TV are the children permitted to watch? What type of programming?

- What is the caregiver's home like? Is it childproofed? Is there adequate room for children to play, or is it crammed with furniture? What kinds of toys and activities are visible? Is there a yard? Do the children spend some time outside each day, weather permitting?

- Does the caregiver take the children on outings? To the park? The library? How do they get there? Are you comfortable letting the caregiver take your child in his/her car? If so, are there an adequate number of acceptable car seats to accommodate all of the children?

Some of the questions you may wish to consider when choosing a *day-care center* are:

- Who licenses the facility and how is it monitored? Most day-care centers display their certifications and accreditations near the front door. If you don't see any, inquire about them.

- What qualifications do the staff hold? Do they have early childhood education diplomas? Other relevant qualifications? Do they have up-to-date first aid, CPR and infant CPR qualifications? If not, is there a nurse on staff?

- Is the facility affiliated with another program into which the child can move when they are older? Sometimes, private schools will have a preschool or infant program attached to them. This can be beneficial if you are considering private school for your child.

- What is the ratio of adults to children in each different age group the center accomodates? Again, different states and provinces have different legislation in this regard, so be sure to check the maximum ratios for your area.

- Is it a faith-based facility? If so, to what extent is the particular faith presented to the children in care? For example, do they tell Bible stories? Sing religious songs? Play with Noah's Ark toys? How comfortable am I with this?

- What are the center's policies on dropping in? Do they permit parents to drop in to observe the children? Can you pick your child up early? Centers with a closed door policy should probably be viewed with some suspicion. After all, what don't they want you seeing?

- What are the staff like? Are they patient, cheerful, and generally positive? Are they interacting with the children, or are they off by themselves just watching? Listen to the tone of their voices as they speak to the children. Are they pleasant and enthusiastic?

- How is the day structured? How much time do the children get to spend outside? What are the outdoor facilities like? How many naps are there? What do they do with children who have outgrown their naps?

- Does the center smell clean? Are the children clean? What are the bathrooms like? Is the outdoor play area free of litter? Does the play equipment look safe and well maintained? How often are the indoor toys washed? Is the center well lit? Is there a source of natural light? Are the windows low enough that a child can see out of them?

- How do they handle food? Do I send a lunch and snacks, or do they provide it? What kind of kitchen facilities do they have? Can I send my child with food that needs to be reheated? Refrigerated? Does the center have a nut-free policy? Are there other allergens that need to be absent from lunches and snacks as well? How is feeding accomplished? To what extent are the children allowed to feed themselves in an age-appropriate manner?

- Are there a lot of cribs, high chairs and playpens visible? Is there any evidence of bottle-propping? These can be signs that the children are not getting the level of adult attention and "touch time" that young children, especially infants, require.

- What kinds of activities are offered? A good day-care center will present a well-rounded spectrum of activities designed to encourage overall child development across a range of skills and competencies. There should be activities to stimulate gross motor control, such as running, follow the leader, dancing, songs with actions, and active games like ring around the rosy or duck, duck goose.

Pagans spend a great deal of time developing their intution and other nontraditional ways of knowing. Use this when you are looking for a caregiver or a caregiving environment for your children. Regardless of whether you are choosing a nanny, a home day care, or a day care center, do not ignore your instincts. Even if everything on these lists tallies up perfectly, if your gut tells you that there is something not quite right, give it a serious hearing.

Child Discipline

Probably the biggest baby debate of all centers around child discipline strategies. In general, most people believe that the purpose of discipline is to define unacceptable behaviors while reinforcing acceptable alternatives. Ultimately, we want our children to be able to make considered, moral decisions on their own, relying on their own inner discipline rather than on external direction. Barbara Coloroso, a popular author of books on children and discipline, gives two basic tenets of good child discipline. First, one should not be willing to treat a child in a way that one would not wish to be treated oneself. Second, the discipline approach must not only work, but it also must leave both the child's and caregiver's dignity intact (1995:11). Many popular writers on child discipline advocate the use of "natural consequences." This is often an appealing position to neopagans because of the extent to which it dovetails with the notion of karma.

A natural consequence is one that follows organically out of the situation. If a child does not come when they are called for dinner, they will be faced with the spectre of a cold dinner. If a child refuses to wear a jacket, s/he may be cold. These are things that are obvious to a child once they occur. Of course, this technique will only work once children are at the cognitive stage where they can connect cause and effect. Most children achieve this milestone between the ages of two and three. Younger children need to be restrained or redirected. If an eighteen-month-old is going for the heirloom crystal, there needs to be someone on hand to say, "Those aren't Brian's toys. Let's go find some of Brian's toys."

Young children also benefit from repetition, since they do not necessarily connect behavior with its consequences. While you may have told a toddler not to touch the stove because the stove is hot and will burn him/her, you may have to tell him/her the next day not to touch the candle because the candle is also hot. A candle and a stove are two entirely discrete objects. It is up to you to connect them in a meaningful relationship.

Time outs, a popular choice for younger children, while superior to corporal punishment in many ways, can still be problematic. It is important that the child not experience the time out as a withdrawal of affection. "As above, so below." Just as pagans would prefer not to believe that the love and protection of the gods is contingent upon perfect behavior, so pagan parents may aspire to create that sense of unconditional love within their families. It must be clear to the child that it is the behavior that is the problem, not the child themselves. It is important to tell the child what it is about their behavior that is unacceptable and has led to the time out. Time outs should generally not exceed one minute for each year of the child's age.

Child discipline has a lot in common with magical will. One of the things that is key to the success of both is your reputation for integrity—that what you will say you will do is actually carried out.

You will often hear people say, "Only reward behavior that you wish to see repeated." Rewards and bribes can be a two-edged sword. While they are often a quick way to obtain the desired results—from a clean bedroom to a quiet mealtime—they can ultimately produce a behavior pattern that many people find unpleasant.

Threats can be similarly damaging. They consistently place the child in the position of being the one with no power. Threats and punishment teach children that those with power have the right to exercise it on those with less power, even when they encounter resistance. It teaches them that adult standards are "right." It also teaches them that the reason one behaves appropriately is to avoid being punished—and that punishment is only an issue if one is caught. Therefore, the focus of their activities becomes not to treat those around them and their environment with respect and tolerance, but not to get caught doing something for which they might be punished. Children learn that they are the appropriate targets for the exercise of power, and they learn to respond out of fear. Probably few people want that sort of relationship with their children.

Children need limits, and they need those limits to be consistent. Children get confused and frustrated when they cannot understand the rules that govern their worlds, or when it appears to them that the rules are arbitrary. Explaining one's "nos" is important. There will be times where the only appropriate parental response is a no, even if it makes us unpopular. But the parent needs to know *why* s/he is saying no, and to convey that to the child.

Children do need to know that their requests have been heard and given some legitimacy, even though you are the parent and they are the child. There *is* an unequal distribution of power, however. There are times when allowing a child to make a choice and experience the consequences is the wrong thing to do. If the consequences are sufficiently severe, parental intervention is appropriate. A young child should not be able to choose whether or not to wear a bicycle helmet or a seat belt. The consequence of that choice might be death or permanent disability. Following the "An' harm ye none" guideline, pagan parents should stop behavior that has the potential of causing harm to the child or others.

MAKING THE CHOICE

Questions you may want to ask yourself when pondering discipline questions are:

- What is the problem that is being caused by the behavior? If one child in the family always dawdles in the morning getting ready for school, with the result that the children all get dropped off at school late and I am late to work, the problem is the lateness.

- Can I work with the child to try to find solutions to the problem? Present the problem to the child, and ask them what they think a solution might be. Write them all down, even the ones that do not seem reasonable. Write your own potential solutions down as well, so that you can look at them together. By removing those that either you or the child find unreasonable, you will often end up with a short list of potential solutions to try. Giving the child some responsibility for finding solutions to the problem teaches them about responsibility for one's own actions, one of the key elements of many neopagans' belief systems.

- When deciding on the consequence of an action, if it does not come with its own natural consequence, is what I am considering related to the nature of the behavior? Would it teach my child something that s/he will be able to use later? Does it reinforce problem-solving skills?

- How important is it for me to teach my child to "mind"? Put another way, do I want to end up with a child (or adult) who accepts authority, or one who questions authority? How will the strategy I am considering support my end goal?

- If I have "applied" a consequence, do I feel good about the outcome, or badly about the outcome? How does my child feel?

- Do my limits and consequences reflect my core values? Do they contribute to teaching my child how to eventually behave as a responsible adult? Many parents say that they need to choose their battles: What criteria do I use when choosing mine?

- What resources other than my own instincts am I relying upon as part of my parenting toolkit? There is a wealth of information out there: Internet sites, books, chat rooms, newsgroups, and other resources on children and parenting. Can I find a few that "feel right"? Ones that reflect the values I hold and seem in sync with the lifestyle of my household? Whatever problem you face with your child, it is likely that someone else out there has encountered it too.

Influences and Exposures

As a parent, you will have at least some ability to control the influences to which your child is exposed. This ability to control things will decrease as your child's social circle widens.

MAKING THE CHOICE: Toys and Books

Questions to ask yourself about toys and reading material include:

- Are there restrictions on what kinds of toys I will allow in my house? Do I want gender-neutral toys, or is the "pink world of girls/ blue world of boys" toy-marketing standard all right?

- Do I want to stick to all-natural materials for infant and toddler toys?

- Do I allow toys with commercial tie-ins, like cartoon characters from television or the movies?

- Do I allow "violent" toys? Guns? What about water guns? Toy sets where characters may have swords, cannon, clubs, or knives?

- What about Barbie? Once seen as a feminist's nightmare, Barbie has been put to work in the past decade. Dentist, doctor, teacher, pet-shop owner—has Mattel pushed Barbie far enough?

- What are my thoughts about "cowboy and Indian" toys? While more popular in Europe than in many parts of North America, many toy companies still produce toys and games that feature rough-and-ready white folks and feathered Indians. Is this imaginative or exploitative?

- How will I respond if someone else gives my child a toy which I do not approve of?

- Are there representations that I would prefer to avoid in books? For example, is an older book series like the Berenstain Bears, which features a working father and a domestic, stay-at-home mother, acceptable, even though it reinforces traditional gender role stereotypes? Would a newer series like the Arthur books, where both parents are seen working, engaging in child care and cooking, better reflect the world to which I want to expose my child? Does this even matter to me?

- Many beloved books from our childhoods contain what is now considered by some people to be morally questionable content. School boards are often divided on whether or not they should use books like *Tom Sawyer*, *Huckleberry Finn*, or *Little Black Sambo*, because they reflect the racist attitudes of their times. Do I think that children should be sheltered from the historical reality of a less just world? If so, until what age? If not, how do I think these sorts of books should be approached with children?

- Do I want my children exposed to mainstream religious literature? What about "subversively" religious literature like C. S. Lewis's Narnia books?

- At what age do I think it is appropriate for my child to be reading books that contain graphic descriptions of sexual activities?

Television and Movies

These media present the same sorts of dilemmas as toys and books, but writ far larger. Most children begin to watch television in their infancy; it is one of the key ways to tell children stories about their world

and its possibilities. And while the jury is still out on whether exposure
to television violence increases the likelihood of subsequent violent or
antisocial behavior in children, young children especially, have difficulty
distinguishing between television life and real life. They are much more
likely than adults to accept all television representations as truthful portrayals of reality.

Many people believe that television promotes conspicuous consumption and a focus on material items as purveyors of status. Fortunately, there is a great deal more positive child-centered programming
available now, particularly on cable channels, some of which have no
commercials. Thanks to technology, you can also pre-record your child's
favorite shows and delete the commercials before showing them. Buying commercial videos of children's programming also eliminates regular advertising, but does mean that you are likely to be bombarded with
advertising for the studio's other products.

Movies have some of the problems of television, but it is somewhat
easier to monitor what movies your child sees, and parents are more
likely to have seen a movie they are going to show their child than any
individual episode of a television program.

MAKING THE CHOICE

Questions you may wish to ask yourself about television and movies
include:

- What kinds of values are portrayed in this movie or program? Do
  people treat each other with consideration and respect? Are there
  portrayals of violence or aggression? If so, how are the situations handled or resolved?

- Are there a variety of people represented, or is everybody white? Are
  traditional gender-role stereotypes reinforced, or are they challenged?
  What sorts of things make the characters happy? Are relationships
  valued more highly than material objects?

- How does this movie or program approach ecology and the world
  more generally? Do I see people walking or taking public transit, or

does everyone have a car, for example? Does my child's viewing include animal programs, which are often very good at talking about human impact on nonhuman habitats?

- Is this program age appropriate? This is often a sticky one when parents have children of different ages.

- How much time do I want my child to spend watching television or movies every day? This is time when the child is not doing other things, such as imaginative play, play with other children, or active play outdoors.

- How often can I schedule time to watch with my child? Watching together provides the opportunity to explain how certain action stunts are done, to question the choices or actions of the characters on the screen, and to generally increase your child's media literacy.

Video Games and the Internet

The current generation of children is more computer savvy than any that preceded it. This is a trend likely to continue as personal computers become ubiquitous in homes, schools and libraries. Many children have been playing educational computer games since before they were two, and continue to use the computer as their primary source of music, information, and entertainment. There is a lot of controversy over what children should and should not be exposed to on the Internet and through video and computer games.

Many of the concerns around children and the Internet have to do with potential exposure to pornography, hate literature, extreme violence, vulgar language, depictions of alternative lifestyles, "how to" information about criminal activities, and adults who prey on children. Another prevalent concern revolves around information disclosure in chat rooms. Most parents have different concerns with children of different ages. While you might not care if your 14-year-old is exposed to vulgar language, you may not want your 6-year-old hearing it.

Computer programs are available that allow adults to monitor their children's computer usage, enforce daily usage limits, and block their access to objectionable sites or even Instant Messengering. These programs are designed to block out the sites you do not want your children seeing, but they will also block information you might want them to have. For example, if you block material with the word *sex*, it is hard to retrieve information about many British tourist attractions because they are located in places like Sus*sex*, Es*sex*, or Middle*sex*. These programs also will block access to sites giving information about safe sex, contraception, and sexually transmissible diseases.

Other parents periodically check the usage logs and histories to see where their child has been. These logs, however, can be erased or altered by your resourceful, computer-literate preteen or teen user. If you choose this route, you may wish to invest in file delete-protection software. Another solution people try is to make Internet access available to children only on a computer located in a fairly high traffic area of the house, like the family room or the kitchen. This way, the child knows that at any moment, a parent may come and look over his/her shoulder.

MAKING THE CHOICE

Some of the questions you may wish to ask yourself about your child's Internet use are:

- Is s/he visiting sites I do not want him/her to see? What kinds of sites are they? How likely is it that my child would come to me and talk to me about something disturbing s/he has seen on the Internet?

- How well have I explained the normal security precautions one needs to take in chat rooms and on generally accessible public venues like newsgroups? How confident am I that my child understands and takes them seriously?

- How do I feel about monitoring my child's Internet usage through reading the logs and records left on the computer? Through using monitoring software? Is it the same as opening my child's mail? Does it violate their privacy in an unacceptable way? Will it do damage to the trust relationship I have with my child?

Concerns about computer and video games tend to center on many of the same issues—that is, violence, nudity, racism, and vulgar language. While most computer games now come with ratings, these alone do not give enough information to make a decision about any individual game. Talking to the staff at a store that specializes in games, reading reviews of the game, and looking for usenet discussion groups about the game in question will provide a much more detailed impression.

In general, games can be divided into a number of broad groupings:

• *Educational games* are often designed specifically for children, and give appropriate age ranges on their boxes. With these games, the crucial element is content. What exactly is being taught, and from whose perspective?

• *Arcade games* are based on popular games such as pinball. They are generally single player, points-based games that rely on hand-eye coordination rather then strategy. While generally fairly harmless, some may feature disturbing themes.

• *Adaptations of board games and computer solitaire* tend not to be very problematic. Many popular board games are available for the computer. Some games can be played online. With any online multiplayer game, you will need to consider to what extent you are comfortable with your child talking to unknown others via the computer. With strategy games in particular, you may want to consider what sorts of activities are rewarded by the game.

• *Sports simulators* tend to mimic the ethic of the sport played in real time. Football is an aggressive, competitive game. There is simply no way you will find a football game where you can win by making cooperative alliances with members of the other team. What you *can* look for in these games is their attitude toward cheating, and their sense of fair play. For example, do they allow you to foul the other team's members without a penalty? Do they promote good sportsmanship?

• *Technical simulators*, such as racing or flight simulators can raise concerns. Flight simulators in particular may involve flying a military mission, where the purpose is to drop bombs on targets, or shoot down enemy aircraft. If this is the case, does the game penalize the player for excessive collateral damage? Is the game environment curiously "de-peopled"? Further, do you want your child exposed to an environment in which the only way to win is to destroy things?

• *Shooters* are the category of game that tends to provoke the most outcry around violence. These are the games that are most focused around the plot of "find and kill." While there may be puzzles to solve or obstacles to overcome during the course of these games, the players' path to victory essentially consists of killing as many enemies as they can. The concern around these games is that they present a curiously amoral universe where violence is almost always a legitimate means of solving problems and victory is impossible except through aggression.

• *Role-playing games* (RPGs), bleed into shooters on one side, and real-time strategy games on the other. In a typical shooter, the player character is generic—the game is driven by action rather than plot. In RPGs, there are mechanisms for customizing your character, and your character is likely to have to spend a substantial amount of game time acquiring skills, equipment, and information. Some of these games are available online in multi-user formats—these are sometimes more like chat rooms with ambience than plot-driven games. In multiplayer game environments, there often is established a set of unspoken, informal norms that are "enforced" by the group, through peer disapproval, for example, of someone who joins the game simply to kill enemies. As in real life, players can be shunned, marginalized or ganged up upon, de-pending on the extent and nature of the informal social control within the game. That being said, there are some multiplayer games that are puzzle-centric and designed in such a way that cooperation is not only possible, but is a required element for success in the game. The anecdo-tal downside of these games is that they are apparently addictive. It is hard to build up a powerful character without spending many hours playing in the game world.

One of the keys to evaluating these sorts of games is to see if there is a class of character that is more favored than others. For example, are you more likely to make it through to the end of the game as a fighter, a bard, or a mage? Another is to look at what classes of activities are re-warded. How do you gain money in the game? Are there ways to advance through the levels that do not involve full-scale carnage and bloodshed? What kinds of mental challenges and puzzles does the game present? What kind of thinking does it promote? The best of these games can be very morally complex, while the worst of them are shooters in fancy dress.

• *Adventure games* usually feature characters less customizable than those of RPGs, and a "quest" orientation. The players are out to find something, explore something, retrieve something, or prevent something, and must successfully complete a number of tasks or solve a number of puzzles in order to accomplish this. Next to the quality of the puzzles, the most important feature of these games is the story that weaves the quest together. Is it a quest purely for the player's benefit, or is there some greater collective good involved?

• *Strategy games* generally provide the player with a world undergoing a particular conflict or crisis. There are a lot of war games that fit into this category. In the war games, a player's strategic choices often are limited by the game's end goal of defeating the enemy, and the fact that the player character identifies very strongly with one particular side. Some of these games are in real time, while others are turn based. As a category, they offer the advantage of requiring the player to engage in strategic long-term thinking and to make choices about the allocation of limited resources. The ability to parse a complex problem and to recognize and address its critical components, as well as to make choices among competing priorities, is a valuable thinking skill in real life. The games' disadvantage is the potential for violence, but in the best of these games, a killing-spree approach, while certainly an option, will not lead to optimum outcomes.

• *God games* are further evolutions of the strategy game. In god games, the player works from the perspective of a powerful, but not omnipotent, overseeing being who can influence and intervene in a simulated world. There tends to be no fixed end goal in these games. This class includes many of the wildly popular "sim" games, in which the player constructs environments where simulated beings live and work. As with other categories, one way to evaluate these games is to view their limits of possibility.

Education

Children's education, particularly their early education, will play a formative role in how they approach learning for the rest of their lives. Experiences that engage and excite them will help to produce positive attitudes, while experiences that bore or frustrate them will create resistance or lack of effort. A child's educational environment should nurture and support the divine within while preparing him/her to be able to recognize and respect the divine within others and within the Earth itself. There are three basic options available to parents for educating their children: public schools, private schools and homeschooling. While there are pros and cons to each approach, it is possible to have a satisfying learning experience in any of these venues.

Some schools have done better than others in integrating students from different racial, ethnic, and religious backgrounds into the culture of the school. This is true both of public and private schools. Unless you choose to homeschool, as pagans, you will have choices to make about how you wish to handle potentially touchy areas of school culture.

Public Schools

Many people have little choice about their children's education. For reasons that may be financial, practical, or ideological, their children are going to the designated local public school. Some boards offer more choice in terms of program offerings than others do.

Regardless of what schooling option you choose for your child, it is important to be aware of what the school is offering in terms of facilities, class sizes, and supplementary programs, all of which will contribute to your child's learning experience. None of these can be taken for granted. While parental involvement is always a bonus no matter what schooling option you select, getting the most out of public education often means a higher level of involvement. Some of the ways in which you can support your public school's learning environment are:

- Getting to know your child's teacher. Does he or she have an e-mail address that they are willing to give out to parents? How often are the scheduled parent/teacher nights? Are there other ways you can keep in touch? For example, does the teacher give children a home-work journal in which you can write comments about things like how easy or difficult your child is finding a particular piece of work?

- Getting involved in the school. Does the school permit parent volunteers? If they do not permit you to volunteer in your child's classroom, they may allow you to volunteer in the classroom for the next grade, which will let you see what's ahead for your child. Are there activities, such as cutting out laminated pictures or shapes, that you could do at home for your child's classroom? Do you have the time to be involved in the school PTA?

- Contributing to the school. Do you have a special skill or interest that you could offer to give a presentation on? Do you have skills that could be valuable to the teacher? Are you willing to publish a monthly class newsletter, for example? Are there things that your child's classroom lacks that you might be able to donate? For example, it is often possible to pick up children's books relatively inexpensively at garage sales or in library-based used-book stores. Does the school have a recycling and composting program? If not, could you start one?

- Getting involved at the higher levels. Do you know who your school board representative or trustee is? Are there issues about your child's school that could be brought to his/her attention? Consider attending school board or district meetings so that you understand what issues are facing the administration, particularly in terms of funding cuts or program closures. If you are unhappy with what you hear in your local district, you can write to your state or provincial department of education. You may need to make a lot of noise to get what you want.

Private Schools

If you have the means and the opportunity, you may choose to send your child to a private school. There are a wide variety of reasons people choose private schools. Some are dissatisfied with the quality of education offered by their local public school. Some fear potential exposure to drugs or weapons. Some prefer a different kind of educational philosophy than the one common in public education. Some choose a private school because of programs offered that are unavailable in the public stream—outdoor education, language studies, music, art, or intensive math and science programs. There is a perception that private schools can attract better-quality teachers, and that students will receive more individual attention due to smaller class sizes. Some parents may send their children to a school that provides room and board, rather than have them attend as day-school students. Many private schools boast of their high Ivy League admissions rates and their students' high SAT scores. Some parents, looking to their children's future, believe that private schools expose students to the "right" sorts of people, thus increasing the chance of upward class mobility. Or the choice may be based on factors as simple as the location of the school, or the presence of on-site before- and after-school care.

There are two basic categories of private school: those that follow a traditional academic model (teacher as authority, same age groupings learning the same lessons at the same time, test-based evaluations, grades given, competitive environment), and those that do not. In the traditional category, there is a lot of variation between schools in terms of what innovations they have made on the traditional model and what elements each individual school has decided to emphasize. In the "alternative" category, there are an extraordinary number of different styles and teaching philosophies available.

MAKING THE CHOICE

It is important to remember though that "private" does not necessarily equate to "better." There are some fine public schools, and some truly dismal private ones. Here are some questions to ask yourself when looking for a private school for your child:

• What is my child like? Is s/he overwhelmed by large groups? Does s/he thrive on competition? What kinds of activities does s/he enjoy most? How does s/he learn: by seeing things, by being told things, or by doing things? Do I have any reason to suspect my child may have a learning disability? Private schools, unlike public schools, do not have to accept all comers, and sometimes winnow out students with "problems" as they work through the program, in order to keep standardized test averages up and so that they can avoid the costs of "special education." Schools that are more oriented to the individual child may be more receptive to a child who is significantly ahead of or behind his/her peers.

- When I visit the school, am I welcome to look around? Can I go into the classrooms? Can I observe the children at play during lunch or recess? If the school administrators are reluctant to show you around, you may wonder what they are hiding.

- How do the children look? Do they appear interested and absorbed by their activities? Do they seem bored? Are there any children sitting by themselves not doing anything? Do the classrooms appear well-organized? Are the teachers engaged with the children or off doing something?

- What opportunities does the school offer for me to be involved in my child's education? How do they communicate with parents? Are they willing to provide me with some names and phone numbers of parents who have children in their school?

- What are the classroom teacher/student ratios? Who is in the classroom on a regular basis in addition to the students and the teacher? Does the school run criminal background checks on its staff?

- If the school claims to be operating from a particular educational philosophy, are they accredited with some organization that enforces and maintains standards for that variety of education?

- What training and qualifications do their teachers have? What is the turnover rate of teachers? (You can often find out this latter point by flipping through the most recent school yearbooks.)

- How does the school conduct evaluations? Are there tests? Do children take any of the standardized "ranking" tests? Are grades given?

Do students know their grades? What provisions are made in the classroom to accommodate students who are either ahead of or behind the class average? Is there homework? If so, how much?

- What methods of discipline are used in the school?

- What does tuition cover? Before and after school care? Transportation? Uniforms? Field trips and activities? Books and supplies? What is included in tuition varies widely from school to school. Some schools will have additional fees, such as enrollment fees or security fees, which can push the cost up considerably. Does the school have a sibling discount policy? Should I need to withdraw my child for some reason, what is their policy on tuition refund?

- Have there been complaints about the school? One way to check is to call your local Better Business Bureau.

Homeschooling

Homeschooling involves choosing to keep your child out of the formal school stream and educating them at home. Once the almost exclusive domain of the strongly religious, homeschooling is becoming a more popular choice among an increasingly broad section of the population who have come to question either the values or the methods of traditional education. Among the benefits of homeschooling are greater control over how your children are taught and what they are exposed to, a substantial decrease in the likelihood that your child will be bullied, and a greater curricular flexibility that allows your child more scope to develop their particular interests.

Some of the drawbacks of homeschooling include the time, energy, and commitment required from all members of the family, an increase in the level of existing family tensions because of the greater amount of time parents and children are spending together, and the availability of support and materials for homeschooling families. Fortunately, the increase in the incidence of homeschooling has led to a phenomenal increase in the accessibility of homeschooling resources—magazines, books, online and offline collectives and support groups, packaged curricula, Web pages, seminars, and the like. Also, some families find that tensions decrease because a child who may have been frustrated and unhappy at school is no longer bringing those feelings back in to the home.

There is a spectrum of approaches to homeschooling, with the "school at home" approach at one end and the "life as school" approach at the other. The "school at home" method essentially reproduces a classroom setting inside the home. There is a set curriculum and a daily lesson plan designed to meet the objectives of that curriculum. There is likely to be record-keeping, documenting that particular lessons have been completed, and there may be testing incorporated into the process. The "life as school" approach, on the other hand, tends to derive its activities and focus from a child's interest in a particular subject or phenomenon. The birth of a sibling could spark a focus on infant development, a new computer game could lead to research on agrarian societies, or a fascination with race cars could turn into a component on engineering tolerances and materials stress. Most homeschooling approaches fall between these two absolute extremes, combining some planned activities with a range of child-led ones.

Among the comments often made by homeschooling parents, regardless of their particular approach, is that their children are able to cover much more material than their peers in traditional school settings because the "hurry up and wait" element is gone. They do not need to wait in line to go outside, wait to be acknowledged to go to the bathroom, wait for other children to get their books and pencils out to start a lesson, or wait until the teacher stops talking to begin an assignment. All this waiting, homeschoolers note, accounts for a good chunk of the average child's school day. Simply eliminating that element, they argue, increases the amount of time that children have to devote to learning activities, whatever the form.

Many homeschooling parents will also argue that much of what children learn in school after about grade three is largely useless. A child needs to be able to read, write, and perform basic mathematical operations, they assert. In their day-to-day lives as adults, they do not need to have memorized the names of every president; they need to know how to find that information. Allowing children to be guided by their own interests will teach them more about finding information than being forced to read and memorize so that their abilities to read and memorize can be tested against those of other children. When, they ask, was the last time your employer gathered all their workers together and gave them a multiple-choice quiz on the procedures manual?

For pagan parents, homeschooling provides a means through which the applied elements of the parents' spiritual practices can be incorporated into a child's basic educational framework. Meditation, visualization, liturgical writing, numerology, and elemental, herbal and other correspondences can be seamlessly integrated into more conventional biology, chemistry, literacy, and numeracy, allowing the child to develop the holistic sense that all learning is, in some way, spiritual learning that is so valued by many pagans. Children who have been homeschooled from the very beginning need not have their creativity, their wonder, their imagination and their sense of the magical stifled by having it labeled "just make-believe."

MAKING THE CHOICE

If you are considering homeschooling your child, some of the questions you may wish to ask yourself are:

- Do my child and I have the temperaments to embark on a homeschooling adventure? How often is our relationship adversarial? Will I resent the additional time my child will be spending at home with me? How can I continue with activities that are important to me? What will this mean for the organization and division of labor in my family?

- Is this a relatively short-term or a long-term project? Am I planning to homeschool only to a certain grade level, or until a planned move, or is this something I plan to continue indefinitely for my child?

- What are the relevant local, state, or provincial regulations regarding homeschooling? While homeschooling is legal, the sort of oversight or reporting that is required to make it legitimate varies widely, even among school boards.

- What are the resources available locally to support my homeschooling? For example, while urban areas will have a plethora of cultural attractions to which one can plan outings—art galleries, dance studios, art workshops, museums, libraries, etc.—rural offerings may be less obvious. Would the local bank be interested in having me and my child in during a slow time to observe how the bank works? Are there opportunities to learn about animal husbandry? Agriculture? Does my town have a major employer? What do they do? How does the economy of the town function? Are there opportunities to witness local government in action, or to get involved in civic projects? Location does not have to be a barrier to creative and effective homeschooling.

- Do I know other homeschoolers with whom I can trade ideas, experiences and resources? If not, how can I locate some? The Internet is an invaluable resource here.

- Are there ways in which I can partner with my local school for some activities? For example, if your child is interested in participating in a national math or spelling competition, a science fair, a college information day, or a track meet, would it be possible for him/her to do so under the auspices of your local school?

- How much money am I prepared to devote to my homeschooling enterprise? Homeschooling can be expensive or inexpensive, depending on the choices you make, but it will invariably require *some* dedicated resources. Purchasing prepared curricula can be pricey, particularly if you have more than one child. You may need to buy another computer or upgrade an existing one. Specially designed learning materials are another cost; however, if you understand the material's intent (preschool materials in particular), you may be able to assemble it inexpensively from garage sales or thrift stores. The good news is that unless you want to study different cultures, languages, and environments by traveling around the world examining them in person, homeschooling is still going to cost less than tuition at a private school.

- What kinds of social opportunities can I make for my child? One of the most frequent critiques faced by homeschoolers is that because they are depriving their children of the opportunity to interact with other children in a school setting that their children will be less able to deal effectively with others as older children and adults. Homeschooling parents point out that the interactions in a school setting are competitive, heavily structured, and controlled, and not representative of the real-life interactions in which their child will later engage. Even so, you should consider social avenues for your child. Is there a homeschooling collective with which your child could do some lessons? Do you wish to enroll them in supplementary classes in music, art, dance, or language? Are they interested in sports? Is there a local children's theater company? Do you have friends with children of similar ages?

• What steps need to be taken so that my child is not disadvantaged in the college or university admissions process? Contact a number of different admissions departments and find out if they have admitted homeschooled children in the past, and what documentation, if any, is required. Do the schools under consideration conduct admissions interviews?

Autonomy and Self-Expression

These will manifest in various ways throughout a child's life—from baby and toddlerhood all the way through the teen years and into adulthood. These issues become most apparent when there is a difference of opinion between what the child wants to do and what the parent wants him/her to do. In these cases, one can look back to the "An ye harm none" guideline.

Your preschooler is determined to go to the grocery store wearing a tutu, cat ears, rubber boots, and a superhero cape. If that is going to be warm enough, is it really a problem? Are you likely to encounter other children at the store who would tease your child? Or would you just be mortified if friends or neighbors saw you there with your child dressed like that? One parent of our acquaintance banished her embarrassment by having a selection of brightly colored buttons made, each of which bore the proud message I DRESSED MYSELF!

Your school-aged child wants to dye their hair blue for the summer. Do you buy them the dye? Do you dye your hair blue too as an act of solidarity? Do you help them with the application so they get a good result? Do you think there is any harm in it?

Your preteen never seems to be hungry at the same time as anyone else in the house. Do you allow the child to eat on his/her own schedule, do you insist that s/he take meals with the family, or both? Letting the child eat when s/he is hungry reinforces the notion that one should listen to the messages one's body gives them. The child may be less likely to develop an eating disorder. On the other hand, in a great many families, family meals are about much more than food. They are the times when the family sits down to share their day and discuss plans, schedules, and current affairs. Can you assist your son or daughter in assembling healthy meals when s/he is hungry, and still have him/her at the table, even if not eating, when the rest of the family sits down? The key to dealing with these sorts of conflicts is to try to find a solution that does no harm, while ensuring that everyone feels heard and respected.

As children get older, differences of opinion can become both more intense and more serious in terms of consequences. It is legally your responsibility to try to prevent your child from smoking, drinking underage, experimenting with recreational pharmaceuticals, and having underage sex. To what extent are these experiences the child's responsibility and the child's opportunity to learn, and to what extent are you responsible for intervening? Families handle these dilemmas differently, based on a wide range of factors, including the extent to which other family members are being affected by the child's activities, the amount of interaction the child has had with agents of formal social control (police officers for example), and the extent to which the child appears willing to change his/her behavior. The potential for harm to the child has to be weighed against the harm to the rest of the family unit or to others who may be involved. The consequences of action have to be weighed against the consequences of inaction. Acceptable limits need to be agreed to by both parties in order for a workable relationship to be maintained.

At some point children become adults and beyond our control. As parents, we need to have already found ways, before they are teenagers, to talk about and resolve issues of competing wants and needs.

Resources

Kids are Worth It: Giving Your Child the Gift of Inner Discipline, by Barbara Coloroso (Toronto: Somerville House, 1995).

WiccaCraft for Families, by Margie MacArthur (Custer, Wash.: Phoenix Publishing, 1994).

Get Out of My Life, but first could you drive me and Cheryl to the mall? by Anthony Wolf (New York: Noonday Press, 1991).

For further information about postpartum depression, visit www.obgyn.net, www.postpartum.net or www.psycom.net.

For more information on breast-feeding, visit medicalreporter.health.org/tmr0297/breastfeed0297.html, www.med.umich.edu/1libr/womens/breast05.htm, or www.4woman.gov/Breastfeeding/bf.cfm?page=227

CHAPTER 5

Money

Money is one thing all members of industrialized societies have in common. Whether money is present or absent in our lives, we must think, plan, and make choices about it. Money is a peculiar thing. Unlike the items used in bartering systems that preceded currency—where one thing of value was exchanged for another thing of value—money has no worth in and of itself. Money is a symbol—it has worth only insomuch as we all agree it has worth and agree to allow its exchange for other items. As people in countries where the currency has been devalued by government writ in order to curb inflation will tell you, the pieces of paper themselves are worth nothing. Yet, money is the central thing around which many people must organize their lives.

As was noted in the introduction, how much money one has relates to the choices one has in terms of even the most basic features of life—eating, living, and making purchases. The social welfare system is less well developed in the United States than it is in most of the European democracies. Social welfare services include such things as government-funded day care, education, health care, disability and old-age pensions, subsidies for families with children, housing subsidies, and unemployment protections. The level of income disparity between the richest and the poorest U.S. residents is the highest of any wealthy nation.

Social welfare in Europe is profoundly different from social welfare in North America. In Europe, it means "the general good of society"; in America, it has increasingly come to mean "government handouts to the poor." While it may seem logical in a tight economic climate to channel resources to the people who need them the most, this has been shown to lead to a hardening of attitudes across class divisions. When social programs and services are universal, everyone enjoys the benefits. Different treatment of the "have nots" from the rest of the population leads to mainstream resentment of "targeted" programs. Targeted programs, directed toward the poorest of the poor, create two groups of people: those who pay but get no benefits, and those who get benefits but do not pay. This creates an environment in which there is pressure from those paying for these programs through taxation to keep the "social relief" available to low-income individuals at minimal levels so that they are never better off than those "hardworking taxpayers."

This approach to social programs also creates the stereotype that people are poor because they do not work hard, or do not wish to work. In fact, there are many places in North America where working full-time at minimum wage will not put an individual above the poverty line for their area, never mind enable them to support a dependent child. Some people are born into poverty, while others enter a state of poverty suddenly, during a protracted period of unemployment or as the result of a divorce, a death, or an illness or injury. Most of the poor would prefer to be working and able to support themselves and their families. Sometimes the work is not there, and sometimes they are simply not in a position to take advantage of it.

Earning Your Money

The work world has changed dramatically over the past 30 years. A lifetime career with one employer, once the norm, is now rare. While real family incomes (income after taxes adjusted for inflation) have gone up somewhat, it more often requires two people in the labor force to earn this income, rather than one. People are working longer at the office, and they are bringing home more work as well. New communication technologies allow for a blurring of home and workplace not previously possible. Cell phones, home computers, e-mail, and pagers all make it increasingly difficult to get away from work. In addition, the number of people who are self-employed or working out of their homes has been steadily increasing. The meaning of work, as well as "work ethic," has been shifting from the dawn of industrial production.

History of the Work Ethic

Before industrial production, the general standard of living was very low, and people worked to achieve subsistence. Once subsistence had been achieved for oneself and one's family, there was no incentive to work more. Consuming goods as an end in itself was not yet a social value. In feudal England and Europe, life was hard in part because production was inefficient. It took much longer than it does today to make cloth, raise food, cook or do almost any other activity. The fastest mode of transportation was a swift horse. The goal was to do the things that needed to be done, but not necessarily in the shortest amount of time possible. Feudal workers had many more holidays than do their modern counterparts.

Industrial production changed things. In order to be profitable, it had to generate a surplus beyond what was necessary to simply cover costs. This meant persuading people to work harder and longer. Wage rates needed to be set low enough that the number of hours that a worker must put in for their family to survive would be sufficient to produce a surplus (profit) for the industrial owners. Having been removed from the land and their traditional source of subsistence, people had to work or starve, and this produced the necessary supply of workers for industry.

It did not, however, produce willing workers content with their lot. Compelling people to work in conditions they would not have chosen for themselves, to give up their time and their control over their own activities in return for a wage barely sufficient to keep them impoverished produced a pervasive dissatisfaction and resentment among workers that—the factory owners feared—might bubble over into violence.

Industrial employers began to attach a positive moral meaning to work so that it would be desired as an end in itself, not merely as a means to achieve subsistence. The message that was drilled into the working classes was that paid labor was the only morally acceptable means of providing oneself with a livelihood. Wage labour came to be described as the way in which one improved one's moral character, and as the way to live a godly life. Submission to the requirements of the industrial employer was constructed as a virtue in and of itself. Those who did not work were portrayed as lazy, uncivilized, and morally bankrupt, a vision that is still promoted by politicians to describe welfare recipients.

Eventually, the notion of the moral superiority of work took a backseat to the idea that by working, people made money, and that by working harder, people could make *more* money. More money meant that people could avail themselves of more of the mass-produced items that they were themselves producing. Increased production led to increased demand, which could then lead to further increases in production. The struggle in the workplace became one not over the freedom and self-determination of the worker, but one over how the profits arising from production should be divided.

Modern Workforce

Today, more people than ever are working part-time, or on temporary contracts that do not include employee benefits. Many of these people are in this position involuntarily. At the moment, there is a labor surplus rather than a labor shortage, as was the case early in the Industrial Revolution. This is why economists bandy about terms like "the natural rate of unemployment" and fret that full employment would put upward pressure on wages. After all, full employment makes it hard for the employers to attract new people for lower wages because there is no pool of desperate, unemployed people seeking whatever job they can get.

The current labor surplus has serious implications, because it means that a larger proportion of the population will find themselves without jobs, and therefore, without the means to provide for themselves, through no fault of their own. Since social assistance plans, particularly in North America, are designed to give the unemployed individual incentive to find paid work by keeping benefits at a lower level than the minimum wage—already below the level necessary for subsistence—a lack of available jobs creates a permanent, chronically deprived social underclass. This underclass is perpetually unable to attain culturally valued goals, such as home ownership, self-sufficiency, and "middle-class" possessions. This forces them either to give up on their goals and accept that they and their children are destined to be poor and marginalized, or to create means that are not culturally accepted, such as involvement in the drug trade. It is widely known that poverty is correlated to poor health, higher birth rates, higher infant mortality rates, shorter life expectancies, and greater incarceration rates, all of which impose additional costs on society.

In addition, the labor surplus has meant that many employers have increased the minimum qualification levels for even entry-level positions. Forty years ago, it was possible to become a bank teller without a high school diploma. Now, most banks prefer to hire people with a college or university degree; if you are hired without those qualifications, you can expect far less upward occupational mobility than you could have in the past. Thus, a labor surplus has the most impact on those people who already have the least choice in occupations.

You and Your Work

The work you do is important. For many people, work is an important aspect of their identity. Your employment absorbs a great deal of your waking time. In general, the more education you have, the more choices you have about your occupation and your workplace. There are many factors that act to limit that choice, however. You may have only one or two big employers in your town. A tight job market means a lot of people stick to work where they can get it, rather than holding out for a possibly better or more satisfactory offer. You may need a job that has benefits, or one that does not pay below a certain floor. You may need the flexibility to organize your schedule around classes or the availability of child care. Some people, both pagan and non-pagan, also limit their employment choices based on the moral implications of working in a particular profession or for a certain company.

For example, a geologist might choose to interpret "The earth is sacred" in a way that causes him/her not to work for companies that engage in strip mining or oilfields exploration. A teacher might choose to work in a child-centered alternative school rather than in a traditional setting because s/he wants to capture more of the sense of "Thou art God/dess" with the children. Someone might choose to work in one of the helping professions (social work, medicine, teaching, etc.) out of a sense of karmic rightness—the sense that one can bring good into the world through one's activities with others. Another may choose to move from a job in a less socially progressive company to something more socially valuable.

MAKING THE CHOICE

If you have the luxury of being able to choose between positions, there may be value criteria you wish to incorporate into your pros and cons list for each position. Ask yourself these questions:

- Is it possible, in this position, to recognize the interconnectedness of all things? To treat others in a way that recognizes their own unique divinity? To reinforce the sacrality of nature and the importance of the care of the Earth?

- Does this employer contribute significantly to the destruction of the environment?

- Does this employer unfairly exploit workers? For example, do they hire illegal aliens and pay them below the minimum wage? Do they farm work out to underdeveloped nations, and if so, what are the conditions those workers face?

- If the workplace is unionized, do they bargain in good faith, or do they utilize the "If you don't accept these concessions we will move your jobs to Mexico, where people will be happy to be making half what you are now" negotiating strategy? If it is not a unionized workplace, has the employer engaged in "union busting"? How much of the workforce is full-time?

- Has the employer ever been involved in a major lawsuit? How did it turn out? Was the company's stance reasonable and appropriate?

- Is the company owned by another company? If so, in what lines of business is the parent company involved?

- How has the employer treated you during the application process? Was your application acknowledged promptly? Were follow-up calls handled in a timely manner? Did they move the interview time or date around at short notice? More than once? You can often get a good idea of how an employer treats its workers by how it treats its *potential* workers.

• What do you know about the leadership style of the employer?

• Do you know of any harm caused by this employer? How comfortable would you be contributing to that harm? Are there things you can do in other parts of your life that would help you mitigate that harm?

• Most important, how would doing this work make you feel about yourself? "As in the universe, so in the soul."

Spending Your Money

Purchases

We all spend money. Spending money is necessary to obtain the basics of life: food, clothing, and shelter. For some people, this is as far as their money will stretch. For those forced to rely on shelters and food banks, the money does not even stretch that far. The majority of people, however, have both *some* income and *some* discretion in even their basic purchases.

The ability to exercise choice in purchasing decisions has been argued by some to be the central organizing feature in late modern capitalist societies such as those of North America and Western Europe. Once societies of producers, they suggest, the developed Western nations have become societies of consumers, where our identities are constructed more by what we have than what we do, and where we define consumer choice as a fundamental right. Those who remember the former Soviet republic recall that at least some of the outrage in North America over state communism was not so much directed at the political oppression that was occurring, but at the *consumer* oppression. In our contemporary society, the ability to make choices about consumption increases in direct proportion to the amount of money one has. Again, the poor are disenfranchised from this process because the means that are available to them are too meager to allow them to participate.

Consumer Culture

Consumption has two intrinsic characteristics in Western society. First, consuming infers ownership. This quality of ownership prevents other people from using one's goods without one's explicit permission. Second, the process of consumption destroys things. Food is used up by the body. Gasoline is used up by a car. Other things can become worn out and no longer fit for consumption.

Sometimes, we may destroy the allure of a "necessary" object through consumption. Think of a record played again and again and again until you are sick of it. You may no longer consider the object fit for use. Clothing, shoes, furniture—even cars—can have their style value worn out; they are no longer the "in" thing to have. If what one consumes is sufficient to satisfy one's needs, one does not constantly require additional goods. But because the free-market economy is based on the notion of continual consumption, new *needs* are manufactured on a regular basis.

One way to ensure constant consumption is to manufacture goods designed to fail after a certain period of time or certain amount of use, rather than making them to last a lifetime. This is called built-in obsolescence. How one defines one's needs, and what one thinks will best meet them, largely determines the purchasing choices one makes.

How You Spend Your Money

Where we spend our money and what we spend it on can have an enormous impact on what corporations deliver to the marketplace. For example, in the early 1970s a major corporation began to aggressively market powdered and concentrated infant formula in developing countries with high levels of water-borne diseases. Hospital and health workers would be given complimentary supplies for use with newborns. Early formula supplementation often meant that the mothers' milk did not come in, and they had to purchase formula—which had to be mixed with unsafe drinking water—rather than breast-feeding their babies, which would have been safer, healthier, and free. Thousands of babies died of water-borne diseases to which they would not have been exposed had their mothers been breast-feeding.

As reports of this came out in the media, a boycott of the company's products was organized by consumers, and eventually spread throughout the industrialized world. The boycott, which ran between 1974 and 1984, caused the corporate executives to rethink the company's controversial marketing strategy. It also impelled the World Health Organization to issue international guidelines for formula manufacturers.

Despite the fact that spending money is an important activity, and one that can cause considerable stress, many people have no idea what they spend money on. Spending on big items, yes: rent or mortgage, taxes, utilities, people remember most of these. But many people do not track casual, day-to-day expenditures, and are puzzled at the end of the month when they find that they have less money than they think they should.

MAKING THE CHOICE

In order to be able to make informed decisions about your spending, you first need to be aware of your existing spending patterns. Here is an exercise that will help you do that.

- Pick one month and record *every* expenditure you make, including coffee from the deli. Do the record-keeping each evening before you have a chance to forget your purchases for the day.

    You will likely be surprised by what you find. A couple of drive-through meals eaten on the run every week can add up to $300 or more in a year; a cup of coffee on the way to work every day ends up costing close to $400 a year. Once you have a month's worth of expenses charted, you need to ask yourself: Is this the way I want to be spending my money? What are the consequences of spending my money this way? Does my spending reflect my priorities—what I believe in, and what I want out of my life?

- You can also look at your spending from a time perspective, as the second part of the exercise shows:

  Take your monthly income and subtract from it all those things you must spend in order to earn it. Include business clothes, income taxes, union dues, transportation costs, additional costs incurred eating at the office, and so on. Now take the time that you spend at work, add the time you need to get there and get home again, and the time you spend doing work at home. Divide the number from the first step by the number from the second step, and you will have your adjusted hourly wage rate in hours.

Here is a sample scenario for spending from a time perspective: You work from 8 A.M. until 5 P.M. You are supposed to have an hour lunch, but you usually eat at your desk and catch up on your work-related e-mail. You spend a half-hour every morning getting ready for work, and it is a 45-minute commute each way. You usually do about an hour of work in the evenings, but none on weekends. So that is nine hours a day at the office, a half hour prep, an hour and a half commute, and another hour in the evening. Daily total: 12 hours. Twenty workdays per month equals 240 hours. Let us say you earn $35,000 per year and pay $7000 in income tax and related deductions. That leaves you with $2334 per month. You spend $30 per week on gas for your commute and an average of $100 per month on business clothes and sundries. That leaves $2114, which, divided by 240, is $8.81. That is your adjusted hourly wage rate—how much spending money you gain from every hour of your life that is devoted to work.

Knowing your adjusted wage rate allows you to ask questions such as "Is what I want to buy worth the amount of *time* it will take me to pay for it?" A $400 leather jacket, in our example, requires almost 45.5 hours of work.

Making informed decisions about spending can empower an individual in many ways. One can decide to spend more, spend less, or spend differently. Spending more can be simple if one has the money. In this consumer- and credit-driven society, however, the key goal for most people is spending less. How one might wish to spend less depends a lot on what one currently spends money on, and what priorities are central to one's pagan life. Following are some suggestions:

Spending Less

- Consider purchasing used items. This is not only easier on your pocketbook, but it is easier on the environment, both in terms of the resources required to produce the item and in decreasing the likelihood of it ending up in the landfill. The well-known three R's of recycling are "reduce, reuse, and recycle," in order of significance in preserving the environment.

- Buy classic cuts and colors. While this may lead to a rather conservative wardrobe, a cream-colored turtleneck and a well-fitting pair of navy wool pants will support all manner of inexpensive, wild, and crazy accessories.

- Think creatively about things before you throw them out or give them away.

- Consider pooling resources with friends and neighbors. Does every single household need to own a lawnmower? You might collaborate with others to purchase items that, while occasionally handy to have, are not used on a daily basis. This will not only save money, but will reduce the overall level of consumption for all the households involved.

- Consider the benefits of a large freezer. Buying the largest freezer that you can afford and that will fit into your space has the potential to save a lot of grocery money. You can buy in bulk while things are on sale and put them in the freezer for later. This will save money, and energy. This is a great coven activity also, because it connects participants to the wheel of the year.

- Consider cooking gatherings. If you find that you use a lot of expensive, prepared foods because you dislike cooking or have little time to do it in, you may want to try to organize one weekend day per month to cook with friends. Cooking, like many other tasks, tends to be less tedious in company. During this day, you can prepare large amounts of food that can be divided out into freezer containers, taken home, and used later. You will save money, and it is a great opportunity to catch up with friends.

- Consider taking a lunch instead of buying lunch at work, and consider buying a drip coffeepot for your desk instead of going out for coffee. These seem like small choices, but you will quickly notice the effect on your wallet.

- Consider your transportation. How many vehicles are there in your household? Maintaining a vehicle is expensive—could you get by with one vehicle, or without one? This latter is generally an option only available to urban core dwellers, for whom basic services are close by and to whom adequate public transit is available. For the money of maintaining a car for a year, you can pay for a lot of taxis, transit, grocery delivery, and rental cars. Bicycling, inline skating, and walking more will all increase your fitness level as well.

- Consider your gift purchases, and how you shop. Do you scramble around at the last minute trying to find the perfect thing? Do you make a list before you go out? Do you find that you end up shopping for many more people than you intended? Do you impulse shop? One of the best ways to reduce the amount you spend every year on gifts is to become a year-round shopper. Rather than head out shopping when the holiday flyers beckon, make looking for interesting sale items a part of your regular shopping. Keep a list of what you have on hand, so things do not get forgotten. With a little bit of organization throughout the year, it is possible to shop at times when the pressure to buy is greatly reduced.

     If you really have an impulse-control problem when shopping—or have a very limited income—and invariably end up spending more than you should, you may wish to consider some of the following tactics:

- Avoid malls. Going to the mall means being confronted with a whole range of stores to browse in other than the one you intended to visit.

ads. There is very rarely a true "once
rs have regular sales seasons, and the
d is likely to come around again.

t time you see it. If it is on sale, find
the sale is over and how many of the
ock. Go back in again before the sale is
ppeals to you.

cially things you do not like, just because they

ds at home. The credit will still be available in
temptation to just "slap it on the card" will be
. If having the card within reach is still too en-
here that you will have to go to considerable ef-
riend's safe deposit box, for example. Some people
to freeze their credit cards into a block of ice in
eir neighbor's freezer.

ies have shown that people are more discriminating
rchases when they are paying in cash rather than on

erently

people want to spend differently, even if that means pos-
g more. Decisions about spending differently often arise
w of what our spending supports. For example, beginning
ical premise that the earth is sacred, you know that you
coffee. You have been buying inexpensive one-pound bags
ans at the local grocery store. However, coffee is often grown
of pesticides and chemical fertilizers as well as cultivation
that rapidly deplete the soil, requiring plantations to expand
ounding areas to remain profitable. In addition, many coffee-
g nations are among the poorest in the world, and the wages
coffee workers are typically too low to provide subsistence for

themselves and their families. You ar
There are alternatives. Would you
pound to get coffee that has been gro
ronmentally sustainable fashion (orga
purchased from worker cooperatives
wage (fair trade)? If that is not affordal
one pound in three?

Spending differently can include buy
to tomatoes, but getting them through
Supporting independent retail outlets and loca
nificant difference in the community.

Spending differently can include adding crit
tors in a purchasing decision. For example, if yo
shirts, and decide that they are of comparable qu
ically buy the one that is cheaper? Would you ch
decision if the more expensive one was made do
somewhere like China, Sri Lanka, or Pakistan?
purchasing decision if one shirt's label indicated
made? How much more are you willing and able to
that are produced in a way you morally consider to
tory? Can you afford to make the choice? No one sh
you are a bad person for refusing to make choices yo
Taking responsibility for your choices is one of the
quences of being neopagan.

Reducing Need

Culturally, North Americans tend to own more "stuff" t
be strictly said to need. This is well documented by advo
"simplicity movement"—which in addition to advocating
in consumption also advocates choosing less complex, mor
nity-oriented lifestyles. Unlike our grandparents, who took
be fixed when they were broken, we tend to throw them ou
new ones. Why? Because it is usually cheaper to buy a new on
get the old one fixed. With many items, the choice in how to

them can prolong their life span, thereby reducing future need for new items. Below are some things to consider:

- *Pay attention to the care labels on clothing items.*

    - Top-loading washing machines and hot dryers can prematurely age your clothes. If you are shopping for a new washer, consider a front-loading model without an agitator—it will be much easier on your clothes.

    - If an item says "hand wash," you may be able to put it in your machine on the delicate cycle, in cold water. Cotton, cotton-ramie, and wool sweaters can be washed this way, but should not be put in the dryer. Instead, these items should be blocked to dry—placed flat, in their correct shapes with their arms folded at the elbows as though putting hands on hips, on an absorbent blanket or collection of towels.

    - Cotton clothes will tend to shrink over time when dried in a hot dryer, with the result that children's clothes get smaller as the child gets bigger. Try drying them just enough to get the worst of the water out, say 5 to 10 minutes, and then hanging them to dry the rest of the way.

    - Leather garments (*not* suede!), especially those worn outdoors, will last better if you treat them with oil once a year. This helps prevent the leather from drying out and cracking.

    - Use the recommended protection on footwear, particularly if you live in a snowy climate.

- *Perform the suggested maintenance.* Whether it is a car, a computer or a toaster oven, it probably comes with maintenance recommendations. These are things that the manufacturer *knows* will extend the optimum performance life of the item.
- *Find out if someone you know is handy.* The less energy you need to expend to get things fixed, the more likely you are to do it.

• *Pick up some domestic and mechanical skills of your own, if you have not already.* These skills can be used to salvage things you might otherwise discard.

Other reasons we tend to own a lot of stuff? There is the "urban planning" reason. North Americans tend to have bigger houses and apartments than do our European counterparts. A "modest Paris flat" is often little bigger than what suburban Americans have for a walk-in closet. In such cramped quarters, one has to be very selective about one's possessions.

Regardless of where we live, many of us are bombarded with advertisements. The purpose of these highly manipulative messages is to sell us stuff—essentially, to seduce us into confusing our wants and our needs. They create an artificial sense of urgency, play on our fears and insecurities, and distort our sense of what is really affordable. Try not to give in to artificially manufactured needs.

Saving Your Money

In this environment, where there is such a cultural push to spend everything you have and borrow to spend more, it is not surprising that savings levels are at an all-time low. For some people, saving is impossible—their incomes do not even cover the basic necessities. It is impossible for some people to spend less than what they earn on a consistent basis. For many others, saving money is either a low priority, or seen as an imprudent use of funds; traditional savings vehicles, like savings accounts and government bonds, pay such minimal returns that the real value of the money saved cannot keep up with inflation. Why save at all?

Saving is part of an overall plan to take responsibility for your own situation, a key component of many pagans' worldviews. It can also help to facilitate your overall life goals. Saving consists of spending less than you earn. If you already have consumer debt, however, your first goal should be to pay down your existing debt before embarking on a savings program. Interest rates on most credit cards, especially department-store credit cards, are much higher than the rates of return you can expect from a savings vehicle. Therefore, it makes good financial sense to retire your high-interest debt before you begin to set money aside for other purposes.

People tend to save for four reasons: to pay for large-ticket items in the short to medium term (less than five years); to meet large, anticipated expenses over the long term (ten years or more); to fund contingencies; and to leave an estate for their children, grandchildren, or other designated people or organizations.

In the first savings category are goals that focus on a single item—saving for a car, a vacation, or a new computer. By adopting a kind of "pay as you go" strategy, people try to avoid taking on consumer debt, which they would then have to pay back with interest. With a short savings horizon (less than five years), this usually involves a savings account or other cash equivalents. These protect the money you put in (secure principal) and are fully liquid (you can take the money out at any time without penalty).

Saving for anticipated long-term expenses includes things such as saving for a large home renovation, for a child's education, or for your retirement. While these might be a long way off, it is not difficult to figure out that they are going to require a lot of money.

There are a variety of financial vehicles designed to help people save for these eventualities. In Canada, you can open a Registered Educational Savings Plan (RESP) as soon as you have acquired a Social Insurance Number (SIN) for your child. In the United States, one similar product is called a Children's Educational Trust. When opening either of these, take care to read the issuer's fine print. What is the money to be invested in? Is there a guaranteed rate of return? Who manages the investments of the plan: you or the issuer? It is important to know these things in order to be able to decide if the plan is a good fit for the range of possibilities you can envision.

The investment mix within the plan should change depending on how long a time horizon you have before you will need to have these funds available. The closer you are to needing access to the money, the less risk you should be willing to accept in your investment mix.

Saving for contingencies usually involves creating a financial buffer against unexpected hardships. How much money do you have tucked away in the event that something untoward were to happen? Three months' worth of income? Six months' worth of income? No money at all? Contingency funds are usually invested in instruments that offer both liquidity and security of principal. After all, if you need money to pay a hospital bill, you cannot really say to the hospital, "Well, this isn't really a good time for me to liquidate. Could you wait eighteen months or so to see if the markets improve?" Many financial experts suggest that you try to have six months' worth of income set aside for contingencies.

One of the most commonly recommended strategies for saving money is to "pay yourself first." This involves setting up a pre-authorized purchase plan (PPP) for some type of mutual fund to coincide with the days you are paid. The guideline is usually 10 percent of your take-home pay. So if you have $750 deposited to your account on the fifteenth and thirtieth of each month, you set up a plan that allows withdrawal of $75 from your account the next day, or the day after. The logic of this strategy says that you will not miss money you never actually see, and that this will impose a savings discipline on people who might otherwise be tempted to spend to the limits of their bank account every month. This is not a strategy to use when you are already carrying debt—direct that pre-authorized payment toward your credit card instead.

Investing Your Money Ethically

If you have sufficient money to consider investment strategies that contain mutual funds or publicly traded corporate stocks, you can choose another means to express your social values.

Just as you can question the social and environmental positions of the companies for whom you work, you can also question the positions of the companies in which you are considering investing. Adding social or environmental criteria to more traditional price and rate-of-return criteria is known as *socially responsible investing*. The choice of criteria is entirely a personal matter, although they are likely to be informed by values and moral position that you hold as a pagan. Screening criteria can include, for example:

- Does this company have a good environmental record? Do they strip mine, clear cut, dump toxic waste, or otherwise commit indignities upon our planet?

- Does this company have a good gender, racial, and ethnic mix at all levels, or do they appear to discriminate?

- Does this company have a good labor relations record?

- Does this company offer same-sex benefits?

- Does this company sell to or buy from the Department of Defense?

- Does this company fund organizations of which I do not approve?

- Does this company produce items I find objectionable? (These could include tobacco products, alcohol, genetically modified food, guns, pornography, SUVs, Barbie, or whatever you might personally find offensive.)

Doing your own ethical screening, while certainly possible, can be both time-consuming and expensive. In the case of mutual funds, you must carefully read everything you are given. If you have questions, ask. Make sure that you are satisfied with the answers you are given. In most cases, you will find that there are no screening policies, and thus, no screening. Funds with screening policies are available from many mutual fund companies, and are not difficult to research online. The investor needs to carefully determine what screening criteria are used by the fund and determine if these are acceptable. Some funds will be a better fit than others.

Corporate shares can be evaluated the same way. Either you can do the research yourself, you can pay a brokerage firm to do the research, or you can take a shortcut, like finding a mutual fund that meets your screening criteria and looking at what companies they hold, and using that as a starting point for your own research. Owning shares in your own right rather than through a mutual fund allows you to participate in shareholder activism, if you so choose. Shareholder activism is a movement through which groups of individual investors come together to get motions reflecting their concerns put onto annual meeting agendas.

If you do not vote your own shares, and you do not assign a proxy, the default is that the corporation itself will act as the proxy for your shares. Complacent and/or inattentive shareholders are to the corporation's advantage, as they increase the likelihood that the corporation will be able to pass any policy it pleases. Consider taking an active stance on how your money is used! You can help create improvements in labor conditions for workers or a commitment to better environmental practices.

While investing money is primarily a way in which to secure your own financial future, it can also be a powerful way through which you can express your values. If enough people choose to invest not only for monetary returns but also for change, there will come a time when corporations will have to listen. One of the ways to stop human-rights abuses and environmental abuses, two points about which many pagans feel very strongly, is to make them bad business. Corporations exist to make a profit—if a concern can gain enough momentum to jeopardize profit, changes will be made.

Even if you do not succeed in changing corporate policies to make the world a better place for its six billion inhabitants, there is a certain amount of satisfaction to be had in living true to your beliefs.

Donating Your Money

If you have more money than you need, you can always choose to give it away. There are a number of different types of gifts you can make. There are "charity begins at home" gifts—gifts of money to relatives or friends who are struggling financially and need a bit of a boost. Somebody probably gave you a break once, and you can always tell your recipient that instead of reimbursing you, they can help someone else who needs it someday—when they are in a position to do so. This style of giving reflects a sense of interconnection among people and with the world, which many pagans feel strongly about. It is also a kind of giving that is consonant with the notion of karma—doing good will bring good back to you as well as bring more good into the world. All of these things keep us connected and strengthen our immediate community.

There are also gifts in support of things from which you benefit. For example, if you like to go to the orchestra, you may support the orchestra by donation, by subscribing to their performances, or by supporting orchestra-sponsored young musicians' scholarships. You may make donations to local hospitals, or if you or a member of your family suffers from a problematic medical condition, you may donate to support research on that particular condition. You may buy hospital or research society raffle tickets. Perhaps you wish to support the political party of your choice. Political donations tend to carry a higher tax-advantage than many other forms of giving.

There are an almost endless number of causes out there competing for your money. Food banks, snowsuit funds, homeless shelters, battered women's shelters, supplementary literacy programs for children and adults, AIDS hospices, crisis lines, wildlife conservation, free clinics, public radio, public television, soup kitchens, organ funds, local arts groups, university alumni associations, wilderness trails, camps for underprivileged children, civic monuments . . . and that is all without leaving the neighborhood! On top of that, there are the international appeals to help avert starvation in the Third World, rebuild schools washed away by monsoons, get medical care to women in heavily patriarchal societies, or rebuild housing demolished by hurricanes. There is an endless string of natural and human-caused disasters that cannot be addressed without funds.

Probably all of these are good causes. The organizations that work to provide adequate food, clothing and shelter both to the low-income segments of our own population and to less affluent populations around the world are unquestionably alleviating suffering and hardship. But we must to ask, to what end? There are families where the food money runs out before the end of the month—*here*, in some of the wealthiest, most advantaged countries in the world. People have to stand in line and give their names in exchange for food, because you can only get food every so often, or there will not be enough food for all the people who rely on the service. In some parts of the country, it is cold enough to freeze uncovered skin in less than fifteen seconds, and there are children showing up at school in holey boots lined with newspaper, and no socks.

When we give money to the food bank or to the "buy warm socks" fund, while we will make a temporary improvement in people's lives, *we are not challenging the circumstances that have led to these conditions.* In fact, by donating to homeless shelters to help people who are poor and often substance addicted, we are making it easier for governments to refuse to deal with the fundamental issues involved.

Fundamental responsibilities of government, which include ensuring that people have access to what we consider basic necessities—food, shelter, education and medical care—are increasingly being turned over to private interests, even for-profit interests. Should somebody be making a profit on the fact that many people do not have enough to eat? This is a value question, and requires a moral judgment. Charity, while it has some benefit, is really only a stopgap measure. Charity permits the status quo to keep right on existing, when what some of these situations need is social change. Social change goes beyond the symptoms of the problem and attempts to address the root causes.

Support for a shelter for battered women gives women today somewhere to go, but it will not stop other women from being battered next week, next month, or next year. Support for education programs about communication, conflict resolution, and nonviolence from elementary school through the end of high school might better help to end the cycle of battering. A check to a disaster-relief campaign to buy food for starving people in the Third World will help feed some people today. A check to a community development organization or a microcredit group (a group that provides small loans to individuals to enable them to start their own businesses) might enable Third World residents to develop small-scale business operations and industries that will leave them less vulnerable to crop failures by diversifying their economies.

Social Change Foundations

In the United States, there are a number of community foundations to which you can contribute. The foundation funds grassroots projects that will facilitate social change in communities, usually through education, organization, and mobilization. Members of the communities in question sit on the boards of these foundations and determine what projects will be funded. Social change foundations can be local or constituency specific, or they can be, like the Funding Exchange, umbrella organizations that give money to other funds or foundations. Goals and constituencies can range widely. For example, the Peace Development Fund provides grants and technical assistance to peace and social justice projects in the Caribbean, Central America and North America; and the Global Fund for Women supports projects aimed at ensuring women's human rights, facilitating their access to the media and other channels of economic communication, and promoting their economic equality. Local foundations include the Crossroads Fund (Chicago), the Fund for Southern Communities (Georgia, North Carolina, South Carolina), the Headwaters Fund (Minneapolis and St. Paul) and the Haymarket People's Fund (New England). Many other local foundations and social change groups exist, and can be found fairly easily by poking about on the Web.

Giving for social change puts the emphasis on reform, which is a fundamental component of many aspects of the pagan worldview. As previously mentioned, Starhawk often uses a chant about the Goddess in her social activism circles: "She changes everything She touches and everything She touches changes." The entire pagan conceptualization of magic is oriented around the notion of change, and many pagan authors reflect this: William Butler states, "Magic is the art of changing consciousness at will." "Magic is the art of causing change in accordance with will," writes Aleister Crowley, and Starhawk writes, "Energy pursues the path of least resistance. Material results are more easily achieved through physical actions than through magical workings.... No magic spell is going to bring results unless channels are open in the material world" (1979:113). Social change organizations open these channels in the material world.

MAKING THE CHOICE

Below are some questions you may wish to ask about foundations or organizations to which you are considering making a contribution:

- What projects has this foundation provided grants to in the past?

- How successful were these projects?

- Were these projects oriented to charitable ends or to social change?

- Are these the kinds of projects that I would consider supporting on my own? Do they reflect issues that I identify as key priorities?

- Does the foundation maintain a large pool of capital and only fund projects out of the income from that capital, or do they disperse most of what they take in?

- How long has the organization been in operation? A brand-new organization may still be building up its resources, which would make your gift especially welcome, but they will not have a history you can examine.

- Does the organization operate alone, or does it work with other, similar organizations as part of a coalition?

- How do the communities being served by the organization feel about it? Do they find that they are being treated paternalistically, or do they feel included in the planning and execution of the organization's projects? Whose priorities are being served?

- You may wish to ask to see a copy of their budget, or their previous year-end report, so that you can get a better idea of how the organization spends the money it receives. How much does the organization spend on overhead? On fundraising?

Planned Giving

Planned giving is often more effective and more satisfying than spontaneous, ad hoc giving. You do not need to have a large amount of money in order to have a giving plan. Decide at the beginning of the year how much money you would like to give. Some people approach this as an absolute number—"I am going to give $500 this year"—while others express it as a percentage of their income—"I would like to devote 2 percent of my income to giving."

Look for groups that match up with your preferences. Many organizations allow donors to choose how to give—all at once, by monthly deduction from a bank account, or even by credit card. You can do your giving all at once, do one gift a month, or use any other method that is convenient for you. If you tend to forget to do things that do not occur on a regular basis, you may wish to write a reminder on your calendar or in your datebook, or you could give a gift on every sabbat. You can give as an individual, a family, or a coven.

Money can be an important vehicle through which to express values, act out moral decisions, and contribute to social change. To do this, you must learn about money, think about the options creatively, and remember that money, while necessary, is not everything. People without money can give time and energy, and people who have money to give should consider giving time and energy as well. Money is like magic: it can get you what you want, it can cause change in the world, but only if your intentions are clear and your mind is focused. Starhawk writes, "A spell is a symbolic act done in an altered state of consciousness in order to cause a desired change. To cast a spell is to project energy through a symbol. But the symbols are too often mistaken for the spell" (1979: 110). Money itself is just a symbol—it has no value in and of itself. Its value lies in what we do with it. Stepping outside of the daily financial autopilot—changing your *consciousness*—can enable you to project your energy through your money in new ways.

Financial Glossary

- *Capital gain:* When you sell an investment for more than the value at which you purchased it, you have generated a capital gain. So if you bought 100 shares of XYZ Corporation at $6 per share, and then sold them for $13 per share, you generated a capital gain of $7 per share, or $700. Capital-gains income is often taxed at a lower rate than either interest or dividend income.

- *Capital loss:* When you sell an investment for less than what you paid for it, you have generated a capital loss. So if XYZ Corporation's shares, which you purchased for $6 each, decline in value to $2 each, and you sell them to avoid the consequences of their value continuing to decline, you will have generated a capital loss of $4 per share, or $400. Capital losses can be used to offset capital gains on your income tax.

- *Cash equivalents:* a short-term investment with a high level of liquidity.

- *Corporate bond:* Corporate bonds operate on the same basic principle as government bonds; they are, however, considered riskier investments, as a corporation is much more likely than a government to go bankrupt and not be able to honor its debts.

- *Dividends:* Dividends are a form of income generated by ownership of shares in a corporation. Corporations may choose to share some of their profits with investors in the form of a per-share dividend—essentially, you will receive a certain amount of money per share that you own.

- *Government bond:* Governments sometimes raise money by issuing bonds. They are a form of government debt. You purchase the bond and receive either interest payments for the life of the bond, or a set, higher-than-purchase value at the time of maturity.

- *Liquidity:* This has to do with how readily an investment can be turned back into cash. A savings account has a high level of liquidity—you go to the bank and you withdraw the money. A piece of fine artwork or jewelry has a low level of liquidity, as the price you will receive for it depends on finding a buyer.

- *Mutual fund:* A type of investment in which the money of many investors is pooled together to buy a portfolio of different securities.

The fund is managed by a professional who invests in stocks, bonds, options, money-market instruments, or other securities. Instead of owning shares in each individual company or a certain value of each type of bond, you will own a certain number of shares in the mutual fund. Shares may be sold back to the fund for that day's price. The advantage of mutual funds for small investors is the diversification you can achieve even with only a very limited amount of money to invest.

- *Volatility:* This has to do with how likely, and how much, the value of the investment is to change in the short term. Volatile investments are appropriate for people who are unlikely to need to sell the investment on short notice in order to meet day-to-day needs. An investment portfolio should not consist solely of highly volatile investments.

Resources

Robin Hood Was Right, by Chuck Collins and Pam Rogers (New York: W.W. Norton, 2000).

Your Money or Your Life, by Joe Dominguez and Vicki Robin (New York: Penguin, 1992).

Investing for Good, by Peter Kinder, Steven Lydenberg, and Amy Domini (New York: Harper Business, 1993).

For more information on socially responsible investing, check out www.socialinvest.org, www.socialinvestment.ca, www.coopamerica.org, or www.soyouwanna.com/sites/syws/socinvest/socinvest.html.

For more information on shareholder activism, visit www.foe.org/international/shareholder/toolsfordemocracy.html, www.kairoscanada.org, or www.equalityproject.org/what.htm.

CHAPTER 6

Community

What do we mean when we talk about *community? Community* is living with, interacting, and sharing space with all things: plants, animals, the natural world, and the human world. Many neopagans consider the word *community* to mean their spiritual community, but in fact the word encompasses so much more. Whether you stay in the same town you were born in or are looking to move, you need to assess what sort of community you want to live in and why. No community is perfect, but you can decide what is a priority and what is not important to you. Perhaps you want to move to a town or city where there is a comprehensive recycling program; maybe you like a vibrant local arts scene; or perhaps you choose to make compromises in order to get the perfect job. All of these issues go into making choices about your community, from the global community we all share to the internal spiritual community you may only share with yourself and the god/desses.

Activism: The World as Our Community

If the earth is sacred, then by extrapolation, so are all things upon it and within it. We have discussed numerous ways in which the individual can work toward honoring and nurturing the world, through choices of clothing, power sources, composting, and even ethical money investments. One could easily go broke and insane trying to support even a small fraction of the worthy international causes that work toward the sort of ethical world in which neopagans would generally like to live. There are two ways to handle this: if you have a little extra money you can earmark for organizations working on causes you support, decide which cause(s) are most important to you and make regular or periodic contributions. The second way of supporting the cause(s) you feel strongly about is to volunteer your time and/or expertise. Most non-governmental agencies and humanitarian organizations are very appreciative of extra hands to stuff envelopes, type correspondence, make phone calls, etc. A sample of the organizations and issues that may resonate for neopagans is included below. Some of the groups mentioned are fairly new on the activist scene, but all have important causes to represent.

AMNESTY INTERNATIONAL

Amnesty International is a nonprofit organization dedicated to ensuring that all human beings enjoy all of the human rights enshrined in both the Universal Declaration of Human Rights and all other human rights standards. Amnesty International focuses on research and action aimed at preventing and/or ending abuses of human rights involving physical and mental well-being, freedom of conscience and expression, and many forms of discrimination. It is worth noting, however, that Amnesty International has historically not considered discrimination based on sexual orientation part of its mandate—one reason why many pagans who are also part of the gay/lesbian/bisexual communities often do not donate to them.

HIV/AIDS ACTIVISM

HIV/AIDS is an epidemic illness that touches all communities. There are myriad organizations, foundations, and charities throughout the English-speaking world you may support through cash donations and/or time volunteered. You might consider seeing if your pet cat or dog is a suitable candidate as a visiting hospital/hospice therapy animal. You could volunteer your time on an information or crisis line, or even lay out the Web page for your local HIV/AIDS affiliate.

In the United States, the American Foundation for AIDS Research (amfAR) is the nation's leading nonprofit organization dedicated to the support of HIV/AIDS research, AIDS prevention, treatment education, and the advocacy of sound AIDS-related public policy. There is also the grassroots AIDS ReSearch Alliance based in California. ARA is the result of blending physicians and activists into one of the leading nonprofit AIDS research organizations in the USA. ARA raises privately donated funds to ensure the pursuit of treatments often deemed unprofitable by the pharmaceutical industry. They focus on compassion and urgency, working to speed up the development of promising new AIDS therapies.

STAND FOR CHILDREN

On June 1, 1996, more than 300,000 people came to Washington, D.C., to attend the Stand for Children March, the largest rally for children in American history. From that march arose a grassroots organization supporting the needs of school-age children in the United States. Stand for Children has managed some landmark achievements in a very short time, including safe after-school programs, dental care for children of low-income families, funding for teen centers, and financial support for additional school support staff, such as counselors, guidance counselors, nurses, and educational aides in schools. They have also managed to lower the class size in many school districts.

CORPORATE WATCH

Corporate Watch works against globalization efforts by corporations through education, network building, and activism. They work to foster what they describe as democratic control over corporations by building grassroots globalization, which they describe as a diverse movement for human rights and dignity, labor rights, and environmental justice. They run a Web site (www.corpwatch.org) that highlights globalization issues and announcements of petitions, activist meetings, etc.

THE RUCKUS SOCIETY

The Ruckus Society's formation in 1995, was sparked by various concurrent events, including the passage of a U.S. federal anti-environmental law and budget cuts at Greenpeace. Ruckus trains and assists thousands of activists in the use of nonviolent direct action. Ruckus trains people in the skills they need in order to practice nonviolent direct action safely and effectively. Ruckus offers physical training as well as classroom-style instruction for action planning, communicating with the media, nonviolent philosophy and practice, and more.

FOSTER PARENTING

Chapter four discusses children and how to raise and educate them as pagans, but there are other ways of reaching out to children within your physical and spiritual community. There are a range of international and local organizations for foster parents. Fostering a child is an immense and rewarding responsibility—please consult the internet! Plan International is an international, child-focused development organization with no religious, political, or governmental affiliation. Plan International works with over a million children, their families, and communities in developing countries to implement projects at the grassroots level in health, education, water and sanitation, income-generation, and cross-cultural communication. Children are sponsored until they reach eighteen years of age.

Locally, children often need a temporary home while their own parents or guardians get their lives straightened out. Other times, they need to be re-homed for a short or long time due to allegations of abuse in their own homes. For orphaned, abused, neglected, delinquent, or disabled children, the answer is often a foster home. Foster parents offer a safe environment for children and are compensated monetarily by various government agencies for the related incurred costs. Today, a foster parent need not be married, or even part of a heterosexual couple.

ADOPTION

Some families do not have biological children for reasons ranging from age to infertility to possible birth-defect issues. Other families have biological children but choose to increase their size by adopting children. The reasons to adopt are myriad, and there are scores of children in North America and overseas waiting for a family to love them and call them their own, permanently. The Internet is filled with both reputable agencies and those of dubious nature; if you choose to look at adopting a child, be cautious as you wade through the available information. The National Adoption Information Clearinghouse is but one source to consult, as is the online site adoption.com. Adoption offers its own unique challenges, as does fostering children, but those who have chosen this path often indicate they would never have it any other way.

Mentoring Children

Consider sparing some time in a mentoring program. A mentor provides young people with support, counsel, friendship, reinforcement, and constructive example. A mentor can make immeasurable contributions to a child's life choices and decisions. Mentors are good listeners, people who care, and people who want to help young people bring out their hidden strengths. A mentor can make immeasurable contributions to a child's life choices and decisions. Mentors, a national organization, was created in 1990 to respond to two comments the founders heard repeatedly from young Americans: No one cares about us, and the American dream is a joke. Mentors (the organization) works at coordinating efforts across the United States so that youngsters and mentors can be successfully paired up.

Big Brothers and Big Sisters is the oldest mentoring program in the United States, having been founded in 1904. It matches adults with children aged 5 to 18 in one-to-one relationships. Little brothers and sisters come to the program through the recommendation of an adult in their lives, such as a teacher, family member, or school counselor. The mentor and child are paired up in order to share experiences and friendship.

The Senior Community

Like Native Americans, the Craft puts a high value on wisdom learned through experience and living. Those who have lived well and long are given an unofficial title recognizing that they are sources of wisdom in our communities: Elder. The traits that combine to make an older person an elder are hard to define, but the phrase "Elders have old eyes" comes close. Miles traveled and years experienced mark a person as a role model and holder of rare knowledge. Often we forget what a valuable commodity experience can be. Elders should be honored and heeded.

Many women in the Craft are recognized as "Crones" when they pass their childbearing years, but there seems to be no widely accepted comparable term for men past a certain age. Becoming an elder is not a time to rest on one's laurels, but rather a time to continue learning and inspiring others. There are many programs in the greater community at large, aimed at those who are 50 or 60 and over, which help protect the rights and health of the elderly, as well as programs that encourage the more mature adult to continue thinking and learning; for if we do not continue to learn, how can we be suitable role models for younger generations?

ELDERHOSTEL

The Elderhostel network is a not-for-profit organization that provides novel and exciting learning-based trips to nearly 200,000 adults aged 55 and over. Elderhostel functions in more than ninety countries, offering participants learning packages including accommodations, meals, lectures, field trips, cultural excursions, gratuities, and medical or insurance coverage. Elderhostel is based on the belief that learning is a lifelong pursuit that opens minds and enriches lives. Age is seen as no barrier to the sharing of new ideas, challenges, and experiences.

AMERICAN ASSOCIATION OF RETIRED PERSONS

Known as AARP, this is a nonprofit organization that addresses the unique needs and interests of persons 50 years of age and older. The organization works to enhance the quality of life for the older adult by promoting independence, dignity, and purpose. AARP also advocates for its membership on topics of interest including the long-term financial stability of Social Security income; the protection of pensions; age discrimination; prescription drug coverage by Medicare, and patient protection in managed-care and long-term care facilities (fighting elder abuse).

Elder Abuse

Elder abuse is a real problem in the modern North American setting and is finally receiving some serious attention from government and private agencies alike. "Elder abuse" refers to intentional, or negligent acts by a caregiver, relative, or any other person causing harm or the serious risk of harm to a vulnerable older adult. Seniors are particularly defined as vulnerable as they are often isolated from their support structures (e.g., living alone), may be living in assisted living, and/or may have increasing impairment of their physical and/or mental faculties.

Elder abuse includes:

- Hurting, or threatening to hurt or injure, a vulnerable elder, or depriving them of a basic need.

- Inflicting mental pain, anguish, or distress on an elder either via verbal or nonverbal acts.

- Nonconsensual sexual contact of any kind.

- Illegally taking, misusing, or concealing the funds, property, or assets of an elder.

- The refusal or failure by those responsible to provide basics such as food, shelter, health care, and protection for an elder specifically under their care.

- Desertion of an infirm elder by one who has assumed the responsibility for their care and/or custody.

In the United States, the National Center on Elder Abuse (NCEA) is a national resource for elder rights and law enforcement, used by legal professionals, public policy leaders, researchers, and the public. The center promotes understanding, knowledge sharing, and action on elder abuse, neglect, and exploitation.

The Wisdom of the Elders

How can neopagans work on honoring not just their Elders, but the elderly within their community? Elders have many stories to tell, about the growth of the Craft in their area, things learned from those who were their Elders in turn, and so much more. Why not bring a tape recorder and record their stories before they are lost to our memory? Now is the time to record the wisdom of leaders such as (for example) Isaac Bonewits, Margo Adler, Starhawk, Zusanna Budapest, Ray Buckland, and many more of our teachers and educators. Ideally, this could become part of an international collection of wisdom for the pagan ages. Similarly, there could be a "how to" series of basic Craft skills taught by different Elders—how to do a candle spell, how to do a cord spell, how to set up a basic altar, etc. It is criminal to lose the information we could continue to cherish as our Elders depart to their deserved time in the Summerlands.

HONORING OUR ELDERS

Because Wicca is a non-centralized religion (e.g., it has no central council or governing body), it becomes hard to choose a way to collectively honor our Elders. Every year thousands of bright-eyed young Seekers come hunting for a teacher in the Craft, and few of them will settle for someone around their chronological age. Despite this, elders are often neglected after they give of their time, energy, and good spirit to teach and lead these young students. Is it any surprise, then, that many of the Elders within the Craft walk away from teaching?

Perhaps we need a designated day to honor our Elders. It would be suitable for a full-moon ritual, and could be focused on thanking those who have given of their time and vision to help us as we walk our own individual paths with the gods and goddesses. Perhaps we could offer gifts to our Elders (food, or something small), or pamper them with a gift certificate for something decadent. Or perhaps we could include a toast to our Elders, seen and unseen, now and forever, in our rituals. Not many Craft groups make their appreciation of their Elders explicit, and perhaps that is something we could consider incorporating into our regular religious practice as a way of underlining the value of both our Elders and the experiences they bring to our lives.

Urban Planning and Choices

Many of us give little thought to where we choose to live and why it is suitable for us. Older communities (e.g. those on the East Coast of North America) are far more "organic" in layout than newer communities further west. Cities and towns of British origin are often laid out on a strict grid system, preferred by the British military engineers. As with much of Europe, old cities are often riddled with little laneways and alleys that start and stop as they please, and meet each other at oblique angles. Often, the first road in a town was cobblestone covered to follow the path the cows perpetually took to market.

New towns and/or subdivisions are usually planned communities which have been laid out by a city planner and/or architects where stores will be situated, what sections will be zoned residential or commercial, how large parking lots will be—all is carefully designed to optimize the designer's vision of a "perfect" community. However, what is perfect to the planner may not agree with your personal view of a good community. You may be in favor of multi-income mixed housing, while a designer may feel that only high-income homes should be in the same area, in order to keep the property values high. It is true that many home-owners fear that lower-income housing may bring down their real-estate values, and that is one reason why mixed-income housing is less popular than many other plans.

MAKING THE CHOICE

Some questions to consider when choosing a community:

- Do I want a lawn? Backyard? Do these things matter to me?

- How do I feel about security in and around my home? Do I want to install a home alarm system? How about a gated community, where my visitors must buzz at the outside gates to be allowed in? Are these things viable concerns where I live, or are they encumbrances to me?

- Many planned subdivisions have both speed bumps/humps, and very curvy, windy roads within the subdivision. The purpose of the curved roads is to slow drivers down (many of these subdivisions are designed to appeal to families with young children), but they often do not achieve their goal. Instead, children and vehicles can collide easily, as curves create "blind spots" for drivers and pedestrians alike.

- Do I like infill as a concept in my neighborhood? (*Infill* is the term for slipping a new home in to an existing street of homes.)

- Would I like an older house with character? Can I deal with the inherent issues older buildings have?

- Would I rather have a newer home with less physical maintenance issues, but also with less "personality"?

Infill can be good for the neighbourhood and the community in general, as housing built into existing areas takes advantage of existing transit, sewer, and road services. If the Earth is sacred and we must respect it, it is practically a crime to see acres and hectares of prime farmland being plowed under to facilitate more homes for suburban dwellers. Infill does not waste land, but puts vacant spots to use. If you choose to live in an urban setting, do you choose a house that has a large "footprint" (the land used up by the building from outside wall to outside wall), or do you opt for a home that is more compact? Using upward space by living in a multi-floor house gives you the same overall square footage but uses up less precious land.

The word *pagan* comes from the Latin word *paganus*, or "country dweller." (Let us point out here that *paganus* has the connotation of "country bumpkin" so it is not historically a complimentary term.) Despite the adoption of the term *pagan*, or *neopagan*, the fact is that we are primarily an urban religious movement. Pagans as *paganus* is a romantic concept, not a lifestyle most modern-day pagans choose to live. Most Wiccans choose to live in larger urban centers where they can shop for magical supplies, eat at restaurants, buy books, visit libraries, and enjoy the other amenities that make cities agreeable to them. Small towns and villages have a slower pace of life and often allow residents more land on which to live, but they also can be places where "everyone knows your business." Large cities may offer more things to do, but they also are more expensive, both in financial terms and in the human cost of living in a fast-paced environment.

MAKING THE CHOICE

Each one of us has to choose what size town or city best suits us and what we choose to get out of our home. Here are a few questions to ask yourself:

- Do I want privacy? Can I achieve this in a large urban setting, where it is possible to know no one but also to have no one who cares for and about me? Could I achieve the same privacy by living on a farm with 50 acres of land?

- Do I want to raise children in the city? Do I want to raise children in a small town?

- How far am I willing to commute to work?

Mode(s) of Transport

Many cities have been good about creating things like bicycle paths, and sidewalks keep pedestrians away from automobile traffic as well as encourage walking. It is quite striking that, the further west one goes within the United States, the less one sees sidewalks. The automobile is king (or queen?) in cities such as Los Angeles, San Diego, Phoenix, Las Vegas, and so on, and sidewalks are often nonexistent. This creates a real challenge to those who prefer to get around on their own two feet.

WALKING

Do you like walking? Is the city you are considering as your home suited to walking? Are there sidewalks, and are they in good repair? If you are looking at an area that gets snow, what is the priority on clearing the sidewalks? In small towns, you can often go for a brisk and enjoyable stroll in the woods around town rather than walking within the town itself. Walking is one of the best choices when your destination is within your walking tolerance: it causes no pollution, costs almost nothing, and is good for your cardiovascular health. On top of all those pluses, walking allows you to move slowly enough to enjoy the view and the wildlife (even in urban areas)!

BICYCLES

The bicycle is an excellent option for many people in urban and rural settings. Most children learn how to ride a bicycle at a young age, even if they need special instruction to learn the related safety tips. Bicycles have the same advantages as walking, with one additional plus: they are much faster than most people can walk. For getting you farther and faster, a bicycle is a good choice as a non-polluting mode of transport. The big key is whether or not your community is bicycle friendly or not. Are there bike-only lanes on the larger streets? How about bike paths to get you from point A to point B quickly and efficiently? How are city drivers about bike riders? Does local law enforcement enforce the rules?

If you choose to get around by bicycle, remember to keep your equipment in good condition. This includes the equipment you wear (such as a bike helmet) and the equipment you ride on. Faulty equipment can cost you time as well as money. Do not forget to make sure your bicycle has a working headlight as well as a working red taillight.

PUBLIC TRANSIT

In larger cities and/or small towns within commuter range of large cities, commuter services become important to investigate as well. Are there buses that service your area? Are they only during traditional rush hours (such as from 6:30 A.M. to 9 A.M. and from 3 to 5:30 P.M.), or can you utilize bus service all day long? Is your urban area large enough to offer 24-hour bus service? If not, do the buses and other infrastructure stop running before the bars close in your jurisdiction? If they do, you may well be looking at inebriated drivers on the roads, a very scary and dangerous thing to have to deal with on an ongoing basis.

How good is the coverage of large and small streets by your public transit system? Do you have rapid transit options such as high-speed rail, a "bus only transitway," or a subway system? Does the city system feed into other urban systems, or is it self-contained? Does your transit system use alternative sources of energy (e.g., propane, natural gas, electricity) or only fossil fuel? Do your city government and/or state (provincial) government help fund your public transit system? Is there any special treatment of riders in the city core? Perhaps there is a great public transit system in your community, but does it work for you personally? If you work overnight shifts, you might be "reverse commuting" into the city in the evening for work and then back home in the morning; will you be able to actually get a bus when you need it?

OTHER OPTIONS

Once you've lived in a neighborhood or city for a while, you may well be able to set up shared rides to and from work or other destinations. Two options are carpools and sharing the travel with friends and/or coworkers. Many large cities offer carpool services both within town and between nearby cities, with notice boards and/or telephone numbers to match up riders and drivers. These help move the maximum number of people with a minimal number of automobiles burning gasoline to pollute our environment. You may also find someone at work or school who drives to the same general area of town as the one you live in: why not ask if you can share rides and costs to and from work with them? Again, this is not only a chance to save some money and avoid polluting the air, but it also allows you to get to know your neighbors and/or coworkers better. Knowing those around you helps build networks of people who can set up other positive groups.

For our environment, unless you are driving a battery-operated or dual-fuel vehicle, driving alone is probably the least positive choice for getting around town. However, there are some people who a) do not like using public transit for personal reasons (e.g. allergies), or who b) have disabilities such that using public forms of transit are not feasible. For some people, it is indeed preferable to have the control and freedom to get to and from their destinations in their own cars. In this case, it is wise to honor the Earth by buying a small car that uses less of our dwindling gasoline resources than a large gas guzzler.

Style of Community

There are many things that contribute to one's choice of where to live permanently. Military families get used to being uprooted every few years, and many jobs also have us on the road, like gypsies, living out of suitcases. Most people, however, prefer to have a stable "base of operations" for their lives, and many individuals never leave the town they were born in. Up until the twentieth century, that was the norm rather than the exception for most people's lives: they were born, lived, and died within ten miles of the same place. In the past, North American culture was agriculturally based.

MAKING THE CHOICE

Here are some things to consider when looking for a community to live in as a pagan:

- What sort of identity do you have, and where do you want to express it? Are you a big-city person? Do you prefer smaller cities, or large towns? Or do you prefer the rural, leisurely pace of life?

- Are most of the functions in town focused around the local church? If so, you might find yourself having trouble fitting in with your neighborhood if you are not a church-going person. In small communities, this can be a real issue, as many municipal decisions will happen at the church strawberry social rather than at town hall meetings.

- If you have chosen to homeschool your children, is the homeschool association where you are considering moving a church- or faith-based one? How diverse are the people in town?

- How affluent is the community? Is the town or city economically depressed? How about the neighborhood you're considering in particular?

Special Considerations

• Are community members of the town or city you are considering known for tolerance?

One of the joys of most large urban areas in North America is their diversity in terms of religion, race, and sexual identity. The more varied the communities within a city are, the greater the chances are that you will not be accosted or ridiculed for being pagan. Usually by the time a community hits a population level of about 500,000, it becomes comfortable to wear a pentacle openly around your neck on public transit. Some smaller communities will simply assume you are a) weird, b) a Satanist, or c) a hard-rock fan, but other communities might think you are an evil-doer and/or a Satanist, and will shun you. It quickly becomes very uncomfortable dropping by the only grocery store when everyone inside stares at you and/or whispers behind your back.

Generally, if you are both of the Craft and practice any sort of alternative lifestyle (openly gay or lesbian, polyamorous, etc.), the larger the city, the less hassle you will have to endure. Most large cities of a million plus population have some sort of "pink ghetto" where many alternative lifestyle people live and enjoy services that are pink-triangle friendly. The smaller the community, the more homogeneous the population tends to be, be they Italian Catholics, Irish Protestants, Finnish Lutherans, or Hassidic Jews. As someone with a different religion and other possible differences, it really does become a good idea to research the tolerance levels of the city or town you are investigating as your new home.

• Is the community you are investigating what one might call blue collar or white collar? Is it "working class"? Do the neighbors care about how their lawns are kept? Do they keep miscellaneous "stuff" in the front yard, the balcony, or in the backyard?

Different things matter to some folks and not at all to others. Drive around the neighborhood you intend to move into and *look* at it. Pay attention to little things, like the level of upkeep of houses and/or apartments in the area. Are the cars parked around the neighborhood new, or are they old beaters? Compare this to your comfort level and hobbies. Use your instincts and speak to people in the community, if at all possible.

- Do you have a plethora of dogs, cats, turtles, and/or snakes? Check the animal bylaws in the community before you move in, to avoid some rude surprises. There may also be bylaws about barking dogs, so check that if you have a yappy (or talkative) dog in your family.

- Will you have anything in common with your neighbors? Do you care?

- If you are fond of spending your free time at home in the buff, how close are your neighbors and their windows? Do you have to pull the drapes to be comfortable in your own "castle"? Are the backyard walls high enough for you to hold a skyclad circle if you so choose? Can you sunbathe nude on your own balcony? What level of tolerance is there for nudity in the community in general? Are there any official or quasi-official nude beaches nearby? For many Wiccans, having the option to go without clothing is important to them as a way of being closer to their natural state of being—make sure the community you are considering as your home will not be scandalized by your actions, unless you feel that the town needs a "good shaking up" and you have chosen to be the instrument of this.

- Are the arts or sports a priority to you, and to the city or town?

  If you love a vibrant music, dance, and/or art scene, you may prefer a larger community over a smaller one. Nevertheless many smaller towns have playhouses and small orchestras, which would give you more of a hands-on experience than would a large city with a music hall or major performance venue. Like the arts, sports can be a rallying point for a community. Would you be happier in a community with a junior hockey or basketball team you could root for, or a city with a team that's nationally known?

- If you work or stay up all night and sleep all day, consider how time-structured the community is. Are there any 24-hour amenities available, such as coffee shops, gas stations and grocery stores?

The community you choose to live in can have a profound impact on how you enjoy your quality of life. When you feel that there are few people "like me," it can make finding community a real challenge. If you like being self-sufficient, perhaps living in a rural area is perfect: you will interact with wildlife more than people. Those who can "telecommute," such as those with certain high-tech jobs, can choose to live almost wherever they choose, as long as they have a reliable Internet connection and can commute to work for the occasional meeting. Some cities feel cold at first but have a warm and embracing ambience when you take the time to scratch below the surface. After all, who has never heard that "New Yorkers are cold people"? In fact, they are some of the warmest, most giving people in the United States, but it can take effort on your part to find their big hearts under the gruff exterior they have had to grow to protect themselves in such a large city. Take your time before choosing a living place.

Communities of Choice

There are many types of "community" one can belong to, and what town or city you reside in is but one type. We call that the *physical* community in which you live. Your family (however you define this) is also a community, as is your spiritual community. How you define your communities will have something to do with your neopagan sensibilities as well as the things you love and live for.

Your geographic community is the region where you live, or the region you identify with. You may consider yourself an Iowan first, and an American second, or vice versa. Some pagans identify themselves as world citizens, viewing international borders as unhealthy and/or artificial constructs. If your job brings you to a new city, you may continue to identify yourself as a Montrealer, or a Michigander, even though you now live in Toronto or Chicago. As discussed in an earlier chapter, many pagans also have imbedded a mythic concept of the "homeland" or "old country" in their identity, so they will be Irish pagans or, as one T-shirt worn at a festival proclaimed, "I AM A W.A.S.P.: WHITE ANGLO

SAXON PAGAN! You may be three generations removed from Italy or Romania, yet you may still identify yourself as an Italian American or Romanian Canadian. This is still part of your geographic community and identity.

Most of us have a smaller or larger collection of kindred linked to us by blood, our *blood kin*. These are the people we had little or no choice in relating with, as they include our parents, siblings, uncles and aunts, grandparents, and other relatives. Your own culture of origin will indicate how far from your nuclear (immediate) family your blood kin is considered to extend. Often, our blood kin are not the family we would have chosen to originate from, whether because we are simply that much different from them, or because there may well have been some level of tension as we grew up around our blood kin.

How close do you want to live to them? For some people, being in the same town is preferable; for others, being in the same state is too close. Although it is unusual, you do have the option of "divorcing" your parents or any other relative if you so choose. Just because you have shared blood between you does not mean you are obliged to have regular contact, or even acknowledge your link with them. It is unfortunate when this happens, but there are times when being away from someone is much better for your emotional health than being close. With some relatives, being far enough away to be in the next long-distance telephone zone is sufficient: you can see them when you want to without driving for days, yet they have to consider the cost before phoning to discuss what they saw on television yesterday... or the health of their bowel movements. For the lucky few, however, our blood kin also become part of our kindred by choice.

A community in which we consciously choose to hold membership is what we refer to as *kindred by choice*: those who have become part of our network of friends from work, hobbies, school, and other venues. Some of your kindred by choice will be close enough that you would offer them a bed overnight if they were passing through town; others will be close enough that you consider them part of your family even though you have no blood ties. It can be very isolating to lose your kindred by choice if one moves; if one dies, it can feel much as if you have lost one of your own limbs. Your kindred by choice will be the people you get the most emotional support from; you can fall out of contact for years but feel as if you spoke "just yesterday" when you meet again. As we grow older, many of us recognize our kindred by choice as our strongest community of all, and the one where we feel most comfortable.

For many in the Craft, life would be intolerable without their *non-human kindred*. Many people have a deep affinity for certain animals, whether as familiars, "overly" familiars, or just as fin or fur friends. Throughout history, witches have been pictured with frogs and toads, cats, bats, and other critters, as their familiars, except that they were usually portrayed as agents of Satan. Having strong feelings for non-human living creatures is not reserved for pagans only, as T-shirts and bumper stickers declare THE MORE TIME I SPEND WITH PEOPLE [men, women], THE MORE I LIKE MY DOG [cat, ferret].

Before you decide on a physical community, check on its bylaws regarding nonhumans. Some communities disallow "exotic" pets (what "exotic" includes will vary widely, from snakes to African pygmy hedgehogs); others have a cap on how many domestic animals may be kept without a kennel license.

Keep in mind that both urban and rural homes have their own unique risks to your four-footed, scaled, feathered, or finned friends. Indoor small animals may get bored or be destructive (clawing door-jambs, peeing in inappropriate places). Outdoor animals run the risk of contracting communicable diseases, including the dreaded rabies, so make sure your pets are vaccinated! Another risk to outdoor pets is larger predatory animals. As a pet mom or dad, it is incumbent upon you to take care of your nonhuman kin, and that includes their health and well-being: make sure there are good-quality foods and toys for them to amuse themselves with.

Remember too that as neopagans with a somewhat shared vision of reincarnation (expressed in aphorisms such as "You shall know them, and love them, and know them again") we are not bound to expect those we have loved to reincarnate necessarily in human form. As in Hinduism, it is completely possible that our former boyfriend or wife may return as a beloved dog or cat. If all things are sacred, then certainly it is incumbent on Wiccans to treat their nonhuman kindred with respect and great love: they are not a commodity, such as a fighting pit bull, but rather, they are our family, perhaps once in the real sense (or will be again).

Spiritual Communities

In some ways the most important of communities is our spiritual one. Neopagans adhere to one Tradition or another for their religious framework and their religious community, but by far the single largest "tradition" in modern paganism is that of the solitary practitioner. Sometimes called solitaires, solitary witches follow a spiritual path unique to themselves. Although covens (usually of up to thirteen people) are the more "classic" image of witch rituals in the public mind, the fact is that far more pagans worship alone (or with one or two close friends) than in coven settings.

Some cities actually have networks and/or umbrella organizations for solitary practitioners, and even the Covenant of the Goddess in the United States has a specific classification for solitary witches as members. Other solitaries may meet through health food stores, yoga classes, or perhaps the New Age and/or pagan bookstore in town. As practitioners network and tentatively make more contacts with those "of a like mind," they may find themselves joining other solitary practitioners in ecumenical-type rituals on the major sabbats. In this way a spiritual community is formed of individual practitioners who might not otherwise have anyone with whom to share their religious joy.

Covens are often far more difficult to find: some traditions are not very public and/or approachable, which makes them challenging to network with. Others are small and prefer it that way, so enquiries into membership will be politely turned down. Membership in an established coven from a Tradition background will of course, buy you a large network of spiritual kin by virtue of your choice of Tradition and/or coven. As an example, there are Gardnerians in most areas of the English-speaking world, as well as in many areas where English is not the primary language. With a proper vouchsafe as to who and what you are, it is possible to travel to other countries, finding co-religionists who might offer you a spare room in their home while you are in town, and even a local tour guide. Membership in a tradition that is well established widens your spiritual community immensely.

MAKING THE CHOICE

Ask yourself the following questions:

• How comfortable am I practicing my religion alone? Would I practice with my spouse and/or children but not with outsiders? Do I prefer the security of a larger group plus a lineage in a long-standing Tradition? Do I care if another witch has ever received an initiation? Being solitary can be lonely, but it is a spiritual choice many many North Americans choose, each for their own reasons. Similarly, a large tradition may offer co-religionists, but it also brings in the ubiquitous "witch wars" and inter-family squabbling which is the hallmark of all families, large or small.

• Is this community or these communities such that I can identify with them as a member permanently? What exactly does this mean? Jews may travel anywhere in the world, yet they can enter a synagogue in any town or city and be recognized and welcomed as co-religionists by other Jews.

• Do I view myself as part of the wider community of people who believe there is something larger than us "out there"? Do I care? Do I have any interest in inter-religious dialogue with Christians, Jews, Muslims, or whoever else wonders what my beliefs mean?

Community and Communitas: Virtual Community

Anthropologists use the word *communitas* (Turner, 1966) to indicate a sort of free-flowing or temporary community where one specific task or interest is all that binds the members together. The concept came out of the study of pilgrimages, and how those on pilgrimage would be joined by their religious fervor and the experience of the pilgrimage itself, but otherwise would have probably never even met and talked. Communitas cuts across financial, cultural, and religious/ethnic boundaries and unites people in what is often a very temporary fashion. Pagan festivals are sites of communitas: you may well be dancing around a bonfire at night, drumming with a doctor from Seattle and a grease monkey from Kansas City. While you are on the grounds of the festival it does not matter what the background of the festival-goers are: you share with them the common themes of the festival, the religious experience, and whatever else you choose to share while there. The festival becomes what anthropologists call a *liminal* place and space: it is, as neopagans often state about a circle during ritual, a place out of time and space, between the worlds, and where the norms and expectations of the outside world may or may not apply. The rules of the festival-space are different from daily space and time, and as a result, you might well spend time and energy with others you would not normally meet in your daily existence. This, then, is the simple explanation of what *communitas* means as compared and contrasted to *community*.

VIRTUAL COMMUNITIES

The Internet has created a massive communitas space, something very new that anthropologists and sociologists (and psychologists as well) have only begun to discuss and study. The land of cyberspace is indeed one of the most liminal spaces human beings can experience and interact within. Cyberspace has no time and no place; it exists in the shared imaginations and moments while any individual is logged into the chat room or website. There are chat channels on just about any and every topic under the sun.

The Internet is the most egalitarian non-place on the globe: it is morning somewhere in the world, and those people will be logging in for a day of chatter and research. Others will be crawling into bed after a day or night of sharing experience and chat as well. People in Australia can sit behind a keyboard and share their magical experiences with others in Germany, Lebanon, and Mexico at the same time. The positive potential of the virtual universe is great, but so are the risks.

Beware of falling victim to the sense that the Internet universe is one of "reality." If the physical world has X percent creeps in it, there is no reason to believe that the percentage of creeps in the Internet world will be lower. Many men and women have been enticed to travel halfway across the continent or the world to meet their "soul mate," "mentor," or even "ritual partner," only to find out that they have been duped. The person "on the other side of the screen" may want sex and nothing more. Worse yet, what if they intend you harm?

There is nothing in neopagan teaching that says "Be naïve and trust everyone." It is true that we depend on both our "inner voice" and psychic abilities, and that the God/desses will care for us, but that is no substitute for a healthy dose of critical thought and cynicism. The virtual world can be fraught with pitfalls, and just because Wiccans would believe that the Law of Three (Karma) will rain revenge upon the perpetrator of something horrible does not mean that we should not take practical steps to prevent something horrible happening to us in the first place. A healthy dose of caution is a good thing in a neighborhood where you are a stranger and do not know the rules of engagement.

Virtual worship online is one of the positive shared things that have come from the Internet's popularity. Many pagans are very isolated from co-religionists, and even if they wanted to share in a public circle for a sabbat or esbat, they might not have the chance to do so because of their location. Online rituals differ slightly depending on who is running them and what their training background (if any) happens to be. There will most likely be someone running the virtual ritual as High Priest and/or High Priestess. It will start at a certain time and some channels will then lock entry to anyone who is not on that channel at the start time; others will keep the channel open, but as you log in there will be some sort of standardized message sent to your screen warning you that the ritual has already begun and the following things are expected of you. A good online ritual can be nearly as satisfying as one in real time with live people in the same room.

Since the Craft accepts that magic is a real force in the world and that it can be directed (much like electricity can be directed, or the flow of a river) at the theoretical level there is no impediment to the efficiency of an online ritual. Rituals involving lit candles can occur at the same time across the world: it is the action of lighting the candle after doing the proper ritual actions that makes the spell efficient, not the timing or shared space. "Magic is alive, Goddess is afoot" does not say that we need to be physically together to do magic. "Thou art God/dess" affirms, in fact, that we have the ability ourselves to create magic and do not need to be in shared physical space to manage this successfully. If magic is envisioned as energy in the universe, then of course an on-line ritual should work. The energy flows from our bodies to the keyboard, from the keyboard through the lines and other electrical conduits to the other computers being used for this magical purpose, ultimately channeled by the High Priest and/or High Priestess, for the required activities in the ritual.

Festivals

Festivals are one more type of communitas even though they manifest within the physical world rather than in the ether of the Internet. These are most often three-day affairs or longer, and are in large part geared toward families as well as single practitioners. Some traditions run their own closed festivals, but in general, most are eclectic and welcome all practitioners of neopaganism—regardless of whether they are solitary or from a Tradition, eclectic, or follow a specific type of orthodoxy. Sometimes festivals will have a specific theme (e.g., Beltaine or Midsummer), but more often they are free-flowing gatherings of co-religionists from the widest possible selection of the neopagan world.

Festivals have been around in North America for about twenty-five years or so, started as small gatherings of friends and acquaintances at campsites. They now sometimes have hundreds of attendees, and often have to rent an entire campground, even taking over large portions of urban hotels. Some festivals raise money in order to buy the land on which they hold their festival, or for other pagan charitable purposes.

Festival-goers come in two general types: those who come to the occasional festival and enjoy them like a holiday, and those who travel like tinkers, following the festival circuit while selling wares, teaching seminars and workshops, or spending their free time at festivals across the continent. Serious festival-goers may make this their full-time employment year round, while the "occasional" festival attendee is often there for a sharing of skills and workshops, plus fun and communitas. For some people the highlight of the week (or weekend) is lazing around the nude beach and feeling safe, or drumming and dancing at the evening's bonfire.

Most festivals feature workshops and speakers, many offered by authors and/or practitioners of notoriety (often called Big Name Pagans, or, facetiously, Big Nose Pagans). Festivals have certain standard activities as well, which usually include concerts, swimming, youth and children's activities, merchants, public rituals, rites of passage, bonfires, and drumming circles.

There are many and varied ways that "community" can be defined, both in the general population and specifically in pagan parlance. What sort of community best suits you and how you find it can be simple or complicated, depending on your individual needs. Whether it is transitory or permanent, virtual or physical, there is probably a Craft community that will suit your needs and lifestyle: you simply need to keep an open mind and try some different ways of defining "community" for yourself.

Choosing to Leave, or When Your Community Leaves You

No matter how hard we try, sometimes we are uprooted from the people we call our community. This can be because of a new job causing you to relocate from where you have lived and set down your roots. Divorce often causes a schism in a community for various reasons. Perhaps you have to move due to financial or mental-health reasons. Along with change, some people may choose to walk away from their friendship with you because the friendship is no longer convenient or rewarding in the same ways.

There are often times when you have to leave your community because of things that have nothing directly to do with your decisions, such as when your family moves. As noted earlier, military families are used to this sort of fairly regular uprooting, as are people in certain types of jobs. For many of us, the strain can be profound on mental, emotional, and psychic levels. Change in any dimension can be a real culture shock. School-age children often suffer intensely, as youngsters are commonly not very kind to newcomers in their school.

The first order of business is learning how to cope with the change of location and/or of community. If you face a physical relocation, a good plan is to hold a goodbye party so you can have a sense of closure about leaving those in your community of friends and co-religionists. Trying to focus on all the positive aspects of your new location and the excitement of meeting new people is another way of coping with the changes. Human beings do not as a rule enjoy change very much, so your best bet is to come up with strategies designed to look for the commonalities and the familiar aspects of your new situation.

Be prepared to do some grieving. It may sound silly at first, but if you worked with a coven, they should have been very close friends to you, much like losing members of your own blood kin. You and/or your children may well go through a sort of grieving process as you miss your old friends, family, and lovers. Whether you are moving across town or across the country, you will probably fall out of touch with some of your kin of choice, which will be difficult. Turn your face to the new challenges of your new location, including looking for new people "of a like mind" who will not replace your old friends, but will augment them and bring you joy in your new community.

Do not be surprised if it hurts *a lot* at first after your relocation. You will need some healing time to deal with the fact that friendly voices are now a long-distance charge away instead of down the street. If you have left or been asked to leave a coven or other circle for whatever reason, it can be excruciatingly painful at first. Pagans expect to experience *perfect love and perfect trust,* so when there is a severing between members of a coven under acrimonious conditions, it can be as painful as losing a beloved blood relative. Often there are recriminations on both sides, stories become inflated in the retelling, and the banishment or expulsion of one member of a coven from the group can ultimately destroy the entire coven structure itself. Do not feel embarrassed by your strong emotions. If you did not feel sad, it would mean you did not care. If you did not care, you were not in the right coven or town.

How do you find yourself a new community? Community is more than just moving to a place: rather, it is moving to a group of people. In a new town, make contacts before you move. See if there are any pagans of your tradition there, or perhaps a neopagan bookstore or discussion group. Are there pagan meet and greets, or meetups, in your area? Check the Internet. You can look for meetups across the United States and around the world at pagan.meetup.com, where information, times, and cities are listed. Additional contact points can be the local feminist bookstore, local health food stores, or the local college or university. Don't forget word-of-mouth: perhaps someone in your tradition or circle of friends can give you the name of someone in or near the area where you are relocating.

When is it time to move on? Sometimes you feel in the pit of your stomach that you have outgrown your town or city, no matter how much you may also love it. Some people describe this as wanderlust, while others say it is simply time to move on. Similarly, despite the fact you may really love the people in your Wiccan study group or coven, it may be time to leave. How can you tell? This is one of the hardest things to decide, since both leaving and staying are in the realm of the unknown. Talk over your pros and cons on the topic with friends you trust. Perhaps you need an unbiased ear: why not discuss this with a teacher or former teacher if you have one whose guidance you trust? If you have a therapist, psychologist, or psychiatrist, discuss your feelings candidly with them: it might well bring to life some hidden concerns, or issues to which you are overreacting.

Ultimately, the decision as to where and when to move from your geographic home or your chosen kinfolk is made by your heart and head in tandem. The Craft tells us to listen to our "inner bell" or "inner voice," yet we find ourselves often doubting that feeling. Try to look at your pros and cons lists with an open eye and heart, since you never know how much better you may find your life when you move on from the rut you may now be mired in. Much of neopaganism is taught and valued because it is experienced: consider your experiences with the coven, your friends, and your job, and then weigh your options fairly. You may find a more pagan-friendly location, because the God/desses are guiding your decisions after all.

CHAPTER 7

The Magic Connection

When Wiccans say "Magic is alive, Goddess is afoot," they are affirming that magic is a real force in the universe. Magic can be viewed in much the same way as electrical power. It is invisible. You cannot see it, as a rule (except in rare circumstances such as a thunderstorm, as a circle is being cast, or when energy is being raised). It is hard to touch even though you might feel a bit of a pulsating sense. You can rarely smell either magic or electricity, yet no one is going to assert that electricity does not exist. So too, with magic: we can manipulate, move, channel it—and see the effects of its use—even if we cannot necessarily point to it.

There is no such thing as "good" or "bad" magic, only good or bad uses. If one follows the analogy of electricity and magic, consider the following scenario. It is 120 degrees Fahrenheit outside and you can literally fry an egg on the front doorstep. If electricity is keeping your home cool and dry, and your mother with high blood pressure avoids stress on her heart by staying indoors, is that "good" electricity? Conversely, if you are cooking dinner and your three-year-old runs into the kitchen and grabs the red-hot electrical element on the stove before you can react, is that "bad" electricity?

Neither possibility has a value judgment assigned as a result of what happens. Magic just *is*. The decisions of the practitioner, and how magic is manipulated by human intention, allows us to call magic good or bad. It is good when used properly and wisely, and bad when misused or put to improper applications. The Wiccan Rede is used by many Wiccans and neopagans as a guideline. As many Wiccans find out, however, living by the Rede is not nearly as simple as some assume it is.

The following short ethical discussion is derived from an excellent essay, "Wiccan Ethics and the Wiccan Rede," by David Piper on the ramifications of turning the Rede from a positive to a negative injuction. (Visit the website wiccanhistorian.home.att.net/bos/wiccanethicsrede. html for the complete text.) Piper goes into far more detail about the pros and cons of the new vs. old versions of the Rede in a short and thoughtful discussion that is well worth viewing and pondering.

> rede (red), *v.*, red•ed, red•ing, *n.* Chiefly Brit. Dial. —*v.t.* 1. to counsel; advise. 2. to explain. —*n.* 3. counsel; advice. 4. a plan; scheme. 5. a tale; story. [ME rede(n), OE rædan]
> —*Random House College Dictionary*, revised edition

The Wiccan Rede basically says, "An ye harm none, do what ye will." This can be interpreted as saying it is okay to do something that will not harm anyone. It does not, however, say anything about those things that do cause harm, except to set an ethical standard of harmlessness as the criteria by which to judge.

Modernization of the Rede's language has given us the translation, "Do what ye will an it harm none." This reversal of the construction takes the first part and puts it after the second, and can be interpreted in modern English as "Do what you want if it does not harm anyone." What this says is that any and all actions that cause harm are forbidden.

One result of this subtle switch in the way the Rede is worded is the injunction that one may never work magic for others, even to heal, without their knowledge and consent. Of course, we are allowed by this injunction to ask if we may pray for a person as a means of obtaining consent. Praying rather than doing a spell sidesteps the prohibitive injunction against ever doing any magic for another without permission, since it violates their free will, including magic aimed at healing an unconscious victim who cannot give consent. Some practitioners collect blanket permissions from the people to whom they are close, which is an agreement that the practitioner may use his/her best judgment to determine whether or not magic might be warranted on their behalf, and consent to its performance if that is the case.

Personal Responsibility

Many younger neopagans have a distressing habit of blaming daily complaints on magical activity, thereby shirking their own role in their destiny. Wicca is not, as a rule, a religious family of practitioners who believe that the gods and goddesses have already decided who we shall be and what shall happen to use from birth to death, as Hinduism is. We were not given life and spirit in order to blame others for our illnesses, poor luck, underemployment, or runny noses.

Pagans, like many other people, will sometimes blame simple things on anyone and anything other than themselves. If, for example, you wake up with a splitting headache and the vague sense that someone is watching you, have you had a malevolent spell cast on you? It is certainly possible; however, it is far more likely that the headache is because you drank too much last night, or did not eat breakfast, or did not get your morning cup of coffee, or perhaps you have not realized how stressed you are at that job interview or final exam you are facing. Perhaps people are watching you because you were in such a state when you got dressed yesterday that put on mismatched socks, or wore your shirt inside out. . . . Perhaps you just have a "cloud" hovering over your head: you are dragging your head, and your shoulders are bowed; you are shuffling as you walk. All this might be below your personal radar, but others may see it and tend to look at you just a little longer as you walk by.

To live as a responsible magical person, you need to remember not to attribute to malice what is easily explained by chance and/or omission. The Wiccan worldview does not fill the universe with bogies and elementals who wish us ill, although we do accept that these things *do* exist. Religions throughout the world have wrestled with why negative things happen, particularly when they befall people we view as innocent or undeserving. Sometimes the randomness of the world or the universe does cause "bad" or "unfortunate" things to happen.

Balance in the Cosmos

One tenet of neopagan practice is not explicit in any of its basic statements about itself, yet is as important as any that we have discussed throughout the book. "The Earth is sacred" is the worldview statement that reminds us that there is a natural world outside of the human being, and that it is valuable, not just to us, but in and of itself. We have discussed how important the natural world is, how the environment becomes an issue to neopagan ethical thought, and that in a non-hierarchical model of the universe, the animal and plant domains are as important as the human sphere of influence.

Neopagans have a relationship with nature—one of living in balance. Neopagans view the natural world as somewhere between benign and nurturing. Neopagans try to live their lives in balance with the natural forces of nature: nurturing where they can, improving where they should, and flowing with the natural world whenever possible. Neopagans try to live lightly on the land and do what they can to improve the health of the natural world around them. For some it can be as simple as recycling a tin can; for others it can be donating to a cause. What neopagans do to stay in balance with the cosmos is individually determined, but they live with a mindfulness of that balance.

Goddess and God

Many Wiccan traditions embody the concept of balance between the forces of the natural world in the personification of the Goddess and the God (or of particular goddesses and gods from particular places and times in religious history). One interpretation of this balance is played out in what is often called the Great Rite, or Wine Blessing. Here the symbolic uniting of an athame and a goblet with beverage is said to represent the Goddess and God in the *hieros gamos*: the sexual union of the two divine figures. Unfortunately, as many neopagans take this as literal rather than figurative or symbolic/metaphoric, there is a homophobic element within Wiccan practice which feels that only a woman can represent the Goddess, and only a man can represent the God.

Increasingly, neopagan philosophers around the world, particularly the more eclectic thinkers, are challenging this attitude. If one looks at the Great Rite as a metaphor rather than a real-time action, one can see how different interpretations of this can occur. Perhaps the Goddess represents the passive or receiving half of creative action? Perhaps the God represents the active, or giving half of this? In Hindu thought the two gender-roles are reversed: the God is passive, and cannot act on his own without having first been energized by his Shakti, or Goddess-partner.

More radical thinkers are moving beyond the physical Earth plane of gender completely. They view the two forces as active and passive, and do not even assign gender roles to them. In this framework, the Great Rite/Wine Blessing can be performed by two men, two women, or even one person representing the union of both forces in one body and one soul. Pre-Christian religions in Europe and the Near East were full of strong goddesses and gods, and many of them did not serve the stereotyped roles of "male" and "female" that Western culture has inherited from Greek philosophy.

GENDER-BENDING

Gender-bending can be appropriate if the practitioner(s) want it to be included. A very traditional group such as a Gardnerian or Alexandrian coven might assume that a transvestite or transsexual person has no place within a magic circle, or that they can worship but not draw down the Goddess or God. In theory, it does become problematic on the physical level as to whether a biological man who has become a woman should draw down the Goddess or the God. Surely this person will know which sort of energy s/he is more comfortable with by now: she has definitely spent enough time deciding that in her daily life!

If however, one embraces the idea that the Goddess and God are beyond "gender" or "sexual assignment," then there should be no problem with a man channelling the Goddess or a woman channelling the God. Much Wiccan theology and thealogy is based on the fact that things are different on different "planes" of existence. Because we live on the Earth, our rituals are understood to be on the "Earth plane" of existence. However, how do the goddesses and gods manifest in the fire plane, or the water plane? There are a myriad of possibilities for role reversals, sex role flip-flopping, and different types of people embodying different faces of the divine when one remembers this.

Any given practitioner is free to choose how s/he views gender bending during sacred rituals. We know that many ancient cultures were fond of having men play women's roles and vice versa, during both secular and religious plays.

The Role of Ritual

Ritual is any sequence of symbolic actions that are done in a certain order to achieve a specific result. This can be saying certain phrases or words over and over under your breath while cleaning up the kitchen (e.g., a chant like "Goddess is alive, magic is afoot"), or a full-blown "bell, book, and candle" production with specific robes, tools, day and hour, and so forth. Ritual can be small or large, simple or complex, a group action, or a single act. Ritual can involve specific motions, music, poetry, and/or text, in order to communicate with the goddesses and gods. If you come from a specific magical Tradition, you have probably learned traditional practices in order to focus energy for a specific purpose—such as healing, celebration, empowerment, protection, and so forth. Choosing to clean up litter off a stretch of highway can be a ritual as much as is a full Beltaine or Samhain ritual. Intention is the key.

Most human beings have daily rituals which may have little to do with their relationship to the divine, the natural world, or other human beings. Patting your cats as you feed them is a small ritual. Shaking someone's hand when you meet them is a ritualized gesture. Bowing to someone in Japan is a ritual. These may be rituals of greeting, or of recognition of status (how low you bow to the person you are meeting, for example). Everyone has a multitude of rituals they participate in: some connect us with the divine, some to each other, and others connect us to the flow of life around us.

Magical ritual is what joins the loosely-knit family of neopagan practices together. "Goddess is Alive, magic is afoot" embodies the belief that there is magic in the world; the fact that Wiccans use this magic in their rituals and religious practices differentiates them from most other religious practices. Reclaiming practitioners may draw their circle slightly differently from a Georgian, and a member of the Wiccan Church of Canada may do things within a set framework, while a self-initiated eclectic may achieve their ritual purpose quite differently; however, the intent used and the framework utilized marks us all as neopagan practitioners.

Some Wiccan traditions have specific times for both major and minor rituals. Rituals are most often expected at the eight great sabbats, as well as minor rituals on each full-moon night. These are not the only times to hold rituals, but they do outline a skeleton "ritual calendar" that most Wiccans follow. When shared with other co-religionists they allow for community sharing, celebration, and additional strength for any magical workings that might be undertaken at that time.

Actually, rituals can be held at any time if the reason is sound. If it is your ritual, you get to decide if it is a good time to hold it. In larger covens, the High Priestess and/or High Priest may decide if a ritual is needed for some specific reason. Most often, small rituals are held by individuals who do a candle spell or similar simple magical working for healing: if someone has been in a car accident, fallen ill with a dangerous medical condition, or perhaps has gone into labor.

If you hear that a natural disaster has hit somewhere far away, and you are moved by compassion and the psychic need to do something, you can do a ritual to help the living, send strength to those giving aid, or ease the suffering of the dying.

It is not appropriate to perform rituals to *compel*. If people are meant to fall in love, they will. Doing a love spell can compel people together who might not be suited for each other after all. Being stuck with someone who is obsessed with being with you can be a nasty thing to cope with! You could have had a hand in putting a friend in an intolerable situation from which they cannot easily extricate themselves. Neopagans are meant to work with the flow of the natural world; do not build a dam to reroute this flow to a location where *you* think it should be. Work *with* it; do not force it, and do not compel it to change course.

Do not perform rituals for things that can be achieved by natural means. The amusing Harry Potter books by J. K. Rowling have numerous examples where spells backfire or go awry when they simply should not have been done at all. For example, do not do spells for a job before you have had the interview. It is certainly appropriate to do a spell asking for "the right job for me," or "a fulfilling job," or something appropriate and vague, but not for "Oh great Goddess, give me this job." Each and every one of us has to be proactive in life. Look at the want ads, network with friends, use Internet sources and whatever other sources you have at hand. Look for that job; don't expect the goddesses and gods to do your work for you. You insult both the divine powers and your own potential by being lazy.

WHERE TO HOLD RITUAL

This depends on the practitioner(s) and the Tradition they follow. For many, holding ritual outside in a covenstead, or specific location in the woods, is impractical for reasons of environment. Living in an urban center often means holding rituals in a living room, bedroom, or (if one is lucky) a dedicated temple room in the house. The gods are not fussy: they do not treat ritual held in a shady glade as any more heartfelt than a ritual held in a small apartment.

Most of the major religions practiced today have some sense of needing to practice their religious rituals in a sanctified place dedicated to this task. Neopaganism as a rule does not require, or even adhere, to the concept of a sanctified ritual space. Because "the Earth is sacred," all places on the Earth are by nature sanctified. Some Wiccan practitioners will tell you that the purification of a circle is done in order to purify the ground, but in most cases it is either to delineate the area where ritual will take place, or it serves to contain the energies raised up in the process (and as some would say, keep negative energy and/or forces out of the circle). The set ritual for beginning a magical working also serves to remind practitioners that they are in a sacred space, and focuses their attention upon that fact rather than changing the essential nature of the space itself.

Some covens establish covensteads. This is less common, simply be-

cause much of the land urban pagans practice on is public and therefore
cannot be "reserved" for ritual on demand. Practicing ritual in outdoor
public locations can also lead to conflicts with those who might want
the space for other purposes, or with those who disapprove of pagan
ritual. Most pagans try to practice outdoors if they can, but are quite
comfortable practicing indoors when necessary. Some practice in their
backyards, while a few are fortunate enough to have dedicated land on
their own property on which to hold celebrations. If you practice out
of doors, remember that there are spirits associated with any given area of
nature, and they should be consulted with and worked with if they are
agreeable to this.

> Rituals should always be performed in harmony with the place you are
> working. Another important consideration at a site is trying to contact
> the site guardian, seeing if your intuition helps you contact it (or them).
> Often they are glad to be considered, and the contact is not too difficult.
> Sometimes they are hostile to certain things (like iron at some old or
> faery sites), which can be avoided once these are known.
> —David Rankine, at www.dragonnetwork.org/magicfr.htm

Never forget to leave location-appropriate offerings. If you work in
the American Southwest, you might want to leave a small tobacco offering at the quarters as thanks for the land and its protection. (This
means pouch tobacco, *not* a cigarette with toxic items like a filter and
paper sleeve!) A good and always appropriate offering is clean, fresh
water, as it is truly the stuff of life. In the Northeast, perhaps a braid of
sweetgrass would be appropriate. Cream and honey have long been traditional in parts of the British Isles and Europe, or a grain confection
(such as a bun or chunk of bread). If you can establish a working relationship with the spirits of the land, you will find yourself with stead-
fast allies indeed.

PUBLIC RITUALS

Some traditions of Wicca view themselves as the "Hidden Children
of the Goddess," and fear reprisals from an ignorant or poorly educated

public who misunderstand their beliefs and practices. As a result, they are often closeted, and do not discuss their religious beliefs with outsiders, nor do they allow curious visitors into their rituals. Often accused of being paranoid or arrogant, these practitioners have a perfect right to "out themselves" to whomever they feel is appropriate, and to keep their religious practices hidden from others. As we have all been given the gift of independent thought and action, so too we have the right to choose when to speak and when to be silent. It is no one's right to publish or announce someone else's religious beliefs, any more than it is a third party's right to expose someone's sexual preference. The person's choice may not be right for you, but it is also not your life path.

There has been a plethora of new seekers in the last ten years, seeking instruction in the Craft and its beliefs. Most of these people have been exposed to the concept of Wicca through the media, movies and books. Some have read a book or two from the local bookstore and have some vague idea of witchcraft as a religion, but are looking for advice and good counsel.

Many larger neopagan organizations run public rituals—they are a form of pagan outreach. Very few organizations have 1-800 dial-a-witch–type phone numbers, and even fewer keep registries of what cities have which covens and Traditions active therein. Public rituals are most often held on the eight sabbats—if a city has a smallish community, they may only offer public rituals on Beltaine and Samhain. Other cities may even have weekly or monthly open circles where anyone may attend for classes and/or ritual. Seekers can be paired up with practitioners or learn enough about Wicca to decide that they want to continue their education with different people. Public rituals allow for a sharing of the sense of community and offer a venue where those who are looking for practitioners may find information and friendly faces.

Open rituals (or at least, semi-public ones) can be found at most large pagan and Wiccan festivals. Sometimes a specific tradition of Wicca will offer to host a given ritual during the weekend, and other times the festival committee itself will set up a grand ritual one night of the festival. These are places where participants from many differing neopagan paths can enjoy the pagan sense of community and religious sharing. There may also be specific rituals held during the weekend for specific purposes, from first menstruation rituals for girls to croning ceremonies for elder women. Some festivals will have a men's drumming circle, or a sexual-diversity ritual time and place.

Magic has as much, or as little to do with your life as you choose. If magic is a real force within the universe, then you must choose how much you want to tap into it. You may wish to keep in mind, however, the old aphorism about putting all your eggs in one basket!

Most experienced members of the Craft ultimately decide to live primarily in the day-to-day world, and turn to magical options only when they seem appropriate or when they are requested, but not as a crutch. It is a bit of a dance, but one that you will become skilled with as you weigh each situation at hand. This is "situationally dependent" ethics, and it is a good description of what proportion magic is practiced in a pagan life. It all depends on the situation.

Choosing Wisely

There is an inscription within the temple of the Oracle of Delphi in Greece: KNOW THYSELF. People would come to the Oracle for a prophecy and the Oracle would answer them indirectly, in symbol and metaphor. Prophecy must be interpreted. Nothing is meaningful when standing alone and without context. This is the central insight of the Oracle.

This book challenges you to make meaningful choices in your life. Know yourself—know what you value and how you want the world to look and feel. Most neopagans come from family backgrounds other than paganism. We are a religion and community still in flux, still growing. Also, we are challenged by a culture not based on pagan values. For that reaason it is hard to know whether a decision is wise because it is familiar or because it is ethical within our new, still-forming value structure.

Knowledge is only the beginning of change, for knowledge alone is not change and will affect only a shift in thinking. Knowledge has to be carried both into and within the world so that it can be enacted, embodied, and shared. This is the key to making change possible. Thinking about things differently might change things for you, but action is important—you must act in different, self-aware ways in order to change the world. Although we do not usually discuss it at this level, it is clear from the discussions in this book that neopagans and witches have embedded within themselves a different worldview than mainstream North America's: now we must start shaping and honing our values and decisions so that they reflect our worldview.

Know thyself, says the Oracle. She teases us to think deeply about who we are so that we may be more effective as people and as Wiccans. We say that we should not harm anything or anyone. We say that our good and/or bad actions will reflect back upon us, often threefold. We recognize that the structure of things on the Earth and the makeup of all things are directly related to how things are structured and constituted among the God/desses. We recognize that the Earth is sacred, and that she is our nurturer. Through this we have a duty of care to tend for the Earth and all things upon and within her. We recognize and acknowledge the divinity that exists in every living person, despite the fact that we may indeed not like some of people. We say that we recognize the presence of the divine as Goddess, and that she is within the world, leading us with her magic until we learn to use that magic wisely ourselves. We recognize some level of rebirth and reincarnation, and look around us for the spirits of those we have loved and known before, in any form.

This book is a form of self-knowledge. It is designed to show various paths we may choose to take, based on how we personally internalize and interpret these aphorisms:

- An ye harm none, do what ye will.

- The Law of Return (karma, or the threefold law).

- As above, so below.

- The Earth is sacred.

- Thou art God/dess.

- Goddess is alive, magic is afoot.

  Plus two others:

- The Earth is our mother: we must take care of her.

- You shall know them and love them and know them again.

Know thyself, and choose thy paths wisely. Walk the earth gently, and keep it in balance. Above all, live your life as a self-aware neopagan. Your path may not be as easy as some others, but on the day that you rest back in the bosom of the Mother in the Summerland, you will be able to look back and know that you lived your life as a pagan, with respect for all life around you.

Selected Bibliography

Adler, Margot. 1986. *Drawing Down the Moon.* Boston: Beacon Press.

Bass, Ellen, and Laura Davis. 1988. *The Courage to Heal.* New York: Harper and Row.

Bauman, Zygmunt. 1998. *Work, Consumerism and the New Poor.* Buckingham: Open University Press.

Berger, Helen. 1999. *A Community of Witches.* Columbia: University of South Carolina Press.

Berger, Helen, Evan Leach, and Leigh Schaffer. 2003. *Voices from the Pagan Census.* Columbia: University of South Carolina Press.

Bloch, Jon. 1998. *New Spirituality, Self and Belonging.* Westport, Conn.: Praeger.

Bonewits, P.E.I. 1971 [1979]. *Real Magic.* Berkeley: Creative Arts.

Collins, Chuck, and Pam Rogers. 2000. *Robin Hood Was Right.* New York: W.W. Norton.

Coloroso, Barbara. 1999. *Parenting with Wit and Wisdom in Times of Chaos and Loss.* New York: Viking.

———. 1995. *Kids Are Worth It: Giving Your Child the Gift of Inner Discipline.* Toronto: Somerville House.

Dominguez, Joe, and Vicki Robin. 1992. *Your Money or Your Life.* New York: Penguin.

Easton, Dossie, and Catherine A. Liszt. 1998. *The Ethical Slut: A Guide to Infinite Sexual Possibilities.* San Francisco: Greenery Press.

Fortune, Dion (pseudonym Violet Firth). 1992. *Psychic Self-Defense: A Study in Occult Pathology and Criminality*. New York: Samuel Weiser. Reissued.

Gerbner, George. 1995. "Television Violence: The Power and the Peril" in Gail Dines and Jean Humez (eds), *Gender, Race and Class in Media: A Text-Reader*. Mountainview, Calif.: Sage Publications.

Harrow, Judy. 1999. *Wicca Covens*. Secaucus, N.J.: Citadel Press.

———. 1996. "The Contemporary Neo-Pagan Revival." In James Lewis (ed) *Magical Religion and Modern Witchcraft*. Albany: SUNY Press. 9–24.

Hutton, Ronald. 1999. *The Triumph of the Moon*. Oxford: Oxford University Press.

Jorgensen, Danny, and Scott Russell. 1999. "American Neopaganism: The Participants' Social Identities." *Journal for the Scientific Study of Religion*. 38(3): 325–338.

Kinder, Peter, Steven Lydenberg, and Amy Domini. 1993. *Investing for Good*. New York: Harper Business.

Kozol, Jonathan. 1991. *Savage Inequalities: Children in America's Schools*. New York: Crown/Random House.

Luhrmann, Tanya. 1989. *Persuasions of the Witch's Craft*. Cambridge: Harvard University Press.

MacArthur, Margie. 1994. *WiccaCraft for Families*. Custer, Wash.: Phoenix Publishing.

Maffesoli, Michel. 1996. *The Time of the Tribes*. trans. Don Smith. Thousand Oaks, Calif.: Sage Publications.

Martin, Judith. 1998. *Miss Manners' Basic Training*. New York: Random House.

Moser, Charles. 1999. *Health Care Without Shame: A Handbook for the Sexually Diverse and Their Caregivers*. San Francisco: Greenery Press.

Orion, Loretta. 1995. *Never Again the Burning Times: Paganism Revived*. Prospect Heights, Ill.: Waveland Press.

Rabinovitch, Shelley. 2000. "Heal the Universe and Heal the Self: Bateson's

Double Bind and North American Wiccan Practice." *Diskus*, v. 6 (2000). Viewable at www.uni-marburg.de/religionswissenschaft/journal/diskus/ rabinovitch.html.

———. 1992. *"An'Ye Harm None, Do What Ye Will": Neo-pagans and Witches in Canada.* MA thesis (unpublished), Department of Religion, Carleton University, Ottawa, Ont.

Rabinovitch, Shelley, and James Lewis. 2002. *The Encyclopedia of Modern Witchcraft and Neo-Paganism.* New York: Citadel Press.

Reid, Siân. 2001. *Disorganized Religion: An Exploration of the Neopagan Craft in Canada.* Ph.D. dissertation, Department of Sociology and Anthropology, Carleton University.

Starhawk. 1987. *Truth or Dare: Encounters with Power, Authority and Mystery.* San Francisco: Harper and Row.

———. 1979. *The Spiral Dance: A Rebirth of the Ancient Religion of the Great Goddess.* San Francisco: Harper and Row.

Tannen, Deborah. 1990. *You Just Don't Understand: Women and Men in Conversation.* New York: Ballantine Books.

Turner, Victor. 1966. "Communitas: Model and Process," in *The Ritual Process.* Edited by V. Turner. Ithaca, N.Y.: Cornell University Press.

Valiente, Doreen. 1989. *The Rebirth of Witchcraft.* London: Robert Hale.

Waldron, David. 2002. *The Sign of the Witch: Neopaganism and the Romanticist Episteme.* Ph.D. dissertation, University of Ballarat.

Wiseman, Jay. 1998. *SM 101: A Realistic Introduction.* San Francisco: Greenery Press.

Websites

Gonzales, Patrisia, and Roberto Rodriguez, "Column of the Americas," "Honoring Our Elders," at www.voznuestra.com/Americas/ _1999/_February/5

Jones, Bear, "Editorials of The Month: Magickal Safety," at
www.witchesway.net/newsletter/january03.html

Kirk, Carol, "The Warrior's Path—Pagans in the Military," Copyright 1999
Carol Kirk, at milpagan.org/PC/the_warriors_path.html

McColman, Carl, "The Pentagon and the Pentacle," at
www.beliefnet.com/story/138/story_13856_1.html#cont

Piper, David, "Wiccan Ethics and the Wiccan Rede," at
wiccanhistorian.home.att.net/bos/wiccanethicsrede.html

Rankine, David, at Dragon Environmental Network:
www.dragonnetwork.org

Rankine, David, at www.dragonnetwork.org/magicfr.htm

www.calcleaners.com/consumers/clothes.html

www.cbc.ca/consumers/market/files/home/overpackaging

www.compostguide.com/?mcpstr

www.consumerreports.org/main/detailv4.jsp?CONTENT%3C%3Ecnt_id=
380163&FOLDER%3C%3Efolder_id=322269&ASSORTMENT%3C%
3East_id=333147

eartheasy.com/live_nontoxic_solutions.htm

www.eere.energy.gov/consumerinfo/refbriefs/ee9.html

www.hms.harvard.edu/oed/themes2/oem/enviro_symptoms.htm

www.milpagan.org/PC/the_warriors_path.html

www.mst.dk/chemi/01081805.htm

www.mybackyard.com/current/26p1.htm

www.organicessentials.com/Benefits.htm

www.prairieghosts.com/ouija.html

www.ruckus.org/about/index.html

www.starhawk.org/writings/truth-dare.html

www.worldwatch.org/pubs/goodstuff/clothing

INDEX

AARP (American Association of Retired Persons), 203
Abortion, 130–31
Abuse, childhood, 97
Abuse, elder, 204
Accidental pregnancy, 130–31
Acupressure, 78–79
Acrylic fibers, 23
Activism, 43–46, 189–90, 198–202
Adoption, 201–202
Adventure games, 159
AIDS activism, 199–200
AIDS ReSearch Alliance, 200
Allopathy, 76–77
Alternative energy sources, 38–40
Aluminum, 34
American Association of Retired Persons (AARP), 203
Amnesty International, 199
An (archaic word), 7
Anger, 87
Animals as kindred, 216
Anonymous interactions, 97–99
"An Ye Harm None" (Wiccan Rede), 5–7, 7–11, 225–26
Arcade games, 159
Arguments, 86–87
Aromatherapy, 79
"As above, so below", 12–13
Asbestos, 30–31
Astral attacks, 88
Attachment parenting, 140
Autonomy in children, 168–70
Ayurvedic medicine, 81

Baking groups, 71
Baking soda, 25
Balance, financial, 57–61
Balance, in Cosmos, 228–30
Bamboo flooring, 29
Beef, 63
Beliefs, hiding, 234
Bicycles, 209
Big Beautiful Women and Big Handsome Men, 83
Big-box stores, 61
Big Brothers, Big Sisters, 202
Birth control, 129
Blood kin, 215
Body, an AIDS and HIV Information Resource, The, 112
Body as temple, 73
Books for children, 152–53
Boundaries, personal, 108–109, 123
Bovine spongiform encephalopathy, 63
Boycotts, 179
Breaking up, 112
Breast vs. bottle debate, 138–40
Bribes in child discipline, 150
Budgets, 57–61
Bulk buying, 70–71, 181. *See also* Warehouse stores
Buses, 209–10
Butler, William, 18

Canning, 70
CAP (Central Arizona Project), 26
Capital gain, 195–96
Capital loss, 196

Carpet, 29
Carpools, 210
Cars, 35–36, 182, 210
Cash equivalents, 196
Casual interactions, 97–99
Celtic reconstructivism, 50
Central Arizona Project (CAP), 26
Ceramic tile flooring, 27–28
Charities, 191–92
Chemicals, 24–27, 31–32
Child care, 143–48
Childhood abuse, 97
Child labor, 60–61
Childlessness, 128–30, 131–33
Children
    adoption, 201–202
    computers, internet, and, 155–59
    discipline, 148–52
    foster parenting, 201
    mentoring, 202
    preparation for, 133–35
    toys and books, 152–53
Chinese medicine, 80–81
Chinese silk, 20
Chiropractic treatment, 78
Chloramine, 25–26
Choices, 6–7
Circles. See Covens
Cities, 206–208, 212
Civility, 97–99
Classes, 121–23
Cleaning solvents and products, 24–25
Closeness, 100–101
Cloth diapers, 141–43
Clothing, 19–24, 185
Coercion, 108
Cohabiting, 100–101
Coloroso, Barbara, 148–49
Communication, 86–87, 99–100, 109
Communities
    communitas, 218–22
    leaving, 222–24
    as neo-tribe, 3–5
    physical layout, 206–208
    qualities of, 211–14
    rituals, 234
    spiritual, 217–18
    virtual, 219–21
Companies, 175–77, 188–90
Complementary medicine, 77–79
Compliments, 98

Composting, 32–34
Computers and children, 155–59
Consumer culture, 177–78
Condoms, 129
Conflict, 117–18
Connectedness, 12–13, 94, 99, 113–14
Connection to the land, 50–51
Consensual sex, 107–12
Consumer culture, 55–57
Consumer purchases,
Cooking, 69–70, 71, 181–82
Co-ops, food, 71
Coping with suffering, 86–88
Cork flooring, 28–29
Corn gluten meal products, 43
Corporate bonds, 196
Corporate Watch, 200
Co-sleeping debate, 140–41
Cotton, 20
Courtesy, 97–99
Covens, 114–19, 137, 217, 223
Covensteads, 232–33
Credit-card debt, 55
Creutzfeldt-Jakob disease, 63
Crib vs. co-sleeping debate, 140–41
Crowley, Aleister, 8, 18
Crystals, 51–52
Cupping, 81

Danish Environmental Protection Agency, 22
Day care, 143–48
Decision making, 6–7
Diapers, 141–43
Disabilities, 84
Discarnate spirits, 89–90
Discipline, children, 148–52
Discrimination, 83
Disposable diapers, 141–43
Dividends, 196
Divinity, 16–17, 17–18, 113–14
Donating money, 190–95
Dragon Environmental Network, 48–49, 51
Duty of care, 10

Earnings, 180
Earth, as sacred, 13–16
EarthEasy, 25
Eco-paganism and eco-magic, 49–53
Education
    homeschooling, 164–68
    neopagan, 121–23

private schools, 161–64
public schools, 160–61
Educational games, 159
Eggs, 65–66
Elderhostel, 203
Elders, 202–205
Electricity production, 38–40
Emotional preparations for a baby, 134–35
Emotional well-being, 85–88
Employment, 174–77
Energy sources (electric), 38–40
Environmentalism, 46–49
Ethics, 1–2
Exercise, 75–76

Fabrics, 19–24
Factory farms, 63–65
Factory outlets, 58
Families, 96–97, 215
Family bed, 140–41
Family support, 136
Fantasies, sexual, 106
Federation of Danish Textile and Clothing
    Industries, 22
Feminine, celebrating, 81–83
Festivals, 219, 221–22, 234
Financial preparation for a baby, 133–34
Financial balance, 57–61
Financial glossary, 195–97
Flooring, 27–29
Fluoridation, 25
Food
    cooking, 69–70
    discounts, 58–59
    ethical issues, 62–68
    frozen, 68–69
    gardening, 71–72
    meat, 63–66, 75
    meat alternatives, 66–68
    milk, 74–75
    storing, 70
Fortune, Dion, 88
Foster parenting, 201
Free-range poultry, 65–66
Friends, 100–102, 136–37
Frozen meals, 68–69
Funding Exchange, 193

Gaia, 13
Games, computer and video, 157–59
Garbage, 32–38

Garbage disposals, 34
Gardens, 42–46, 52, 71–72
Gardnerians, 14, 217
Gemstones, 51–52
Gender roles, 228–30
Genesis, 14
Geothermal energy, 39–40
Gifts, 182, 190–95
Glass, recycling, 34
Global Fund for Women, 193
Glycols, 23
Goddess and God ritual, 228–30
God games (on computers), 159
Government bonds, 196
Grains, 74
Grass lawns, 42–46
Great Rite, 228–29
Groves. *See* Covens
Guns, 91–93

Halal meat, 66
Harm, 9–11
Harrow, Judy, 10–11
Harvard Medical School, 20
Heinlein, Robert A., 16
Herbs, 52–53
Hiding pagan beliefs, 234
HIV/AIDS activism, 199–200
Home day cares, 145
Homeschooling, 164–68
Honesty, 96, 100
Honoring elders, 205
House rules, 103–104
Housing, 206–208. *See also* Living together
Humanity, 14
Hurt, 9–11
Hydropower, 39

Identification with neo-tribe, 4
Identity, 214–15
Immanent divinity, 16–17
Impulse buying, 56, 182–83
Income, 56
Indian silk, 20
Indoor air quality, 26–27
Industrial production, 173
Infant formula, 178–79
Infill development, 207
Inherent spirituality of humanity, 14
Interconnectedness, 12–13, 94, 99
Internet, virtual communities, 219–21

Internet and children, 155–59
Intimacy, 100–101
Investing, 187, 188–90

Karma, 5, 11–12
Kindred, 215–17
Kirk, Carol, 92
Kosher meat and cheese, 66

Labor, child, 60–61
Labor surplus, 174–75
Laminate flooring, 29
Landscaping, 42–46
Law of Return (karma), 5, 11–12
Law of Thelema, 8
Legumes, 75
Linoleum, 28
Liquidity, 196
Living together, 102–104
Love, 116–17
Lovelock, James, 13

Mad cow disease, 63
Magic
    and change, 193
    ethical use, 226, 231–32
    nature of, 225–26
    relation to divinity, 17–18
    rituals, 230–35
Magical relationships, 112–14
Maintenance, 185
Maquiladoras, 60
Massage therapy, 79
Masturbation, 106
McKay, Floyd J., 61
Meat, 63–66, 75
Meat alternatives, 66–68
Medicine, 76–81
Menstruation, 81–82
Mentoring, 121–27, 202
Mentors (national organization), 202
Military service, 91–93
Milk, 74–75
Money
    consumer purchases, 177–79
    donating, 190–95
    financial balance, 57–61
    reducing spending, 181–82
    saving, 186–88
    spending differently, 183–84
Morality, 2, 3, 6

Motor oil, 36
Movies, 153–55
Moving, 222–23
Mutual funds, 189, 196–97

National Adoption Information
    Clearinghouse, 201–202
National Center on Elder Abuse (NCEA),
    204
Native plants, 45–46, 52–53
Natural consequences, 149
Natural fibers, 20–21
Natural stone flooring, 27
Natural wood flooring, 28
Nature, attitudes toward, 13–16
Nature spirits, 233
Naturopathy, 80
NCEA (National Center on Elder Abuse),
    204
Needs, reducing, 184–186
Neo-tribes, 3–5
Ninefold Law of Return, 11
Nonhumans as kindred, 216
Non-meat alternatives, 66–68
Nuclear family, 96–97
Nutrition, 74–75

Off-gassing, 26–27
Omnivores, humans as, 67–68
One Law. See Wiccan Rede
Organic cotton, 20
Organic meat, 65–66
Organic waste, 32–34
Ova-lacto vegetarians, 67–68
Overpackaging, 36–37

Pacificism, 92
Packaging, 36–37
Paper, recycling, 35
Parenting
    adoption, 201–202
    back to work vs. stay at home debate,
        143–45
    breast vs. bottle debate, 138–40
    cloth diapers vs. disposable debate, 141–43
    crib vs. co-sleeping debate, 140–41
    foster parenting, 201
    preparation for, 133–135
    support, 135–138
Partnerships, sexual, 105
Partnerships, working, 119–21

Payment for teachers, 126–27
Peace Development Fund, 193
"Perfect love and perfect trust", 116–17
Personal responsibility, 227
Pets, 216
Planned giving, 194-95
Plantings, 44–45
Plastics, recycling, 34
Pliny the Elder, 30
Political activism, 43–46
Polyamorous relationships, 110–12
Polyester, 22–23
Poultry, 64–66
Poverty, 172
Praying, 226
Pregnancy, accidental, 130–31
Preparation for a baby, 133–35
Prepared foods, 68–69
Private schools, 161–64
Psychic care, 88–91
Psychic Self-Defense (Fortune), 88
Psychic shields, 90
Psychic vampires, 89
Public rituals, 233–35
Public schools, 160–61
Public transportation, 209–10

Rankine, David, 51, 53, 92
Rape, 108
Rayon, 21–22
Recycling, 32–38
Reform, social, 193
Reiki, 80
Relationships
    with divine, 112–14
    ending, 112
    sexual, 105, 106, 107–12
    teacher/student, 121–27
Relatives, 215
Relocation, 222–23
Respect, 95–96, 127, 131–33
Responsibility, personal, 227
Rewards in child discipline, 150
Rings. *See* Covens
Rituals
    gender roles, 228–30
    location, 232–33
    public, 233–35
    traditions, 230–32
    virtual, 220–21
Role-playing games (RPGs), 158–59

Romantic thought, 15–16
Roommates, 102–104
RPGs (role playing games), 158–59
Ruckus Society, The, 200–201
Rules, 2–3
Rural living, 207

Sabbat cycle, 14
Sacred marriage, 120
Sacred spaces, 232–33
Sales, 183
Sales opportunities, 59–60
Salvation Army, 57
San Francisco Sex Information, 111
Saving money, 181–82, 186–88
Scarleteen, 111
Schools. *See* Education
Scratch and dent products, 58–59
Seasons, cycle of, 14
Secondhand stores, 57
Self-awareness, 236–38
Self-esteem, 86
Self-expression in children, 168–70
Self-identification with neo-tribe, 4
Self-respect, 82, 86
Seniors, 202–205
Sense of place, 49–51
Septic tanks, 41–42
Sex
    birth control, 129
    consenting, 107–12
    masturbation, 106
    sexual partners, 105
Sex roles, 228–30
Sexual favors, 126–27
Sexuality and U, 111
Shareholder activism, 189–90
Shields, psychic, 90
Shooters, 158
Shopping, 60–61, 71, 183
Sick office syndrome, 26–27
Silk, 20–21
Silver, 52
Simplicity movements, 184
Simulators, 157–58
Sin, 8
Situational morality, 3, 6
Small towns, 207
Social change, 192–94
Socially responsible investing, 188–90
Social welfare, 171–72

Society for Human Sexuality, 111
Solar power, 40
Solitaires, 217
Spells, 231–32
Spending, 177–79, 181–84
Spiritual communities, 217–18. *See also*
    Covens
Spirituality, inherent in humanity, 14
Spiritual practice in children's education,
    166
Spontaneous entities, 90
Sports simulators, 157
Stand for Children, 200
Starhawk, 47, 82, 193, 195
Staying at home vs. working debate,
    143–45
Steel, recycling, 34
Step-parenting, 130
Sterilization, 128–30
Stone floors, 27
Storing food, 70
Strabo, 30
Stranger in a Strange Land (Heinlein), 16
Strategy games, 159
Stress, 85, 134–35
Student/teacher relationships, 121–27
Suffering, 10–11
Support for parenting, 135–38
Synthetics, 21–23

Teachers, elders as, 205
Teacher/student relationships, 121–27
Technical simulators, 157–58
Teenagers, 169
Television, 153–55
"Thou art God/dess", 16–17, 98, 221
Threats in child discipline, 150
Threefold Law of Return, 11
Tile flooring, 27–28
Time outs, 149
Tires, 35–36
Tolerance, 212
Toothpaste, 25
Toxins, household, 31–32
Toys, 152–153
Transporatation, 182, 208–10
Transvestites, 229–30
Trothes. *See* Covens
Trust, 96, 116

Truth or Dare (Starhawk), 82
Tubal ligations, 128–30

UNICEF, 60–61
Urban planning, 206–10

Valiente, Doreen, 7–8
Values, 1, 190, 192–94, 236–38
Vasectomies, 128–30
Veal, 64
Vegans, 67
Vegetarians, 67–68
Vegetation for green space, 44–45
Vehicles, 35–36, 182, 210
Video games, 155–59
Vinegar, 25
Virtual communities, 219–21
Virtual worship, 220–21
Volatile organic compounds (VOCs),
    26–27
Volatility, 197
Volunteering, 199

Wages, 180
Walking, 208–209
Wal-Mart, 61
Warehouse clubs, 59–60
"Warrior's Path, The" (Kirk), 92
Warrior Way, 91
Waste, 32–38
Weber, Max, 15
Weeds, 43–44
Weight issues, 83
Welfare, 171–72
Western medical practice, 76–77
Wiccan Rede, 5–7, 7–11, 225–26
Wild plants, 52–53
Wind power, 39
Wine Blessing, 228–29
Wisdom, 205
Witch's Creed, The (Valiente), 7–8
Wood flooring, 28
Work, 173–77, 180
Working partners, 119–21
Working vs. staying home debate, 143–45
Workplace, 137–38
Worship, virtual, 220–21

Xeriscaping, 45–46